بسم الله الرحمن الرحيم

ALSO BY ABDAL HAKIM MURAD

Muslim Songs of the British Isles: arranged for schools (2005).
Bombing without Moonlight: the origins of suicidal terrorism (2008).
Commentary on the Eleventh Contentions (2012).
Tartīb ashʿār wa-adhkār al-Ḥamdiyya ʿalā uṣūl al-Qalādina (2017).

ABDAL HAKIM MURAD

TRAVELLING HOME

ESSAYS ON ISLAM IN EUROPE

The Quilliam Press

Third impression (revised) 2023

The Quilliam Press Ltd
14 St Paul's Road
Cambridge CB1 2EF

ISBN 978-1-872038-20-9
EPUB ISBN 978-1-872038-21-6
MOBI ISBN 978-1-872038-22-3

Printed in Turkey by Mega Basım

Contents

INTRODUCTION

A song for dear Mona, a jubilant song!
  Huzza for the little Manx nation!
So cheer loud and long, full-hearted and strong,
  Ye Manxmen of every station.

SHEYKH-UL-ISLAM ABDULLAH QUILLIAM BEY

'ISLAM UNDERSTOOD BETTER than anyone that a universal truth is worth more than local particularisms,' wrote Emmanuel Levinas,[1] and this is obvious in this most post-axial and unparochial of monotheisms; but paradoxically it is for this same reason that Muslims find themselves at home everywhere, for this same universalism of Islam enables a local rooting which recognises that 'wheresoever you may turn, there is God's Face' (Qur'an 2:115). Following its Abrahamic nature and Muhammadan example Islam has shown itself an intrinsically portable religion with a strong historic culture of migration, *hijra*, and of migrants, *muhājirūn*. The Man of Praise, like Abraham, was himself a refugee and an asylum-seeker, arriving destitute in his new shelter; the *hijra* bisected and defined his entire Prophetic career. Yet he came to conceive a love for Madina as well as for his native city, and this *Dār al-Hijra* turned into his permanent and authentic home. In this combination we find a paradigm which characteristically shapes Muslim identity: to Mecca we turn in prayer and pilgrimage, but we fully belong in all places, since 'the whole earth is made a mosque for me' and the healing signs of God's presence are everywhere, even, as for Quilliam, out on the windswept Isle of Man, geographically so remote from the *Dār al-Islām*.

1 Emmanuel Levinas, tr. Seán Hand, *Difficult Freedom: Essays on Judaism* (Baltimore, 1990), 179.

Such is this Muslim sense of belonging that believers feel more at home in a place than any atheist could, since to lose contact with God is immediately to forfeit one's sense of connection to a place of His making; it is to feel one's roots and identity shrivel; there can be no truly English, German or Russian atheist. From this kind of Muslim perspective Lenin was not Russian, Douglas Murray is not British and Sam Harris is not American; they seem to wait in a forlorn foreign encampment even when officially at home. By contrast, to become Muslim, or to arrive from an Islamically Abrahamic place, and to maintain that traditional sensibility which perceives God's signs superabundantly everywhere, is immediately to see the land with understanding, and hence to begin to grow roots and to adorn and engage the earth. Such, very roughly, is the Islamic theory of Abrahamic mobility: unlike Israel's wanderings in exile, which await the Messianic intervention which will take the people to a home greater than all homes, Muslims travel from one home to an equal other, and do not cherish a return to the Mother of Cities, except as visitors. They migrate Abrahamically; but every country, for them, is a promised land.

The present set of polemical essays seeks to explore and to theorise in the contemporary context this natural and longstanding habit, framing itself against the resurgent European fashion for seeing Islam as irreducibly foreign. Rooted in classical Muslim perspectives it is unlikely to please minds shaped by most contemporary Muslim discoursing on politics and society as this has been cast since the mid-twentieth century and applied, often with catastrophic results, by 'Islamic movements' of various stripes, and which continues to shape the thinking of several Muslim leaders in the West. Neither will it be acceptable to the subaltern classes whose self-esteem as Muslims has collapsed beneath the bullying might of secular hegemons, and who have—usually in great spiritual misery—raised the white flag of surrender. Instead these squibs are offered to that growing band of dissident souls unconvinced by materialist accounts of the human situation but who also recoil from those who love to see Islam as a system keen to divide and dichotomise, rather than as an all-embracing *dīn*. In short, it is for vagrants, nostalgics, dissidents and dervishes of conscience, who today are unsupported by any global infrastructure or national polity. But it considers this nomadism and friendlessness to be almost a sign of authenticity in fractured and anxious times of nationalism and pandemic, for as the hadith says, 'blessed are the strangers'.[2]

The essays which follow roughly adhere to the helpfully imprecise paradigm which has become known to Western Muslims as 'Traditional Islam'. Most are versions of talks given in a variety of contexts to audiences of disparate academic or devotional expectations, and their tonal inconsistency reflects that. Often they began life as keynote lectures and so adopt a wide-ranging and synthesising method. Their sequence is of arguable clarity. They all, however, attempt to explore ways in which 'Traditional Islam' can claim to represent a more intellectually and morally coherent response to the present emergency of Muslim integration than either secular scientism or Islamism. It should be underlined that Traditional Islam, as understood in these essays, is not an anachronistic exercise in resurrecting medieval rulings and applying them uncritically in the modern world; instead it is a return to the civilisation's time-honoured root-epistemology, the *uṣūl*, and an employment of the cumulative wisdom of the Muslim centuries in all its amplitude (*madhhabs, taṣawwuf, kalām* and more) to extend the continuous narrative, the *traditio*, of the *umma,* here attempting to devise an uncompromising theory of Islamic belonging in the European homeland of the late modern *mêlée*.[3] In such a context, this entails a rejection of the emotive anti-Westernism of the fundamentalists. It also entails an insistence—and here is a second trigger warning—that integration and harmony must take place on Islam's terms; since non-Muslim think-tankers, social administrators and

2 Muslim, Īmān, 232.

3 For more thoughts on 'Traditional Islam' see Abdal Hakim Murad, *Commentary on the Eleventh Contentions* (Cambridge, 2012), 33-4.

party politicians have no jurisdiction in internal matters of Muslim belief, outlook and practice. In this respect the essays are inspired by the work of Charles-André Gilis, who insists that the Muslim relation to secular societies must recall the non-negotiability of Truth (*Ḥaqq*), and the equally vital need for the virtue of truthful honesty (*ṣidq*) in our interpretations and in the forms of our desired conviviality.[4]

The approach is also traditional in its attempt to be strongly contextual and realistic. Positivity towards majority non-Muslim societies and a proper engagement in their civic structures must be seen by Muslim minorities not only as desirable but as a necessity (*ḍarūra*) in the post-Srebrenica environment. Europe is surging rapidly in a nationalist direction, and Muslims are viewed by increasing numbers as a Dark Other fit only to be securitised and stigmatised, and perhaps, in the dreams of some, banished from Europe's walled garden. Fundamentalist and Islamist narratives of polarity and contrarity thus represent a direct threat to Muslim flourishing in Europe, complying as they do with the enemy's cruel image and recruiting zealots for his cause. However the turn to Traditional Islam cannot primarily be strategic, but instead should adopt a firm rejection of two contemporary Muslim weaknesses: firstly, reactive identity-religion with its desire for status and revenge driven by ego (*nafs*); and secondly, a declining reference to the presence, power and compassion of God, a slackening which leads to what I capitalise as Fearfulness. The decay of *taṣawwuf* and the consequent externalising of Islam have for many yielded an increasingly stiff and exoteric system preoccupied with boundaries and dichotomies, defensive and unhappy, and we will need to show how this has happened, and why Islam's other contemporary travails cannot be overcome until these two attitudinal lapses have been corrected.

This is, hence, not a call for reform so much as an attempt to repair what has been deformed. Alienation must be healed with

4 Charles-André Gilis, *L'Intégrité islamique, ni intégrisme, ni intégration* (Paris, 2004).

authenticity, and certainly not with a different alienation which unconsciously replicates many of the features and failures of modernity, of which it is in many ways simply a transposed version. John Gray in his *Al-Qaeda and what it Means to be Modern* borrows Karl Kraus' teasing remark about psychoanalysis to see radical Islamism as 'a symptom of the disease of which it pretends to be the cure.'[5] Slavoj Žižek makes the same point, noting that despite the standard Islamophobic narrative, extreme Islamism presents a radical discontinuity with the Muslim past, and the adoption of Enlightenment or counter-Enlightenment strategies of working for a utopia by violent and terroristic means. Like other such projects, it wants 'capitalism without capitalism', 'without its excess of social disintegration, without its dynamics in which "everything solid melts into the air".' For Žižek, the American cultural order presides over the globe so absolutely that the Jihad versus MacWorld characterisation is not enough, the reality of Jihad has become a MacJihad.[6]

Integration, then, but through something authentic and honourable which is neither MacWorld nor MacJihad. This will be rooted not in the ideologies which are reflexes of the ruling ideology, but in a trusting sense of what the neglected libraries contain across the immense range of the *Dār al-Islām*, both in their *fiqh*, which reveals that a project of 'minority *fiqh*' is in fact unnecessary, given the wisdom and flexibility of the existent mainstream tradition,[7] and also

5 John Gray, *Al-Qaeda and What it means to be Modern* (London, 2003), 26.

6 Slavoj Žižek, *Welcome to the Desert of the Real* (London and New York, 2002), 146.

7 The case is made by Amjad M. Mohammed, *Muslims in Non-Muslim Lands: a legal study with applications* (Cambridge, 2013). See also A. Caeiro, 'Theorizing Islam without the State: minority *fiqh* in the West', in M. Diamantides and A. Gearey, *Islam, Law and Identity* (London, 2011), 209-235. With the seemingly inexorable rise of state-curated religion in majority-Muslim countries and the progressive restriction of free religious education and mosque assembly, it is evident that minorities in the West often enjoy greater freedoms than those available in the Middle East or other Muslim-majority regions; and this undermines the basic premise of most 'minority *fiqh*' discourse.

the *taṣawwuf*, the inner technology of fighting that 'greater enemy' which is 'the ego within you',[8] an initiatic tradition essential to moral advancement which is currently being combated, unsurprisingly, by modernists and fundamentalists alike.

The believer hears God, and is heard by Him (*samiʿa'Llāhu li-man ḥamidah*), and is thus an Ishmaelite, 'heard by God' and 'hearing Him'. We will reflect, then, on what it means to be properly Ishmaelite, which is to be free of self, for one has heard something higher; if scorned by the 'laughing' followers of his younger brother Isaac, 'Ishmael' will seek something better than retaliation: for him, Isaac too is fully a prophet, and his line is blessed rather than unchosen. Inclusivity is vital to the meaning of the Ishmaelite charism and of the *khatm*, the Sealing of prophecy. But Ishmael carries another role: the followers of Isaac have been, from early times, often 'Ishmaelophobic': readers of Genesis have habitually concluded that he is ethnically impure, his mother being African; that he is a wild donkey, that he is *ferus homo,* cast out as the paradigmatic refugee, despised and marginalised.[9] Serb irredentists call him *balije*, gypsy. In our time the Muslim is once again demonstrating the nature of Ishmael's charism: while to be despised and marginalised is not his rightful role and should not be acquiesced in, it is unsurprising and should not occasion panic. The rich take tea in Margate while the Ishmaelites drown in the Channel, and there is a certain Prophetic expectedness to this. Palestine, which Žižek calls the 'symptomal knot', is where the division and the world's Separation Wall seem physically to begin, with the privileged on one side, and the

8 Abū Ḥāmid al-Ghazālī, *Iḥyā' ʿulūm al-dīn* (Riyāḍ, 1434/2013 edition), IX, 206 (K. al-Murāqaba wa'l-muḥāsaba, murābaṭa 6).

9 E.g. John V. Tolan, *Sons of Ishmael: Muslims through European Eyes in the Middle Ages* (Gainesville etc., 2008), 142-3; Norman Daniel, *Islam and the West: the making of an image* (Revised edition Oxford, 1993), 100-1, 151. Thinkers of the Reconquista and the Inquisition considered it natural to expel Ishmael and Hagar, since Abraham had done the same: Mary Elizabeth Perry, *The Handless Maiden: Moriscos and the Politics of Religion in Early Modern Spain* (Princeton, 2005), 178-9.

Ishmaelites, and hence all impoverished victims of global inequality, on the other.

A theology of Islam in Europe, considering the low status and prestige of most Ishmaelites in the rich but disturbed continent, must take the Abrahamic bifurcation as the indicative grounds for inspiration: again, not to retaliate with a reciprocal exclusion, but, as we explain in Chapter Seven, with 'something better'. The scandal of true religion is that God stands with the outcast, and this must be particularly true in our age of immense and still growing inequalities of power and wealth; and Ishmael's truth is thus detestable to the elites: the master-Islamophobe Milo Yiannopoulos wears a T-shirt bearing Paris Hilton's alleged commandment: 'Stop Being Poor.' Yet retaliation against this in kind is both unwise and unscriptural; 'something better' has to be found.

A constructive Ishmaelite theology in Europe, which, as we will suggest at several points, opens up the prospect that our communities will slowly be understood by their neighbours as God wishes, as a therapeutic rather than an allergenic presence, must also be aware that ours is a continent of extremes. As Mark Mazower observes in his *Dark Continent*, democracy seemed triumphant in 1918 but had collapsed across Europe only twenty years later. He shows that the roseate view of liberal democracy as the most obvious and necessarily victorious intellectual outcome of Enlightenment reason and of Darwinist reductionism is arbitrary: the two other outcomes, Communism and Fascism, claimed the loyalty of very many, and might well have prevailed. But 'not even the murderous record of the twentieth century has yet, it seems, diminished Europe's capacity for self-delusion.'[10] Europe tends to lurch from thesis to antithesis and back again, and the current quick rise of xenophobic populism reminds us that it remains, as Tomás Masaryk once described it, 'a laboratory atop a vast graveyard.'[11]

---

10 Mark Mazower, *Dark Continent: Europe's Twentieth Century* (London, 1998), xiv.

11 Mazower, 10.

The continent's paroxysmic episodes during the twentieth century reflected a deracinating trust in science and an enmity towards monotheism, tendencies which have been reinforced further in recent years; and our theorising of life on the continent will need to take note of the strange and very extreme point which European secularity has now reached. We need to evolve a theory to deal with the large-scale absence of any faith, and we struggle to find authority for this in our old libraries (Chapter Eight). Europe's Bible has been replaced by Darwin's *Origin of the Species*, and competitive individualism has become the energising force of its societies; and in our populist and nationalist age the *Origin* seems eminently suitable as a founding document for an atheistic continent, many of whose twentieth-century thinkers recalled that the subtitle of Darwin's book was *The Preservation of Favoured Races in the Struggle for Life*. This secularity couples with a post-religious hedonism and a decline in family and neighbourhood life which damages our communication with our neighbours, many of whom seem to have abandoned rule-based ethics in favour of the slogan 'Do as thou wilt; Love is the law'.[12] Jordan Peterson has written convincingly on the psychological and social consequences of this shift to individualism.[13]

The decline of religion and of philosophical metaphysics has left little to be certain about, and of the ancient ternary 'mind-body-spirit', the third has atrophied while the first is assailed by postmodernism and neuroscience, so that only the body seems to remain. And thus we inhabit an age preoccupied by tattoos and cosmetic surgery, of dieting and fat-shaming. Craving certainties and codes to define in- and out-groups, and lacking the possibility of metaphysics, late modern society is turning the body into a credal object, so that entire human identities seem to radiate from it. Some of the more recent body beliefs are handily weaponised by identitarian social justice warriors in order to demonise traditional religious groupings in society, which are often unsure how to

12 Aleister Crowley, *The Book of the Law* (New York, 2004), 12.

13 Jordan B. Peterson, *12 Rules for Life: an antidote to chaos* (London, 2018).

respond. In 2014 Facebook offered new users the choice of fifty different genders, and conscientious doubts about their reality or the neopronouns which denote them are met with a startlingly furious and aggrieved polemic.[14] The body, not the divine, is now redolent with charisma, and wrongful thinking about it has become the late modern equivalent of blasphemy. This new normal is again without precedent in Islam's historic experience of engagement with others, and requires of Ishmael some careful new reflection. Again, the theology which ensues will need to be rooted in compassion rather than in arrogance and anger; we must cultivate the *futuwwa* instinct which wishes to see the best in all of God's creatures, to understand their hurt, to see His image behind the veil, and mercifully to rescue and to restore.

So these are essays conceived in the context of an age of anxiety and declension. For many years the strong alternative to Islam has been the upbeat religion of Progress. That colossus is now crumbling, not only in its most intensified socialistic manifestations, but systemically, since technology now unmistakeably threatens the entire species with destruction through climate change, artificial intelligence, transhumanism and posthumanism.[15] The sovereign human will on which Enlightenment humanism was grounded

---

14 For a list of some new genders see Angela Nagle, *Kill All Normies: online culture wars from 4chan and Tumblr to Trump and the Alt-Right* (Alresford, 2017), 70-72.

15 Martin Rees, *Our Final Century: a scientist's warning* (London, 2004); Reza Negarestani, *Intelligence and Spirit* (New York, 2018). See also the remarkable century-old prescience of Guénon: 'As the danger of these inventions - even of those not purposely designed to play a fatal part where mankind is concerned, and which nevertheless cause so many catastrophes, not to mention unsuspected disturbances in the terrestrial environment – as this danger, we say, will no doubt continue to grow to an extent that is difficult to foretell, it is permissible to suppose, without too much improbability, that the modern world will succeed in bringing about its own destruction.' René Guénon, tr. Marco Pallis and Richard Nicholson, *Crisis of the Modern World* (London, 1975), 89-90.

is deconstructed by philosophers of mind and denied by brain science.[16] Only the body beliefs vibrantly motivate us; and they and their commandments are often at war with one another.[17] This collapse of Enlightenment positivism seems to open a way for alternative and more spirit-oriented epistemologies; however it also entails mortal threats to minority existence, as values evanesce and the ancient conviction that virtues need a metaphysical anchorage, repeated in modern times by Iris Murdoch and Charles Taylor, slips from Europe's mental grasp. In the warning of a Bosnian intellectual: 'a secular-liberal model means that the Other will only be tolerated provisionally. Once the opportunity presents itself, such a situation always risks degenerating into greater or lesser outbursts of violence.'[18] There are signs that the liberal-democratic Europe of openness and inclusivity is now in full decline, and that this decline will be intensified following the Covid-19 pandemic, as technologies of surveillance and authoritarian centralism become normalised. And yet in conformity with the Prophetic counsel, Muslims will prefer optimism, while still hobbling their camel against contingencies.

So the book is theological rather than sociological, and sits in the small genre of internal Muslim writing on Ishmael's search for settled status in Western minority situations. In some ways it takes its inspiration from the first British Muslim community, whose authors, like the Manx patriot Abdullah Quilliam, coupled an intense love of their own country and its provincial landscapes and folkways with a fervent Qur'anic commitment, a cohabiting which in those days when all Islam was Traditional Islam did not seem incongruous or difficult.

The book, directed to insiders, assumes a knowledge of the

16 Daniel Wegner, *The Illusion of Conscious Will* (Boston MA, 2017).

17 If gender is a matter of self-identification, what remains of classical feminism?

18 Rusmir Mahmutćehajić, *Bosnia the Good: tolerance and tradition* (Budapest, 2000), 48.

standard Islamic jargon and narratives, and where Arabic terms known in the West appear (*jihād, fatwā, sharīʿa*) these are used in the usual Muslim sense, rather than in the sense familiar in the Western public conversation. Some definitions of technical terms are included in the Index. Although this is not an academic volume, it is equipped with a large armature of annotation, given that many of its claims are contentious and will be expected to be properly evidenced; the footnotes may also help those looking to do some further reading.

Chapter One began life as a lecture given to the Oslo Litteraturhuset (20 March 2011); Chapter Three was given at Cardiff University's Centre for the Study of Islam in the UK (19 September 2012); Chapter Four was delivered at Cambridge's Divinity Faculty (12 February 2003); Chapter Seven was the 2019 Karimia Institute Trust Building Forum lecture, University of Nottingham (16 April 2019); Chapter Eight was given at the Catholic Academy of Berlin (16 April 2013); Chapter Nine began as the Aziz Foundation Distinguished Lecture, Senate House, London (19 November 2018); Chapter Ten was given at the 2nd Biennial PCI Nahdlatul Ulema Belanda International Conference, Radboud University Nijmegen (19 June 2019); Chapter Eleven was given at a National Zakat Foundation event in Canary Wharf, London (6 May 2016).

I am grateful to the Aziz Foundation for financial support during the period of research leave necessary to complete this book.

The citation from 'The Rock' by T.S. Eliot (*Collected Poems 1909-62*) is by kind permission of Faber and Faber Ltd.

CHAPTER I

Can liberalism tolerate Islam?

MUST ONE BE liberal to belong to Europe? For all the polite multiculturalist denials, this question is being put to us more and more insistently. The European Union, as it struggles to articulate a common civilisational as well as economic vision, regularly toys with grand statements about Europe as a vision of free human community whose success validates the universal model now being urged upon the rest of the world. European liberals, with their Enlightenment, civil society, democratic institutions and human rights codes, sometimes seem to self-define as a collective secular Messiah, willing and ready to save the infidel. To resist is, by implication, to align oneself with an unregenerate, sinful humanity, an abrogated covenant, an Old Testament. This liberal religion of progress often finds it difficult to respect dissidents, although in theory they are proudly tolerated in a European Union whose official motto is 'United in Diversity'.

Yet we Europeans exist in fact in the middle of a difficult argument. We are constantly quarrelling with ourselves over definitions of belonging. We can unite to build an Airbus, but will we really unite around a moral or cultural ideal? What, after all, are the exact historic and intellectual criteria for European civilisational cohesion? Moreover—and this now looks like the continent's greatest concern—how might Ishmael fit in?

Possibly it helps to consider Europe's furthest roots. Homer tells us how Europa, the daughter of the King of Phoenicia, was abducted by Zeus, duly ravished, and borne off to the island of Crete, where she gave birth to the Europeans. There is something interestingly emblematic and transgressive about this myth of origin: a Lebanese maiden torn from the breast of Asia and deposited in a corner of the continent which eventually bore her name. The beginning of our story is a violent European colonial raid upon Asia, an unhappy migration, and a confiscation of identity.

Perhaps we can trace back this far—and Europe's literature begins with Homer's stories—the continent's ambiguity about its self and its values. But Europe only finds herself, and discovers the boundaries of her soul and body, long after this classical prologue ends. For the Romans it was the Mediterranean which defined the core of their terrain and their commercial and religious life. Rome embraced equally the European, African and Asian shores of the Middle Sea. But while it saw its culture as superior, it rarely sought to impose its philosophies on others. So we will hesitate to accept the tempting thought that in our time, ancient history has been reborn: America is Rome, Europe is Athens, while Islam is an endlessly troublesome Judea. Ancient Rome had no systematic programme of universalizing its values, even within the bounds of its political sway, and still less did it encourage other nations to accept its pieties or its social beliefs.

When Islam appeared in the seventh century the African and Asian shores were suddenly lost. Thrown back on its own resources, 'Europe' sought to define itself, then as it does now, as the rather small remnant of antique soil that the Saracens had missed. From this defensive beginning Europe came to nurse ideas of its unique and universal rightness.

In 1939 Henri Pirenne launched the famous thesis which claims that it was when the Arab, Berber and convert advance into France was finally stemmed that the Franks and hence the Europeans gained their first intimation of a sense of self.[1] The first use of the term

1 Henri Pirenne, *Mohammed and Charlemagne* (New York, 1939). From the European Muslim perspective Islam's first arrival is interesting as a creation-myth: like most of his soldiers Ṭāriq appears to have been a convert, and was invited to Spain to liberate the Jews and to avenge the 'rape of Florinda'.

Europenses comes in 754 in a chronicle describing Roland's defeat of the invading Saracens at Poitiers.[2] Charlemagne's capital at Aachen seemed symbolically to straddle both banks of the Rhine, making a nonsense of the old Roman frontier; Europe was starting to form a reality as a counter to Islam. The Teutonic barbarians who had brought down Rome and who now ruled in Gaul and Germania as they had ruled in Italy and Spain, now claimed to be heirs to the imperium. The almost obsessive cult of the Latin language and classical mythology which characterised European education from that time until well into the twentieth century shows how anxious the Germanic and other 'European' peoples were to see themselves, rather than the Saracens who controlled most of the old Roman world, as the true heirs of antiquity. When the Ottomans conquered Constantinople in 1453 Sultan Mehmet II adopted the title of Roman emperor, but Christian Europe rejected this out of hand. Rather as Genesis momentously rejects Abraham's first son in favour of the 'laughing one', so Europe's self-understanding seemed to have been united in nothing so much as its fearful repudiation of Islam's claims to legitimate participation in the blessings bestowed by antiquity, and by those gentile patriarchs, Plato and Aristotle.

As a matter of fact—and this is not widely noticed by advocates of European exceptionalism—Islam was for much of its history the principal heir of the Greek world, intellectually as well as geographically. Avicenna was a more distinguished Hellenising philosopher than was any Christian. Yet traditional Europe will no more see Islam as a rightful inheritor of Athens than it will allow Ishmael legitimate authority over Jerusalem. The reason has been the concept of Christendom. Christian monks contrived to see themselves as the true interpreters of Hellenism, for all their borrowings from Ibn Rushd and Ghazālī. Rome, the major remaining Christian metropolis of the classical world in the Occident, was assumed to be the inheritor of that world's riches, which had somehow migrat-

2 David Levering Lewis, *God's Crucible: Islam and the making of Europe* (New York, 2008), 172.

ed West, rather than remaining in their places of origin in Antioch, Ephesus, Cyrene and Alexandria. Even though he was Aristotle's master-interpreter, the Saracen remained an interloper and an upstart. Thanks to the same *furor Teutonicus* which had baffled and brought down Rome, the Franks kept the false inheritors at bay, and even, during the Crusades, found themselves united as Europeans in a counter-attack that brought Jerusalem again into Christian hands. From that time until the present, most Europeans, followed by their children in the ethnically-cleansed Americas, have been sure of their sole proper possession not only of ancient Semitic prophecy but also of the legacy of Athens, with which it cohabited in a series of complex though often unstable liaisons.

An older Orientalism once claimed that Islam, the larger Semitism, sniffed briefly at Greece but then turned away from it. This is the persistent legend of al-Ghazālī sounding the death-knell of Greek philosophy in the world of Islam, which survives among some polemicists even today. Hellenism, according to the likes of Ernest Renan and Leo Strauss, could find room only in the European inn; Islam, with its burden of scriptural literalism, treated it as a resident alien at best. This applied not only to metaphysics but also to ethics and the art of politics, notably Plato's brief Muslim apotheosis on the pages of al-Fārābī. Strauss has had many admirers: significantly, Donald Rumsfeld and Paul Wolfowitz were among them, together with various essayists inhabiting Europe's new Islamophobic right. Even Pope Benedict's unhappy 2006 lecture at Regensburg seemed geared to presenting the Muslims as improper partakers in the classical legacy of rationality and rights which, according to this Europhile heir to the Holy Office, is Europe's alone. Yet the best recent scholarship, such as the work of Robert Wisnovsky, has belied this political and papal confiscation: we are now very likely to see Juwaynī, Ghazālī and Rāzī as great advocates of a critical but profound instrumentalising of Greek dialectics.[3] Greek ethics, too, lived on powerfully on the pages of Miskawayh,

3 Robert Wisnovsky, *Avicenna's Metaphysics in Context* (Ithaca NY, 2003).

al-Rāghib al-Iṣfahānī, and al-Ghazālī. In political thought the old themes also enriched Muslim discussions in manuals of statecraft studied carefully by Ottoman, Safavid and Moghul emperors and their viziers. And if Plato was modified drastically by the *Sīra*, that was no bad thing, given what Popper had to say about his vision of society. Plato offered a rigid and stratified political ideology, whereas the *Sīra* opened the door to a legal tradition largely indifferent to social class, which proved pragmatic and highly responsive to context and human variety.

The recruitment of ancient philosophy, including those strands in which modern liberal thinking claims its remote beginnings, did happen differently in Muslim lands and in the Western world. That may be one reason why Athens, in Europe, finally defeated Jerusalem, and philosophy of an increasingly secular bent overcame theology. Aquinas, whose *Summa Contra Gentiles* was written to help secure Christian theology in lands conquered from Muslims, proposed a symbiosis of philosophy and scripture which has, for most Europeans, now outlived its credibility: the permanent balance which was successfully achieved in Islamic thought proved difficult for Europe. The same Christian interval in Europe which laid claim to the classical age, a claim which seemed to be supported by the Pauline and Johannine Hellenizing of Christ and by the antique culture of the patristic authors, eventually faltered, to be replaced by the whirl of post-Enlightenment European history and crisis, succeeded more recently by vibrant paganisms, polemical scientism, or an often militantly secular republicanism. Hence the remarkable decision by the drafters of the European Constitution to include a quotation from Thucydides, and to pass over the Christian centuries in silence.

In this newly post-Christian continent, which seems to have embraced Gibbonesque views of the decline of antiquity as a triumph of barbarism and religion, a new class of crusading atheists (Richard Dawkins, Anthony Grayling *et alii*) now assails faith for its supposed unreason and an inability to deliver a peaceful and just society. The past contained violence and religion, and therefore, we are told, a secular future is likely to be peaceful. Ethical liberal arguments against religion are now much more commonly heard than older objections to faith grounded in the problem of evil or the implausibility of Leviticus. This was energised in the late nineteenth century, when all reasonable people seemed to abhor Pope Pius the Ninth's *Syllabus of Errors*, which anathematised the Enlightenment notions of religious freedom and of the separation of church from state. As article 80 of the *Syllabus* proclaimed, one could be excommunicated for holding that 'the Roman Pontiff can, and ought to, reconcile himself, and come to terms with, progress, liberalism, and modern civilization'.[4]

Since the Second Vatican Council of the early 1960s (frankly described by Ratzinger as an 'anti-Syllabus') Pius IX's anathemas have been hard to remember, and even the Vatican is reinventing itself as an advocate of precisely the modernist opinions—or many of them—that a century ago might have resulted in the withholding of the sacraments and hence a sentence of eternal damnation. Its support for Darwinism, for the separation of religion and state, and for religious freedom, are three iconic examples of this seeming conversion to the idea of Progress.[5] Modern democracy's triumph is so complete that many Christians today can hardly appreciate the old and fierce Christian opposition to it. However the turn has provided ammunition for the secular polemic against traditional faith: religion seems to have disavowed its former code.

Thanks to assorted *voltefaccia* the Europe that historically made itself a unit by keeping Muslims at bay, or by eliminating them (in Spain, Portugal, Provence, Sicily, the Balkans, Crete, Circassia and

4 David I. Kertzer, *The Pope Who Would be King: the Exile of Pius IX and the Emergence of Modern Europe* (New York, 2018), 340.

5 Romano Amerio, *Iota Unum: a study of changes in the Catholic Church in the XXth century* (Kansas City, 1998); for a Muslim criticism of the process see Karim Lahham, *The Roman Catholic Church's position on Islam after Vatican II* (Abu Dhabi, 2008); Abd ar Razzaq Yahya, *La papauté contre l'islam : Genèse d'une dérive* (Paris, 2011).

the Volga), has now substantially let go of the distinctiveness of the religious vision of society that allowed that to happen. Liberalism, whose crooked genealogy entails a reading of distant concerns in ancient Athens, and whose Lutheran tributaries, claimed by some Americans, may be only imaginary,[6] has replaced the older theocratic thinking, which lingers on only in fringe ultramontane and royalist circles. Secularity is largely the invention of the continent which was the cradle of Christian monarchism; today, indeed, in a world of faith in which there may be secularism abroad, but not secularity, it almost seems to be a European monopoly. 'God's continent' has been transformed into the global crucible of an increasingly fierce materialism.

Partly due to this anti-theistic culture, as the desk pilots in Brussels look ahead they know that the future expansion of their Union must always be to the East, not the South. The *drang nach Osten* of Euroland may within thirty years bring Europe, intelligibly enough, to Minsk; but Tangiers, barely twenty miles across the sea which in classical times was a thoroughfare and not a barrier, is generally admitted to be psychologically a far foreign land. Ishmael may be Abrahamic and also Hellenistic in his theology, but his recognition of Isaac as a brother is less reciprocated than ever. Hence we find that today, as regularly in the Christian past, Europe's arguments about itself, whether right-wing or left, often end in terms of

6 Contemporary liberalism claims a partial rooting in John Locke's *Second Treatise*. It is piquant to reflect that Locke was, in his time, accused of Muslim sympathies by his traditionalist, theocratic enemies, who suspected that his opposition to the Trinity and the Incarnation, and to church hierarchy, were derived from Muslim sources. The same churchmen also suspected that his belief in liberty had roots in Islamic, Ottoman practice; for in that time, Englishmen saw that Empire as a successful multi-religious state, where despite the official privileges granted to Muslims, it was possible to be a subject of the ruler without following his religion. And this was precisely Locke's great contribution to Western political philosophy. Cf. John Marshall, *John Locke, Toleration and Early Enlightenment Culture* (Cambridge, 2010), 393-5; Nabil Matar, 'John Locke and the Turbanned Nations', *Journal of Islamic Studies* 2 (1991), 67-77.

its relationship with its significant and negated Other: the Saracenic and Turkish realms, now identified with the problematic principle of religion itself. Experiencing a crisis of identity Europe recreates its own solidity by again self-defining against Islam, now seen as the very type of conservative piety, or, as Meyda Yeğenoğlu sees it, treating the Muslim Other as 'a categorical opposite, a radical denial or negation of itself.'[7]

Following the great geographical discoveries Europe broke the bounds a triumphant Islam had imposed upon it, and the outflanked Islamic world was, to its chagrin and confusion, progressively summoned to submit to European patterns of government and economic life. Today most elites in the postcolonial Muslim world are, substantially, Europeans themselves, and are no longer recognisable adherents of local specificities. Publicly or discreetly they take upon their shoulders the mantle of Progress and the battle against substantive faith; their ancestors become the Others against whom they primarily self-define. Sometimes their fervent dislike of the indigenous makes them seem even more royal than the foreign king.

With such converts Brussels has no significant quarrel, although it regularly puzzles over the deep corruption and often the cruelty of the westernised classes in the former colonies. But dealing with those *Animal Farm* regimes raises no more than a human rights issue. The elites are called to adhere to the constitutional and humanitarian norms, as well as the secular protocols, of post-monotheistic Europe. Yet as the Eurocrat is nervously aware, and as early twenty-first century events showed, those elite converts can resemble a fragile membrane stretched over a mass of cultural difference. The 'Arab Spring' demonstrated that the Muslim world, and perhaps the larger non-Western world, is reminiscent of the polar seas. The ocean, at no great depth, is alive and moving, a mass of liquid; while on the surface plates of congealed ice uneasily coexist. Tensions be-

7 Meyda Yeğenoğlu, *Colonial Fantasies: towards a feminist reading of Orientalism* (Cambridge, 1998), 6.

tween, say, Morocco and Algeria, are disputes between cold, empirical, Europeanised classes, not between the often devoutly religious populations beneath them, for whom the boundaries drawn by past generations of colonial cartographers are usually experienced as painfully discrepant with local linguistic and ethnic reality. Secular elites, tactically invoking selected liberal values, hold down a mass of holy and civilisational sentiment. This subaltern secularity is as carceral as the authoritarianism of the Islamist utopias: the nation-state simply becomes a prison. The holding-down can be so violent that on occasion traumatised terrorists emerge to horrify the world, and to confirm, in turn, Western policymakers in their uneasy support for the regimes.

This tension, between the highly autocratic elites which enjoy this paradoxical support from European liberal governments, and the still substantially religious masses with their desire to enter the public square, to shape decision-making and to hear accurate news, has now become so kinetic that the ice is melting and the sea breaking through in very many of the Muslim states which look over the sea to Europe. The Arab Spring is a social and political equivalent of climate change. The outcome is often a type of crisis for the liberal conscience, or a sudden and carefully-timed *volte face*: as we saw when on January 14 of 2011 the French president offered President Ben Ali of Tunisia a contingent of riot police to shore up his rule, while the next day, when it became clear that the popular uprising had triumphed, France refused Ben Ali the right even to enter its airspace. *Dès qu'on a des ennuis, elle n'est plus votre amie …*

As they fret over birthrates and immigration, Europe's theorists are well aware of this. Hence the fractiousness of, for instance, the recurrent European debate over Turkish membership of the European Union. When it came to power the Erdoğan government presented liberals with a paradox. Less fiercely secular than its predecessors, it was keen to curb the military's projection in the political realm. The generals, with their tight-lipped laicism, had claimed for decades to be the guardians of Ataturk's project to recreate Turkey in Europe's image; yet Europe is no longer the fascistic continent it was becoming in the 1920s and 1930s when Kemalism looked to it for inspiration. Hence the teasing conundrum for the Eurocrats. Many European liberal statesmen, particularly in the core 'Charlemagne' states of France and Germany, oppose Turkish membership on grounds that are clearly to do with Europe's ancient habit of self-definition as something that, ultimately, is not Muslim. On this view, Europe may be economically inclusive, and passionately liberal and libertarian, but ultimately, to be itself, it must be exclusive of outsiders, and of Muslims above all. The old Crusading cry of '*Chrétiens ont droit et païens ont tort*' has simply been modified by replacing the Christians with gender activists, usurious bankers, and human rights commissioners. In 2004 Frits Bolkestein, EU internal market commissioner, was voicing a very widespread sentiment when he cried that if Turkey joined the EU, 'the liberation of Vienna [from an Ottoman siege] in 1683 would have been in vain'.[8] The UK's 2016 Brexit convulsion was energized by claims that Turkey would join the EU, prompting fears that a tsunami of migrants would overwhelm British health and social services.[9]

It is not impossible that Turkey will be admitted, perhaps after two or more decades. Yet the current proposals envisage Turkey's exclusion from the Amsterdam Treaty in respect of the country's Muslim population. Citizens of historically Christian EU countries will be able to live in Turkey, but to allow Turks to emigrate freely to Europe would be too much for electorates to contemplate. This, currently, seems to be the kind of compromise that Ankara will be compelled to accept: again, Ishmael accepts Isaac, but not *vice versa*. Other arrangements with Muslim nations such as Albania, Bosnia, and perhaps Azerbaijan, may well impose the same condition. A Europe increasingly at ease with minaret and *niqāb* bans, and which has not forgotten its ancient and deepest definition as non-Sarace-

8 'Open the gates of Vienna', *The Spectator*, 18 September 2004.

9 Tom Baldwin, *Ctrl Alt Delete: how politics and the media crashed our democracy* (London, 2018), 210.

nic, is very apt to be comfortable with structural discrimination on this scale.

Having thus charted our odd situation, let us deal with the question. To be Europeans, must we be liberals? Does liberal Europe's implicit insistence when drawing its outer borders on the partial or total exclusion of Islam have implications for internal definitions of belonging? If we inspect the bland Euro banknotes, the product of extended and somewhat desperate searches in the 1990s for a shared European symbol, we find that the key image that was finally agreed is the outline of the continent itself, which blurs into nothingness wherever it reaches places inhabited by Muslims. The vague bridge drawings were inspired by 'seven ages' of European culture and design, but naturally there was no risk of annoying real Europeans with any trace of a Moorish arch to recall the 'first Renaissance' in Cordoba. For Brussels officialdom there is implicitly no more appropriate symbol of Europe than one which indicates non-Muslimness. What, therefore, should a European Muslim think of himself or herself when using this currency? Does a conscious exclusion at the frontiers on religious grounds have implications for internal solidarity and belonging? Must liberal Europe, to be ironically faithful to its liberal beliefs, create a subtle internal firewall against Muslim converts and migrants and their bafflingly religious progeny?

For all the brave talk of European unity, the reassuring reality on the ground is that there is no consensus at all. The French model, grounded in Enlightenment anticlericalism, claims a fierce exclusion of religious affiliation of any kind from its concept of belonging. This does not concern Islam alone, but was made clear more than a century ago in the Republic's response to the *Syllabus of Errors*: a law was passed preventing priests from mentioning the papal document from the pulpits. Thus was a process established whereby secularity could win important victories over freedom of speech.[10] And

10 Which has more recently surfaced in the form of censorship of Muslim literature, including, since 1994, the pamphlets of Ahmad Deedat.

Catholicism, though the victim of a deep anticlericalism, was at least seen as indigenous. In the republic's more recent travails with Islam, an empathy with Maronites, the dirty war in Algeria and a general official disdain for religion have made the exclusion of Muslimness in the name of Republican laicity particularly natural and emphatic, and Jim Wolfreys' book *Republic of Islamophobia* offers an impeccable and troubling study of this ideology.[11] Hence the constant susurration of French media rage against Muslim difference, and the broad-based consensus among liberals that women who wear the *niqāb*, or Parisian Muslims caught praying together in public places, should be detained by the police.

The United Kingdom is generally more reserved in its willingness to irk and coerce its minorities, and Boris Johnson, on assuming the mayorship of London, retreated from his earlier pungent discoursing on Islam and found it politic to recall that his Turkish great-grandfather had memorised the entire Qur'an. But the recent British Ofsted assessment of the poor quality of 'citizenship' training in faith-based secondary schools may indicate the shape of things to come. Even without the troublesome Muslims, Ofsted confronts a hard uphill struggle. 'Citizenship' has formed part of the National Curriculum only since 2001, and Ofsted confirms that instruction in this rather nebulous subject has been extremely patchy across the board; in fact, it is said to be the worst-taught subject in the nation's schools.[12] So bad is the situation that one in

11 Jim Wolfreys, *Republic of Islamophobia: The Rise of Respectable Racism in France* (London, 2018).

12 *Citizenship established? Citizenship in schools 2006/09* (090159), (Ofsted, 2010). The situation is said to have improved somewhat since that time; however the tension between the inculcation of doctrines deemed conducive to 'social cohesion' and the underlying culture of individualism ensures the ongoing frailty of the curriculum. More effective, and of more interest to pupils, would be the inclusion of a requirement to research and create family trees, enabling young people to learn the names and identities of their relations; an emphasis on knowing one's neighbours would also aid actual, rather than merely abstract and theoretical, social cohesion.

ten pupils in Britain apparently do not even know what citizenship classes are, even though they have attended them. Few engage actively with the liberal issues and body beliefs raised in citizenship training. The reason seems to be the general apathy towards politics and ideology current among many teenagers, the result, perhaps, of the escapist content of commercial youth entertainment, together with larger public perceptions that old definitions of sovereignty and national selfhood are being inexorably eroded by globalisation and the Internet. Only sixty-four percent of British pupils identify themselves as 'British', and even fewer as 'European'. Reflecting the crisis in this subject area a revised curriculum was promulgated in 2014; however the problems remain.

With his basilisk gaze directed evidently at the Muslim schools, where citizenship training is allegedly also in disarray, the Chief Inspector of Schools says: 'We must not allow recognition of diversity to become apathy in the face of any challenge to our coherence as a nation. We must be intolerant of intolerance.'[13] By coherence here is meant doctrinal uniformity, or what the Chinese leadership calls 'harmonization', the suggestion being that failure to convert to the elite's current raft of social beliefs, and to adhere to beliefs current, say, thirty years ago, is a sort of treason. The older British constitutional principle, dating back at least as far as John Locke's *Letter Concerning Toleration,* which held that the state's certainties should not be imposed on the population, which should be allowed the right of difference and dissent, has been overruled in a quite remarkable and very un-British way.

Here the official finger seems unconsciously to rest on the Achilles heel of secular liberal ethics. If we must be intolerant of intolerance, then can liberalism tolerate anything other than itself? Gilis observes that the rhetoric of integration rests on a claim of 'openness to the Other', yet liberalism 'has never been able or wished to

13 'We must resist this culture of anti-British segregation', *The Guardian,* 31 July 2005.

integrate with anything which did not resemble itself.'[14] If Europe defines citizenship in terms of adherence to a set moral template, with all else defined as intolerable, how can Europe ever positively experience real difference, which more often than not is bound up with good (or bad) religion? Lévi-Strauss includes in his list of factors which ensure the entropy of the secular West a theory of 'coalition of cultures': globalisation confiscates the energising presence of the substantively different Other.[15] Herbert Marcuse takes a similar view of the vitally galvanic role of minorities in consumer society. However Ishmael has not been welcomed as such an Other, but is instructed constantly to adopt the social beliefs of the dominant mass culture; and this seems to be the real meaning of 'integration.'

Of particular concern to British Muslims has been the government insistence that the 'values' of citizenship are simply to be handed down by the state rather than justified in universally-accessible rational terms. The National Curriculum for citizenship requires that as well as learning about the British constitutional, legal and economic system, pupils must be invited to embrace a certain set of social beliefs, but at no point are they to be exposed to the reasons for professing those beliefs.[16] There is an Association for Citizenship Teaching, but again this seems to regard the social beliefs to be inculcated as so self-evident as not to require any analysis. Pupils are 'partners', but only in the shared compulsory journey towards entirely unexamined conclusions.[17]

Muslims are not the only religionists to fall victim to this coercive-liberal definition of European authenticity. A memorably iconic test was applied in 2004 when the Italian jurist Rocco Buttiglione was forced from his candidacy to be a European commissioner when it emerged that he supported the Vatican's teachings on homosexuality. Despite his insistence that his belief in the sinful-

14 Gilis, *Intégrité islamique*, 51.

15 Claude Lévi-Strauss, *Race and History* (Paris, 1952), 41-2.

16 *Citizenship Programmes of Study, key stages 3 and 4* (Department for Education, 2013).

17 www.teachingcitizenship.org.uk

ness of homosexual practice would not affect the decisions he took in public life, the tight consensus of European officialdom obliged him to resign. The Italian Justice Minister, Roberto Castelli, objected in a futile way, by calling the ban 'a decision which reveals the true face of Europe, a face which we do not like. It is fundamentalist, and this is entirely wrong.' But his suggestion that an intolerant secular religion was now becoming a European orthodoxy elicited only frowns. Liberalism, in the new Europe, increasingly seems only to be itself if it is intolerant of dissent.[18]

In the UK, a series of laws including the 2010 Equality Act have underlined the state's growing assurance in continuing to tolerate private religious belief while regulating some forms of religious expression where these are deemed to clash, for instance, with the 'protected category' of sexual orientation. Following the 2009 case of a Christian marriage registrar in Islington who was refused exemption from performing same-sex civil partnership registrations, and who consequently lost her job, it became clear that liberal legal culture, in its current stage of evolution, establishes

> the willingness of courts to prefer sexual-orientation equality as a state aim even if this interferes with religious freedom. If a religious individual or association cannot, in good conscience, provide the public service without sexual-orientation discrimination then the solution is that they should withdraw from the public activity.[19]

There is no reason to suppose that the same 'othering' and hence 'de-Europeanising' of ethically-dissident religious adherents will not be applied to ensure that the conservatively religious, and others who hold traditional social beliefs, will be excluded from serving not only as marriage registrars, but as teachers, diplomats, and prac-

18 Simon Hix, *What's Wrong with the European Union and How to Fix It* (Cambridge, 2008), 38–9.

19 Maleiha Malik, 'Religion and sexual orientation: conflict or cohesion?' 67-92 of Gavin D'Costa, Malcolm Evans, Tariq Modood and Julian Rivers (eds.), *Religion in a Liberal State* (Cambridge, 2013), p.86.

titioners of other vocations in which the expression of the state's body beliefs is required as a contractual obligation. The Western polity has now found a comprehensive doctrine again, which progressively excludes conservatives and other dissidents from the tolerated 'overlapping consensus', thanks to what Guénon sees as the 'equalitarian passion for uniformity.'[20] The same culture of censorship and exclusion is growing in multinational corporations also.[21] Few liberal theorists have properly considered the longer-term implications of such an exclusion for social cohesion and for the public perception of already-disliked faith communities; or if they have, they have not shared their thoughts.[22]

Despite an ongoing awareness of an older history of ecclesial chauvinism and the alarming spectacle of church collaboration during the Bosnian *klaonica*, Muslims have watched with concern this striking proof of how categorically Europe has walked away from its traditional Christian moral compass and identity. It is concerning that European citizenship today is becoming a matter of conformity to sacrosanct social beliefs (in the Buttiglione case the historically very un-Christian notion that conscientious non-acceptance of homosexual practice is so wicked that those who hold such beliefs must be excluded from public office). As Buttiglione himself remarked, 'The new soft totalitarianism which is advancing wants to be a state religion. It is an atheistic, nihilistic religion, but it is a religion that is obligatory for all.'

It is possible that this enforcement of 'shared' social beliefs

---

20 Guénon, *Crisis*, 90.

21 For instance the case of James Damore, an engineer sacked by Google for circulating a memo on the scientific evidence for behavioural gender differentials. Damore received threats, but also anonymous expressions of support from scientist colleagues afraid to express their views publicly. *Daily Telegraph,* 8 August 2017.

22 Research suggests that pro-integration coercive liberalism prompts negative reflexes and polarities which in fact hamper integration and social cohesion. See Nicole Stokes-DuPass, *Integration and New Limits on Citizenship Rights* (London, 2015).

through legislation, social engineering in schools and a convergent media culture will become more intense, despite its evident clash with principles of freedom of conscience. In 2009, Nick Clegg (later the British Deputy Prime Minister) said that children attending faith schools must be taught that alternative sexualities are 'normal and harmless'. Special lessons, he opined, should be required of such schools to encourage this belief.[23] Many will recognise in this pattern a reversion to historic European norms, alien to Islam, of imposing a uniform doctrinal system on the king's subjects: *cuius regio, eius religio*. Liberalism of a particular socially-prescriptive kind seems to be filling the void left by religion, and Europe being the historic land of the divine right of kings, creed here has often been more closely bound up with politics than it was in traditional Muslim polities. In this case, the critique of a particular expression of *eros* now functions as a blasphemy, or, in the argot of campus codes, a 'speech violation'. Other blasphemies include, for instance, the idea that men and women are suited to different tasks, that the death penalty is a just punishment for murder, that parents have the right to use corporal punishment to discipline their children, and that unbelievers are less pleasing to God than believers. The list is quite a long one, and it seems to be growing. George Steiner's well-known *Nostalgia for the Absolute*, in which he proposes that Europe's major modernist ideologies (Freudianism, Marxism, Nazism) functioned as ersatz religions to fill the space vacated by Christianity, now needs to add the twenty-first century system of social and body beliefs to its catalogue of new secular faiths.[24]

Society abhors a belief-vacuum. After the Second World War, Europe and America went very different ways regarding truth: Europe lapsed into what Heidegger called *gelassenheit*, just letting things be, a mood which eased the otherwise outrageous collapse into postmodernism. America, whose heartland did not suffer Allied area bombing or Nazi death camps, remained confident

23 *Daily Telegraph*, 13 January 2010.
24 George Steiner, *Nostalgia for the Absolute* (Toronto, 1997).

about God and family values, allowing a continuing religious alternative to the secular monoculture and an ongoing tolerance of variant social beliefs. But as the European continent increasingly defines itself not as a traumatised convalescent from war but as a potentially mighty unit, it needs shared religious or para-religious beliefs. Like America it tends to fix on Islam as its significant Other, but while America launches religiously-driven foreign wars,[25] Europe is preoccupied with *internal* cohesion, framing laws that in the United States would be strange: to shut the *ḥijāb* out of sight, to ban minarets, to bully or arrest those who pray on the streets, to criminalise the religious slaughter of animals, and to penalise in general the public expression or teaching of conservative morality and faith. In other words, the federal and cross-racial unity which in America is bought by external wars against Muslim opponents is possible in a less imperial Europe only by putting Muslims at the centre of an *internal* war of values. Liberal beliefs are often referenced very explicitly as a means of defending Europe's purity from Islam: in 2019, Hungary's Viktor Orbán was commended by visiting Myanmar premier and 'Asia's best-known feminist' Aung San Suu Kyi for his country's policy of opposing Muslim immigration.[26]

The 2020 Coronacrisis is likely to increase Europe's sense of unease over demographics and difference, as nations retreat into themselves and conspiracy theories bloom. If Léon de Pas' 1997 'Europa and the Bull' statue, which stands outside the European Council building in Brussels, symbolically revives the ancient myth as a symbol for the continent's core modern anxiety: that Europe may be sleek and powerful, but requires the importation of an Arab fertility if it is to survive, then Muslim demographic replenishment is likely to become even more salient as a political touchstone for postviral politicians courting a bruised and resentful electorate

25 Tim Winter, 'America as a Jihad State: Middle Eastern Perceptions of Modern American Theopolitics', *The Muslim World* 101 (2011), 394-411.

26 https://qz.com/1636655/aung-san-suu-kyi-and-viktor-orban-discuss-muslim-migration/

anxious about decline: minorities are always first in the firing line.

Many Muslims, from their vantage-point in Europe's ghettos, observe this correctly. But they then conclude that the true believers by definition have no allies. Some Salafist perspectives, in particular, seem unable to accept the possibility of partnership with non-Muslims.[27] Yet Fearfulness and xenophobia seem both scripturally unnecessary and practically unwise. If Europe continues to secularise, while her mosques remain full, then Islam is likely, without any planning or even forethought, to become the leading monotheistic energy across much of the continent. Our function in such a future must be therapeutic, not pathogenic; Gilis concludes that French militant laicity reveals Islam's providential function in Europe as a divinely-planned witness to the sacred, and as a conservator of what Europe has lost. Ishmael's presence is no accident.[28] However as a minority travelling into this unheralded and widely-challenged future we will be well-advised to seek allies and partners, and the indications are that these are most likely to be found in the churches.

We should note that the pressure being brought to bear on Muslim communities relates to social, not metaphysical, beliefs. No-one in Brussels is greatly exercised by Muslim doctrines of the divine attributes or Prophetic intercession; but they do care whether or not Muslims believe in a certain type of feminism. This places Muslim believers in a historically new position. It should be possible to forge close friendships with other Europeans who also have the courage to blaspheme against the Brussels magisterium. We may differ with conservative Catholics and Jews over doctrine, but we are all facing very similar challenges to our social vision. Signor Buttiglione could easily have been a Muslim and not a Catholic martyr.

---

27 David Commins, *The Wahhabi Mission and Saudi Arabia* (London, 2006), 40-70; Namira Nahouza, *Wahhabism and the Rise of the New Salafists: Theology, Power and Sunni Islam* (London, 2018).

28 Gilis, *Intégrité islamique*, 25-30.

Here a clear burden of responsibility rests upon the shoulders of Muslim leaders. It is in our interest to seek and hold friends. We are not alone in our conscientious scepticism about many liberal orthodoxies. The statement by Bishop Michel Santier of the French church condemning the official punishments imposed on women who wear the *niqāb* is an important sign of the possibility of cooperation. The challenge is going to be for Muslim, Christian and Jewish conservatives to set aside their strong traditional hesitations about other faith communities and to explore the multitude of moral goods that they hold in common. To date, clearly, the interfaith industry has failed to catalyse this, partly because it tends to be dominated by liberal religionists. We are more and more willing, it seems, to discuss less and less, implicitly or explicitly bowing our heads together to the moral consensus of a secularised and individualistic culture.

However an *alliance sacrée* between orthodox believers in different religions would deflate the potentially xenophobic and Islamophobic possibilities implicit in the new process of European self-definition. If Europe defines itself constitutionally, as it evidently should, as either an essentially Christian entity, or as one which is at least founded in belief in God, then the fact of Muslim support for core principles of Christian ethics would give Islam a vital and appreciated place and would demolish the old polarity. But a purely secular Europe will always see Muslim values as discrepant problems on the margin, of failures of conformity to be tolerated or punished according to the electoral needs of the politicians. The relationship with European Jews is no less critical. If Orthodox Jewry—currently gaining in numerical strength—can make common cause with Islam over key moral issues, many chauvinisms and suspicions which currently exist on both sides will be seen as self-injurious. At stake is the survival of healthy diversity, of the right to a conscience, and to what Jonathan Sacks has called 'the dignity of difference.'

CHAPTER 2

Muslims and National Populism

> I know that everything essential and great originated from the fact that the human being had a homeland and was rooted in tradition.
>
> MARTIN HEIDEGGER

A CONRADIAN VOICE of sanity against the presently intensifying mood of anti-Muslim feeling across Europe is offered by the Catholic novelist Jacques Neirynck. His novel *The Siege of Brussels* imagines events in the Belgian capital in the near future. In this nightmare of Europe's becoming, official Christianity has become a ghost, with its cathedrals reduced to the status of museums where Mass is celebrated only to satisfy the curiosity of Far Eastern tourists. The Cardinal-Archbishop bears the mock-eucharistic soubriquet of the 'Real Absence', as his hyperliberal theology, anxious to placate all sides, proves unable to mobilise Christian resistance to the new Flemish chauvinism.

In Neirynck's future the triumph of the New Right has presided over the opening of concentration camps and the expulsion of the country's Jewish and Muslim communities, who are given twenty-four hours in which to shoulder their possessions and walk in single file towards the south. Despite the enfeeblement of the official church this is an ostensibly religious as well as demographic backlash, under the Crusading cry 'Dieu le veut!', blessed by a supposed 'cultural and religious restoration' which favours the Jansenist crucifix, whose Jesus is suspended so low that his arms appear to embrace only a small elect. Nationalist priests call for 'surgical strikes which will cut out the tumour,' and go on to bless the siege and bombardment of the Muslim ghetto, as Brussels slowly transforms itself into a second Sarajevo. The drama ends with a Muslim surge which liberates a concentration camp, thereby provoking the panic-stricken flight of the Flemish militias, finally revealing the fragility of the far right's commitment as well as the unreality of its Christian rhetoric.[1]

Despite its upbeat ending, Neirynck's fable seems alarmist and improbable; yet it is written on a Flanders battlefield where Turkish and Maghrebian immigrants, joined by a significant convert community, already provide a prominent lightning-rod for the insecurities of other Belgians of all social classes, unnerved by unemployment, terrorism, an unsettled national identity and the daily visibility of the non-white Other. In the real Belgium, Flemish populists are not reticent in identifying Muslim newcomers as a type of Covid infection against which native antibodies must react. Filip Dewinter, the senior figure of the *Vlaams Belang* which in 2019 became the second-largest Flemish party, has called for the hermetic closure of Belgium's borders, and, Qur'an in hand, instructs his parliament on the need to end Muslim immigration, for 'Islamophobia,' he insists, 'is a duty.' This is to be accomplished by the progressive deprivation of state benefits and citizenship rights, and the creation of specific immigrant areas within cities to improve levels of surveillance. Islam itself is to be prohibited, 'because this religion is anti-Belgian and anti-European.'[2] Voters, often unsure whether the party is of the left or of the right, are uninterested in its economic programme, and are mainly attracted by its anti-establishment and anti-immigrant rhetoric.[3]

1 Jacques Neirynck, *Le siège de Bruxelles* (Paris, 1996), 250.

2 Frédéric Larsen, 'En Belgique, l'extrême droite s'installe dans les coulisses du pouvoir,' *Le Monde Diplomatique*, February 1992.

3 Stephen D. Fisher and Marc Swyngedouw, 'Electoral change, party composition, and the position of the extreme-right in the Flemish party system', nuff.ox.ac.uk, p.6; Teun Pauwels, *Populism in Western Europe: comparing Belgium, Germany and the Netherlands* (London, 2014), 100-113.

Of the emblematic tropes raised in Neirynck's Belgian cautionary tale, let us begin with the idea of Islamophobia as a structural parallel to anti-Semitism. Notions of Islam and Judaism as religions of law, with Christianity and the putatively Hellenistic and 'Aryan' culture which opposes them in its advocacy of the 'spirit', are very ancient, but remain vibrantly alive.[4] For Schopenhauer, who stands almost at the head of today's European tendency to praise Christianity for secular reasons, St Paul imports ultimately Vedic principles of self-mastery into monotheism, and hence supplies a perfect antithesis to the narcissistic Judaic matrix. This idea of the selfish, earthbound and lawbound Semite locked in eternal conflict with his free neighbours was for a long time one of the most dominant intellectual paradigms in Europe.[5] Among Generation Identity activists, 4chan warriors and vloggers it effortlessly transposes into the new context of Muslim immigrant difference; after all, Islam originated among Arab 'Semites', whose primal stamp it is thought obscurely to bear.

One purpose of Neirynck's fable is to underscore the parallels which thus exist between the old anti-Semitism and the new Islamophobia, something which Slavoj Žižek has also noted.[6] When Christian Worch, the German 'neo-Nazi' leader, was asked: 'Is Islam a greater threat than international Judaism—especially after 11 September?' he simply replied, 'The enemy is changing.'[7] Antisemitism as anti-Jewish prejudice is a very longstanding European tradition, a 'longest hatred' which is now only erratically fading. Time-honoured discourses of a Jewish 'enemy within' or

---

4 For a recent reformulation see Kenneth Cragg, *Semitism: the whence and the whither, 'How dear are your counsels'* (Brighton, 2005).

5 Achim Rohde, 'Der Innere Orient. Orientalismus, Antisemitismus und Geschlecht im Deutschland des 18. bis 20. Jahrhunderts,' *Die Welt des Islams* 45 (2005), 370-411; for a foundational Orientalist typologising see Léon Gauthier, *Introduction à l'étude de la philosophie musulmane. L'esprit sémitique et l'esprit aryen: la philosophie grecque et la religion de l'Islâm* (Paris, 1923).

6 Žižek, *Welcome*, 151.

7 Cited in Nick Ryan, *Homeland: Into a World of Hate* (Edinburgh, 2003), 294.

of Hebrew 'contamination' are no longer acceptable in cultivated circles, although there are unmistakeable signs that notions of Jewish financial or political cabals, or of a general disloyalty, remain widespread.[8] Europe has not yet, however, come to terms with its other historic chauvinism, which has only recently even found a name: 'Islamophobia'.[9] This is a fiercely contested term which, at the least, ought to denote an emotive dislike of the Islamic religion as a whole, rather than of its extreme interpretations; or rather, we might more usefully define it as the assumption that extremes and aberrations favoured by some Muslim adherents have normative status. It cannot denote 'a type of racism', since such an intersectional definition would, by importing baggage from older race-relations paradigms for polemical purposes, underrate the wish of many religious groups to be considered as collectivities defined entirely by belief rather than race. An ungainly distinction is sometimes proposed between 'colour racism' and 'cultural racism', and the latter coupling will be intelligible to academics and other elites; but most religious practitioners, journalists and ordinary citizens will be unconvinced, and may even react strongly against it. Since around nine percent of British Muslims defined themselves as 'white' in the 2011 census, and most Swiss Muslims are 'white', notions of Islamophobia as racism-linked may turn out to be a form of racial discrimination in themselves, implicitly de-Islamising or marginalising the ancestrally European Ishmaelite on 'racial' grounds. Furthermore the old image of the sensationalist white journalist demonising helpless non-white minorities has been complexified by the appearance of a growing cohort of empowered anti-Muslim writers of non-white origin: to call someone like Ayaan Hirsi Ali a

8 Uriel Heilman, 'Dual-loyalty bias worries US Jews', *Jerusalem Post,* 12 June 2005: 'One out of three Americans believes that American Jews are more loyal to Israel than to the United States'.

9 For the early history of the term see John E. Richardson, *(Mis)Representing Islam: the racism and rhetoric of British broadsheet newspapers* (Amsterdam, 2004), 20-28.

'cultural racist' is hopelessly awkward. In any case, for the Qur'an, which sets the pace for the Muslim discussion, one cannot understand the enmity of the Prophet's enemies unless one observes that it was axiomatically rooted in *dīn,* not tribe. The new faith had divided brother from brother and family from family, for the sake of a God majestically indifferent to 'race'.

A more Islamically-viable definition runs as follows:

> An exaggerated fear, hatred and hostility toward Islam and Muslims that is perpetuated by negative stereotypes resulting in bias, discrimination and the marginalisation and exclusion of Muslims.[10]

Here we stand on less controversial and less ideological ground: such a prejudice palpably exists, and needs to be distinguished from moderate or even serious dislike, which should always be allowed a voice, and can even prove reactively beneficial. Still, even with this better definition the word 'Islamophobia' remains infelicitous. To avoid this ugly Arabo-Greek coinage, which seems problematically to insist on an analogy to other 'phobias' and suggests that the enmity is always and essentially an expression of fear (*phobos*), we might propose a more indigenously Islamic term: 'Lahabism'. This immediately offers more clarity and links modern-day psychic enmities to the recognisably comparable chauvinisms of pagan Mecca. Abū Lahab, the oligarch of Quraysh, had initially promised protection to the nascent Muslim community, not out of religious respect but because the honour code of his tribe imposed rules of hospitality. Made angry by Muslim difference and increasing

10 Definition by the Center for American Progress, cited in Sayeeda Warsi, *The Enemy Within: a tale of Muslim Britain* (London, 2018), 137. Another sensible definition is offered by Bangstad: 'indiscriminate negative attitudes and sentiments concerning Islam and Muslims' (Sindre Bangstad, *Anders Breivik and the rise of Islamophobia* [London, 2014], 18). For a defence of the 'cultural racism' definition see Tariq Modood, *Essays on Secularism and Multiculturalism* (London, 2019), 76-88.

numbers he then turned against the faithful and hurled furious brickbats at them, lampooning (*hijā'*) the Man of Praise and raising anti-Muslim feeling wherever he could in the City and among the wandering tribes.[11] In this fanatical *hijā'*, in his slogan *tabban lak*, 'may you perish,' we find the true dark beginnings of anti-Muslim hate, a latter-day version of the scorn which seems invariably to attend prophets and sages. Lahabism is based not only on fear, but more significantly on self-centredness and arrogance, *kibr*, *superbia*, greatest of the seven deadly sins.

But whatever the definition, Europe has hardly begun to purge its subconscious. Despite Copernican transformations in Christian views of 'infidels', even the churches continue to harbour intransigent voices of the type scorned in Neirynck's fiction. In Italy, an Archbishop of Bologna has called for the closure of the country's mosques and an end to immigration by Muslims, who are, he believes, 'outside our humanity.'[12] In 2019 Cardinal Robert Sarah, Prefect of the Vatican's Congregation for Divine Worship, echoed the feelings of many conservatives when he spoke out against Muslim immigration to Europe. Provocatively challenging the more hospitable policy of Pope Francis, he was quoted as follows:

> If the West continues in this fatal way, there is a great risk that, due to a lack of birth, it will disappear, invaded by foreigners, just as Rome was invaded by barbarians [...]
>
> If Europe disappears, and with it the invaluable values of the old continent, Islam will invade the world [...] And we will totally change: culture, anthropology, and moral vision.[13]

---

11 'Abū Lahab', *Integrated Encyclopedia of the Qur'ān*, I, 89-91.

12 'No offence meant, Pope tells "defective" religions', *The Guardian*, 2 October 2000.

13 https://www.valeursactuelles.com/clubvaleurs/societe/cardinal-sarah-leglise-est-plongee-dans-lobscurite-du-vendredi-saint-105265; *Daily Mail*, 4 April 2019; for other examples see Abd ar Razzaq Yahya, *La papauté contre l'islam*.

What should we make of such adversions to Europe as the first and paradigmatic Christian continent, which remain frequent? The Christendom idea seems to be the most obvious and historically-entrenched ground for the enmity, and perhaps supplies further support for the idea of the hatred as structurally cognate with anti-Semitism. In Austria the Freedom Party, founded by former SS *Brigadeführer* Anton Reinthaller, and the steady growth of which has allowed its nominees recently to occupy the posts of vice-Chancellor and Ministers of the Interior and Foreign Affairs, loudly invokes God in its electioneering. Yet in practice the Austrian Catholic church has shown itself as strongly supportive of asylum-seekers and refugees, and the party has been forced to adopt the very secular election battlecry *Daham statt Islam*, homeland rather than Islam, together with the feminist slogan *wir schützen freie Frauen*: we protect free women.[14] From its perspective, the new Turkish invaders are un-Austrian more than they are un-Christian, a very visible aspect of an alienating modernity which seems to threaten the country with the confiscation of its identity and with social disaster. Even though most local clergy have sharply denounced it, this sub-Christian populist party attracts a third of the vote of this stable, prosperous Catholic democracy, and despite electoral volatility it seems well-placed for further growth.

Such sentiments become more abusively religious when one travels towards Europe's East. The object lesson of the complicity of many Orthodox clerics in the Yugoslav wars of succession will be rehearsed in Chapter Four. In Athens, official plans to create the first dedicated mosque for the city's quarter-million Muslims have been consistently opposed by the Orthodox hierarchy: Bishop Seraphim of Piraeus, where the very humble structure is to be created, calls the plan 'a disgraceful and humiliating sacrilege'.[15] In Kamchatka, at

14 Zsolt Sereghy, '"Vienna must not become Istanbul": the secularization of Islam and Muslims in Austria', in Yasir Suleiman (ed.), *Muslims in the UK and Europe I* (Cambridge, 2015), 178. Note also that churchgoers in Belgium are statistically less likely to support the national populist Vlaams Belang: Pauwels, 105.
15 https://greece.greekreporter.com/2013/04/04/bishop-seraphim-wants-athens-mosque-stopped/

the furthest end of European settlement, the Orthodox bishop has backed opposition to the construction of a mosque for the region's small Muslim community. The mosque would be 'a direct insult to the religious and civil feelings of the Slavic population,' according to its local opponents, and would encourage further Muslim immigration, with the result that 'given their mind-set, they won't let us live normally here.'[16] In Tatarstan, Muslims complain that the new Metropolitan of Kazan has requested the transfer of the site of the new Kazan Kremlin mosque to Orthodox control.[17]

However in Western Europe, as Neirynck underlines, the cross brandished by the new populist parties tends to be a Klansman's cross, a symbol of absence rather than of presence. Overwhelmingly —as with Nazism—Europe's new mood of national populism[18] is a secular evolution, reflecting rather than challenging a very chronic spiritual recession across the continent, and recalling the atheistic mood of most twentieth-century totalitarianism. Pegida UK, launched in 2016, was co-chaired by Anne Marie Waters, a lesbian rights activist and feminist, who reportedly calls for the mass expulsion of Muslims and a policy of systematic mosque closure. Her position is not Christian, however, and she has even served as a director of the National Secular Society.[19]

Western European populists advocate 'Judeo-Christian civilisation' without wishing to practice either religion themselves. Calling himself a 'hard-shelled materialist,' Niall Ferguson still laments

---

16 'Muslims under fire in Russian Far East,' *Japan Times*, 7 August 2000.

17 Dominic Rubin, *Russia's Muslim Heartlands: Islam in the Putin Era* (London, 2018), 138.

18 The serviceable but still contested term; for an argument that the movement's internalising of feminism actually puts it at odds with populism see Sara R. Farris, *In the Name of Women's Rights: the rise of femonationalism* (Durham NC, 2017), 57-77.

19 James Bloodworth, 'Meet Anne Marie Waters – the Ukip politician too extreme for Nigel Farage,' *New Statesman* 18 August 2017; David Willer *et al.*, 'Taking racism seriously: Islamophobia, civil liberties, and the state', at opendemocracy.net.

the 'moral vacuum our dechristianisation has created,'[20] a vacuum which opens a space for the unpleasant values and beliefs of newly-arrived Muslims. Alain de Botton, clutching the 'God-shaped hole' in his European heart, commends Comte's attempt to create an ersatz religion offering atheist rituals and sociality.[21] Something similar underpins the spiritual nostalgia of 'Christian atheist' Douglas Murray, who condemns Islam in the name of a heritage whose religious centre he can no longer inhabit. The consistency of anti-Muslim sentiment is again evident in all this: unconfessed envy is, as the Qur'an indicates, a significant component of Lahabist emotion.[22]

The xenophobes (who, when they still care about 'race', are not 'racists' now, but 'ethno-separatists') stand therefore mainly on Western Europe's secular side, the territory which the Enlightenment predicted would yield reason and equal rights and respect for all. One champion of this hard Enlightenment secularity is the Dutch politician Geert Wilders, who since founding a Freedom Party and declaring independence from 'the elite' in 2004 has combined an intensified feminism and Zionism with a particularly strident anti-Muslim rhetoric. He compares the Qur'an to Hitler's *Mein Kampf,* and insists that there is no 'moderate Islam'. Wilders zealously campaigns for a ban on sales of the Qur'an, for a 'head-rag tax' of a thousand euros a year, and for a ban on mosque construction, and has tried to persuade his parliament that Jordan should be renamed 'Palestine', in accordance with the desires of the Israeli right which wishes to deny forever the Palestinian right of return.

---

20 Niall Ferguson, 'Heaven knows how we'll rekindle our religion, but I believe we must,' *Daily Telegraph*, 31 July 2005.

21 Alain de Botton, *Religion for Atheists: a non-believer's guide to the uses of religion* (London, 2013), 300-7.

22 'They wish to turn you back to disbelief after you have believed, out of envy; but you must forgive and forbear until God brings His destiny to pass' (2:109).

In 2018 he energetically backed President Trump's decision to move the US embassy in Israel to occupied Jerusalem.[23]

Norway, perhaps because it too is a liberal and secular bastion, has been fairly quick to follow the lead of the Dutch. The 1997 elections saw the sudden appearance of the anti-immigrant Progress Party of Carl Hagen, which by 2013 had grown strong enough to join the coalition government as the third-largest political party in the country. In the same year the party voted for same-sex marriage and same-sex adoption. As well as being staunchly feminist the party supported Israel in Operation Cast Lead, and wishes to move the Norwegian embassy to Jerusalem. Sylvi Listhaug, the party member who became Minister of Immigration and Integration between 2015 and 2018, tells Muslims: 'Here we eat pork, drink alcohol, and show our faces. You must abide by the values, laws and regulations that are in Norway when you come here.'[24] Her party leader Siv Jensen alarms her compatriots with theories about a covert Islamisation of Norway, even though Muslims represent no more than three percent of Norway's population.[25]

In liberal and secular Denmark the rapidly-growing ultranationalist DPP has likewise become mainstream, again benefiting from widespread popular anxieties about globalisation and a focussed dislike of Muslims. Its folksy leader Pia Kjaersgaard who ran the party from 1995 to 2012 opposed entry into the Eurozone, railed against 'welfare cheats', and was famous for her outbursts against Islam. The same line has been taken by her successor Kristian Thulesen Dahl, whose policies, including a commitment to cutting Muslim immigration, ensured that his party almost doubled its vote in 2015 to secure second position in the Danish parliament.[26] A 2018

23 Roger Eatwell and Matthew Goodwin, *National Populism: The revolt against liberal democracy* (London, 2018), 73; Pauwels, 114-27.

24 Peter Walker in *The Independent,* 21 October 2016.

25 http://news.bbc.co.uk/1/hi/world/europe/8008364.stm; Walker, op. cit.; Bangstad, *Anders Breivik*. Breivik himself began his Islamophobic career in the party (Bangstad, 3-5).

26 Simon Tisdall, 'Danish rightwinger Kristian Thulesen Dahl rides high on

poll indicated that 27% of Danes agree with one populist leader's policy that observant Muslims should always be denied Danish citizenship. Her power base is primarily among middle-class professionals.[27]

Similar to these Scandinavian coercive-liberal formations is the Swiss People's Party, which has become the largest party in the country's parliament, and has in fact won the largest share of the national vote ever achieved by a Swiss party. Including many upper-echelon professionals, and supportive of the 2009 referendum in which 57.5% of voters supported a ban on minaret construction, the party is associated with anti-refugee and anti-Muslim sentiment and the promotion of liberal social beliefs throughout society.[28]

The French *laïciste* legacy which for two centuries has propounded a kind of secular fundamentalism finds itself locked in a particularly titanic battle with Muslim difference, angrily banning *ḥijāb* and long skirts in schools, and the public wearing of 'burkinis' and the *niqāb*, while the National Front's Marine Le Pen deploys feminism as her discursive weapon of choice against the Muslim presence in the country.[29] In Germany sixty percent of the population now claim that Islam does not belong in their country, a view publicly supported by the minister of the interior;[30] in the 2017 elections the anti-Muslim *Alternative für Deutschland* party won almost 13% of the vote.[31] In Italy, Matteo Salvini even becomes angry at the Arabic surname of the winner of the San Remo song competition.[32]

The 2018 study of national populism by Roger Eatwell and Matthew Goodwin points to a new style of politics rising fast across

---

populist tide', *The Guardian,* 19 June 2015.

27 *B.T.* (Copenhagen), 16 September 2018.

28 Martha C. Nussbaum, *The New Religious Intolerance: overcoming the politics of fear in an anxious age* (Cambridge MA, 2012), 43-8.

29 Jean Baubérot, *La laïcité falsifiée* (Paris, 2012), 93; Farris, 33-37.

30 Eatwell and Goodwin, 277.

31 Eatwell and Goodwin, 153.

32 'Salvini cuestiona al representante italiano de Eurovisión', *La Vanguardia,* 11 February 2019.

Europe: Lahabist, feminist, pro-Israel, pro-gay, and Eurosceptic, which cannot be simply classified as right-wing, since it adopts key egalitarian causes and thrives particularly in countries with strong liberal traditions (Le Pen's 2017 campaign slogan was 'Neither Right Nor Left'). New ideologies such as militantly anti-Islamic 'femonationalism' and 'homonationalism' form an increasingly important ingredient in the mix, again thwarting characterisations of political Lahabism as naturally conservative or right-wing.[33] The bestselling author Milo Yiannopoulos considers himself a Zionist right-winger, but also uses his militant homosexuality to proclaim gays as a vanguard class vital to protect the West from Islam.[34] Muslimness is the major unifying topic for these movements and is always the target of choice. Europe, newly unchristian, has strangely returned to its self-defining medieval custom of treating Islam as its main point of reference; the Pirenne Thesis has found a second wind.

Here in Britain the same tendency has to some extent been paralleled in the ideology of the British National Party, whose fortunes, however, have proved more volatile. As though to distance itself from the racism which lies at the roots of some of its discourse, a recording issued by the party, entitled 'Islam: A Threat to Us All: A Joint Statement by the British National Party, Sikhs and Hindus', described itself as 'a common effort to expose and resist the innate aggression of the imperialistic ideology of Islam'. As with many of its Continental allies the BNP gained popularity by rowing back on racist language, by adopting a vague narrative of Christian identity, and by attempting to forge alliances with non-Muslim Asians and

---

33 Farris, *op. cit.*; Jasbir K. Puar, *Terrorist Assemblages: homonationalism in queer times* (Durham NC, 2007). Puar's purpose is to evidence and parse 'the racism of the global gay left and the wholesale acceptance of the Islamophobic rhetoric that fuels the war on terror' (p.xi). For Le Pen's reaching out to LGBT groups see Eatwell and Goodwin, 67; for femonationalism in Norway in the context of the Breivik attacks see Bangstad, 117.

34 Nagle, 65. Yiannopoulos is atypical of the national populists, however, as he opposes many key feminist beliefs.

blacks.[35] The result was documents such as an 'Anti-Islam Supplement' of the BNP newsletter *Identity*, which ended with an appeal to 'Join Our Crusade'. The then chairman of the BNP, Nick Griffin, waded in with discussions of 'The Islamic Monster' and the 'New Crusade for the Survival of the West'.[36] The BNP's fortunes have since waned, although the appeal to identity and civilizational depth as a defensive line against the growing Ishmaelite presence remains, articulated in smaller groups such as the English Defence League,[37] and has been subtly internalised in much mainstream political and media discourse. A recent Chatham House survey shows that most British people want to see an end to all Muslim immigration.[38] Nonetheless, British populism remains less flagrantly Lahabist than most of its European counterparts, perhaps because some of its concerns have been directed most forcefully not against Muslims, but against the European Union through the UK Independence Party.

Across the continent traditional parties and narratives are facing an unprecedented challenge. Liberal discourse appears either to be failing, or in indicative ways to be morphing into a coercive liberalism of a remarkable and poorly-understood kind. Almost everywhere Muslims are observing the unsteady but unmistakeable rise of a fairly cohesive new political movement. Essentially populist and enabled by hardening economic stratification and the loss of godly and folk identity, it responds to the presence of migrants and refugees with an appealing smorgasbord of attitudes. It is not anti-democratic, and in fact favours the reinvigoration of democracy

---

35 Nick Lowles, 'Sleeping with the enemy: Griffin ponders black membership', *Searchlight*, February 2002; Ian Cobain, 'Racism, recruitment, and how the BNP believes it is just "one crisis away from power"', *The Guardian*, 22 December 2006; Nigel Copsey, *Contemporary British Fascism: the British National Party and the Quest for Legitimacy* (London, 2008).

36 www.bnp.org.uk/articles.html

37 Craig J.J. McCann, *The Prevent Strategy and Right-Wing Extremism: a case study of the English Defence League* (London, 2019).

38 Eatwell and Goodwin, 111.

through instruments such as referendums. It tends to be femonationalist and homonationalist, Europhobic, Zionist, and implicitly or explicitly committed to denying key civil rights to the Ishmaelite Other. As in the heyday of anti-Semitism its ranks are swelled by believers in conspiracy theories, notably the Great Replacement Theory: 31% of British voters for Brexit believe that Muslim immigration is part of an elite plot to make Europe an Islamic continent.[39]

As with the old anti-Semitism, insecurities about demographic change and hence the Other's sexuality supply an important component of this.[40] Muslims tend to have larger families, with the average Muslim mother in Europe giving birth to 2.9 children in comparison to the non-Muslim average of 1.9.[41] The virility of Muslim men as perceived in popular culture merges with this deficit to occasion widespread and often primitive anxieties: in Switzerland, where the national birthrate in 2017 stood at only 1.54 babies for each Swiss woman, the minaret ban is popularly and jocosely analysed by Muslims along Freudian lines. Testosterone levels and sperm counts are known to be steadily contracting across the Western world.[42] Further, the often-noted prominence of women in the national-populist leaderships is sometimes thought to represent the consequence of unconscious envy: the Ishmaelite offers a fecundity, a family life, and a physical consummation which

---

39 Esther Adler, 'Study shows 60% of Britons believe in conspiracy theories,' *The Guardian*, 23 November 2018; Natalie Nougeyrède, 'Europe is in the grip of conspiracy theories,' *The Guardian,* 1 Feb 2019.

40 During the Bosnian conflict, Islamophobic nationalist anxieties about fertility differentials seem to have facilitated the centrally-organised practice of rape; see Tatjana Takševa, 'Genocidal rape, enforced impregnation, and the discourse of Serbian national identity,' *Comparative Literature and Culture*, 17.iii (2015), art 2.

41 https://www.pewresearch.org/religion/2017/11/29/europes-growing-muslim-population/

42 T.G. Travison et al., 'A population-level decline in serum testosterone levels in American men,' *The Journal of Clinical Endocrinology and Metabolism* 92 (2007), 196–202.

is imagined to be less and less available from 'indigenous' men.[43] Like some other themes in Europe's Islamophobic symphony this draws on some very ancient terrors about the East and its atavistic and sexually dangerous religions, which might be traced back as far as Euripides' *Bacchae*. Whatever its etiology, the consequences of this anxiety about biological, demographic and sexological futures are becoming politically significant.

There is a further wind filling the sails of Europe's unease, which we might describe simply as the 'persistence of Ishmael'. The unreflective Lahabist mantras of 'the Crisis of Islam', or 'What Went Wrong?' conflict with an unnerved sense that Ishmael, for all his travails, continues to find religion indispensable. A Cardiff University research study on religious nurture in Muslim families shows that Muslims are generally rather successful in passing their beliefs and practices on to the new generation. The research showed that seventy-seven percent of adult Muslims 'actively practise the faith they were brought up in, compared with 29% percent of Christians and 65% of adherents of other religions.'[44] Again, these numbers directly challenge most sociological theories and allied prognostications, and arouse deep anxiety and bafflement in many secular hearts. In almost every European country the most striking example of what Lord Sacks calls 'the persistence of faith' is offered by Ishmael.

Where are the reasons? One ironic factor in the endurance of belief among the Muslim young might be Islamophobia itself, and the concomitant sense of inhabiting a beleaguered counter-culture. An eighteenth-century French visitor to England recorded this thought:

43 Reasons for the Muslim male eminence in this area are popularly said to include lower levels of pornography addiction, stronger male self-confidence, and less use of antidepressants.

44 J. Scourfield, C. Taylor, G. Moore, and S. Gilliat-Ray, 'The Intergenerational Transmission of Islam in England and Wales: Evidence from the Citizenship Survey', *Sociology* 46 (2012), 91-108.

> I find the Catholics much more zealous in England than in France: they are more scrupulous in their religious observance: it is because they are discriminated against. It is the disposition of all men in all countries to like doing what is forbidden.[45]

Perhaps more convincing than this essentially negative-reactive exegesis, and to make of Islamic persistence a sign of hope rather than anxiety to our secularised neighbours, we might invoke Charles Taylor's characterisation of our time as one of expressive individualism, an extension of the eighteenth-century fondness for the pursuit of the self's convictions irrespective of social convention, in a search not only for self but for truth, and even (though this is out of fashion) transcendence. The ongoing religiosity of the Muslim young may well be, paradoxically, the fruit of the self's rebellion: against parental folkways but also against the homogenising demands of the coercive liberal state and what Taylor calls the felt flatness of secular modernity. There is something edgy and exciting about an urban Muslim identity, with its hoodies, street credibility and talk of Palestinian freedom, which defies the stuffy disapproval of powerful liberal elites. But there is something of an inner complementarity here, as religion is experienced as God's hospital. Taylor points to the failure of the churches to attract young people because although these are certainly the sign of an alternative social imaginary, they reject, as he suggests, the Dionysian.[46] He does not note the Islamic exception in Western cities here, but we might observe that the Dionysian is precisely the principle that, for a Nietzsche hazardously looking for his superman, marks out Islam's 'virile' superiority over Christianity. Ian Almond has published interestingly on this.[47] Islam is perceived as holistic, as assertive,

---

45 La Rochefoucauld, tr. Norman Scarfe, *A Frenchman's Year in Suffolk: French impressions of Suffolk life in 1784* (Woodbridge, 1988), 68.

46 Charles Taylor, *A Secular Age* (Cambridge MA,2007), 503.

47 According to Almond, Nietzsche's critique focuses not on the non-existence of God as such, but on the uselessness of a certain 'life-hating', i.e.,

as affirmative of life, incorporating the body fully into faith. Thus it appeals to those seeking an alternative paradigm, a counter-culture to both secular instrumental modernity and to its Christian opposite; perhaps reminiscent of Marcuse's revolution against inhibitors, but with boundaries understood as *fiṭra*-compliant and thus instinctual. Ishmael is, after all, the heir 'according to the flesh'.[48] Although the vertical integration of Muslim discourse and mosque culture is poorly-advanced, and the leadership does little to lead the young, the timeless beauty of Islam's basic forms of life and its distinctive mind-body holism evidently inspire very many, and can furnish a magnetic witness in the context of a post-religious conurbation.

The appeal of the Sunna to those seeking an integrated and holistic counter-culture is evident in an age of anxiety, atheism, and fissiparous inner lives. 2018 was the year in which sales of antidepressants in secular Britain reached record levels. However the media only unhappily and reluctantly reported research at Mannheim University, which had applied the widely-known Satisfaction with Life Scale to adherents of different world views. This study of almost seventy thousand respondents showed that Muslims, of all groups, are the most satisfied with life, which they interpret in terms of the overall oneness or coherence of their worlds. In second place were those Christians who self-identified as neither Catholics nor Protestants; while Buddhists came third.[49] The results, published in the *Journal of the American Psychological Association*, run counter to the usual media image of the angry Ishmaelite and the shrouded, miserable Hagarene, but give a good account of our hypothesis that the holism of the Sunna, in which body, mind and spirit are experienced as aspects of a unity, and bodied forth in the form of the Muslim prayer, is making Islam a permanently serious

'Christian', concept of God. Ian Almond, *The New Orientalists: postmodern representations of Islam from Foucault to Baudrillard* (London, 2007), 7-21.

48 Galatians 4:29-31.

49 'Muslims have the highest life satisfaction,' *Daily Mail,* 10 April 2019.

option for younger, independently-minded dissidents in atomised modern cultures. Ishmael's resilience is thus real, a persistent irritant to an already confused Europe and an accelerator of the national-populist reflex.

However sinuous its tributaries, Europe's diverse but discrete populist turn represents the most significant new tide in the tempestuous and sometimes catastrophic history of the continent's politics, albeit one which is weakly noted by elites, perhaps because those elites may explicitly or covertly sympathise with many of the same xenophobic grievances, or may be either confused or reassured by the inclusion by the coercive-liberal parties of a large fraction of socially progressive language and policies. Across the continent, *ḥijāb* and *niqāb* bans smack Muslim communities into remembering their own deplorability, but claim their justification not in racist but in feminist beliefs. Carelessly dismissed as 'far-right', 'racist' or 'fascist', the new populism is often something quite different: xenophobic but pro-Israel, and in most cases firmly convinced of the modern body beliefs and the need to impose them by law. Deeply fearful of reproductive differentials and further immigration, it warmly embraces the 'Eurabia' fantasy of the inexorable Islamisation of the continent,[50] and connects to a fading European identity by maintaining what Jonathan Lyons has shown to be 'a comprehensive idea of Islam' whose key tropes stretch back at least a thousand years.[51] Europe no longer knows what it is; but it clutches with increasing intensity to a time-honoured conviction about what it is not.

* * *

The Muslim reaction to this new polemic has so far been indistinct. Most mosques continue to function as 'race temples' created as enclosures for single ethnicities,[52] and their mono-ethnic and in-

---

50 For a defence of this theory, with some interesting historical analogies, see Niall Ferguson, 'Paris and the fall of Rome,' *Boston Globe*, 16 November 2015.

51 Jonathan Lyons, *Islam through Western Eyes: from the Crusades to the War on Terrorism* (New York, 2012).

52 In the UK, 95% of mosques have single-ethnicity managements (Tariq

trospective leaderships are generally unfamiliar with any novelty occurring outside their silos. Such communities did not come to Europe to converse but to work, and this mentality continues to secure their unhappy silence. Extreme, *tanfīrī* believers, by contrast, treat the enmity as a useful although unsurprising proof of infidel inveteracy, and use it to widen their recruitment. Elite Muslims twisted by the usual inferiority complexes (their parents and grandparents having acclimatised their minds to colonial-era social Darwinist doctrines of the inevitable rise and rule of the benign West) now feel disorientation, even panic, as the cultural climate changes and liberal neighbours turn against them. Some react by discarding their identity and joining the chorus of Furies, hoping to find healing in what on some level they still know to be treason. Others simply keep a low profile, hoping and perhaps praying for better times.

There are more authentically Muslim strategies of response. Despite the rise of *tanfīr* and the continued prominence of race-temple Islam in community leadership, and despite the leaders whose highest ambition is to have their photograph taken beside an MP, one observes considerable numbers of ordinary believers dealing with the belligerent tropes in mature and morally impressive ways. Most, particularly those able to recall the spiritual virtues of an older Islam, recognise the urgency of the need for restraint and forbearance, and even for the kind of reparative response which is to be discussed in Chapter Seven. This must be further accompanied by a compassionate awareness that the suffering of secularised Europe, which casts around for inner repair after having endured the ripping-out of its historic cardiovascular system, is for many thoughtful individuals a truly intense and agonising trial, and is fur-

Modood, *Essays*, 7). Internal disagreements along ethnic and micro-ethnic lines are common and very destructive; see Amine El-Yousfi, 'Conflicting paradigms of religious and bureaucratic authority in a British mosque', *Religions* 10 (2019), 564. Evidently a race temple can also be dominated by white converts, as was notoriously the case at the Ihsan Mosque in Norwich during the 1990s; this is no less inimical to the spirit of Ishmaelite religion.

ther exacerbated by the continued erosion of comfortingly familiar landmarks by globalisation, visible demographic change and the new social beliefs. Humans are creatures of habit and are naturally conservative, and many, even most, Europeans feel disempowered by impersonal global forces, and denuded of meaning and context by the new digital and multicultural environment.

To point out the absurdity of scapegoating migrants and other Others for this deep and traumatic alienation will not defeat Lahabism and the other rancid pathologies of rejection. Painstaking Muslim corrections of formal and factual misunderstandings do not reach the heart of the matter; even when defeated, memes of Muslim viciousness will simply be replaced by others, of which cyberspace in particular harbours a limitless store. In part this is because anti-Muslim prejudice exists, as Yeğenoğlu suggests, primarily as a 'cultural representation of the West to itself by way of a detour through the other.'[53] Muslim atavism is true because anxious Western self-definition requires it to be true; it is a structural meta-truth unassailable by mere factual dissent, just as traditional anti-Semitism paid scant attention to realities in its creation of a folk devil against which Christendom reassuringly defined its identity. The traumatic dissolving of the Western Same is rendered less agonistic by the uniting and sense-giving sight of the single Semitic or Saracenic Other; even to acknowledge that Islam has internal disparities and gradations might be a reminder of the Same's own internal divisions and hence, implicitly, its vulnerability.

Diagnosis is not enough, however, nor the prescription of individual remedies for each case of inflammation; preventive medicine is always preferable. Muslim communities need to understand the pain which many Europeans feel in their spiritual and cultural exile, and find Islamic reasons not to patronise and moralise, but to sympathise with and respect their sense of loss and nostalgia for a more straightforward, homogeneous and comforting world. French author Michel Houellebecq's novels *Atomised* (1998) and *Platform*

---

53 Yeğenoğlu, 1.

(2003) consider modern society as a concatenation of unhappy individual particles caught in a Brownian motion with no discernable direction, source, or teleology; the lost *vieille France* is inaccessible, and only the body's hedonic functions give citizens a healing sense of continuity with what is humanly important. Youth, beauty and money are the sole true determiners of human worth and fulfilment. Parisians still intuit, in spite of everything, the reality of gender difference, of region, of religion, of culture and of family, but have been denied the philosophical or vernacular language which might legitimise their conviction that these are strong themes which ought naturally to shape the contours of life. Censored and frustrated, aware that their lack of faith and tradition matters, they learn to enjoy their atomised world, uniting only against Ishmael, the sole remaining subscriber to a metanarrative, however absurd and unpleasant his religion might seem to be.

To pray for this atomised Europe is thus the first duty of Muslims here, an activity more interesting by far than simply praying for one's own protection or requital, as the Fearful do; or drafting more legislation, as the sociologists advise. A *tawḥīd* and *daʿwa*-rooted Islam, secure in God's providence, will overpower any primitive mammalian fight-or-flight reflex, and will seek to understand and empathise. The Other becomes a kinsman of the Same when the language is not 'I' and 'Thou', but '*ummat al-ijāba*' and '*ummat al-daʿwa*': humanity is either from the *umma* that has 'responded', or the *umma* that is 'called'; and when we see neighbours in that designation we set aside clashing sociological nostrums and communalist paranoia, and remember the essential and non-negotiable Prophetic duty of a summons directed to all members of the Adamic tribe. And this can only happen when we understand those Others, and present the consummated Abrahamic truth as a specific remedy for the pains which they experience. Only this strategy, centred on religion and its founder as 'mercy to the worlds' (21:107), is likely to achieve permanent results.

This is where theology outnarrates sociological analysis. Unhappy Europeans see us in our strangeness, but within ourselves we do not doubt that Ishmael belongs, since the whole earth is God's. Cornish coasts, the Masurian lakes, the quiet Danube, are already our home, because we love their author and read their purpose. Our neighbours, however, those who are 'subject to the summons', increasingly feel themselves to be foreigners in their own lands; many are the modern citizens David Goodhart calls 'Anywheres' because they are uprooted from their own ancestral landscape, from which the time-honoured meaning has been drained.[54] When they visit the cosmopolitan cities the faces of passers-by seem worryingly different to them and fail to evoke childhood memories of a familiar local scene. Superficially Muslims look like outliers and visitors, even though deeply they belong, because they belong to God. Equally superficially, the secular 'indigenous' seem to belong, because of a genetic inheritance, and because they hold the keys to power and status and accept the regnant social beliefs; but in their depths they are alienated, since the sanctity which is the deep meaning of formerly enchanted landscapes has been veiled from them. To be alienated from meaning is effectively to be alienated from everything. Thus it is Godlessness and modernity, not immigration, which have turned the Somewheres into Anywheres; and so Ishmael, comporting himself as a believer, is not in fact inseparable from the problem, and should be able to function as remedy, not pathogen.

To make *daʿwa* to the type of atomised and sorrowful *étranger* described by Houellebecq will require several procedures. Firstly, the polarised and xenophobic discourse of the *tanfīrīs* and other Fearful in our communities must be eliminated in favour of the more difficult and authentic virtue of empathy and compassion. Hate speech wins no souls, while 'gentleness always makes a thing beautiful'.[55] 'Had you been harsh and hard of heart, they would have scattered

54 David Goodhart, *The Road to Somewhere: the new tribes shaping British politics* (London, 2017).

55 Muslim, Birr, 78.

from round about you.' (3:159) The impulse of the Fearful is typically to distribute badly-printed Zakir Naik pamphlets, imagining that disdain will somehow melt unbelieving hearts.[56] Alternatively they cling to parliament's skirts, begging for more legislation to suppress the hostile voices; and yet they have no strategy for dealing with the hostility itself, nor any willingness to suppose that they themselves should be open to self-scrutiny and change. But however blinkered their stubbornness, the *daᶜwa* ordinance cannot be abolished; and every human circumstance requires engaging with human spirits, even the most inflamed of which are never irrevocably closed. The Man of Praise, surrounded by intense and manifestly lethal enmity, never ceased to hope for the softening of hearts, and would frequently pray, 'O Lord, strengthen Islam with Abu'l-Ḥakam or ᶜUmar'.[57] Islam's great missionary successes have been the consequence of a similar optimism about monotheism's magnetic power.[58]

---

56 For *tanfīrī* success in exacerbating Islamophobia see Mohamed-Ali Adraoui, 'Salafism in France: ideology, practices and contradictions', 364-83 of Roel Meijer (ed.), *Global Salafism: Islam's new religious movement* (London, 2009).

57 Martin Lings, *Muhammad: his life based on the earliest sources* (Cambridge, 1991), 86.

58 Contrast the modern *tanfīrī* insurrections, driven by rage against the 'coalition' invasion of Iraq in 2003, with the Muslim response to the Mongol invasion of Iraq in 1258. In the present time, terroristic responses have led to the division and destruction of a Muslim land; in the earlier time, the Sufi preaching of the likes of Sayf al-Dīn Bākharzī, accompanied by respect for aspects of Mongol life, ended with the conversion of the invaders. The lesson is clear: *tanfīr* leads to catastrophe; *taṣawwuf* leads to astonishing victory. For the *ṭarīqa* preaching and patient wisdom which melted the Mongol hearts see A. Bausani, 'Religion under the Mongols,' pp.538-549 of the *Cambridge History of Iran,* V (Cambridge, 1968); T.W. Arnold, *The Preaching of Islam: a history of the propagation of the Muslim faith* (Westminster, 1896 and reprints), chapter 8; Devin DeWeese, *Islamization and Native Religion in the Golden Horde: Baba Tükles and Conversion to Islam in Historical and Epic Tradition* (Philadelphia, 1994).

The Fearful, often incredulous at the idea that the Other might recognise the truth carried by Ishmael, must be confronted with the evidence of the readiness of European activists, particularly on the Right, to see the value of our doctrine once Islam is made accessible and the *tanfīrīs* are out of sight. Take, as an example of this remarkable and moving ʿUmarī *metanoia*, the case of Werner Klawun, an MP for Germany's far-right National Democratic Party, who converted with the help of Goethe's great 'Sufi' poem the *West-östlicher Divan*. He was followed in 2018 by AfD politician Arthur Wagner, who promptly resigned his party membership. In Holland, former MP and Wilders colleague Joram van Klaveren converted in 2018, following The Hague right-wing city councillor Arnoud Van Doorn, who had announced his conversion in 2013. There are also undisclosed Muslims (the so-called 'submarines') in the populist parties, and others who are seriously studying the Ishmaelite way.

Many Muslims, particularly those swept up by the anti-tradition ideology of most sociologists, would prefer to see these conversions taking place on the Left, as was indeed normal a generation ago. Tage Lindbom (d.2001), chief theoretician of the Swedish Social Democratic Party, and Roger Garaudy (d.2012), former chair of the French Communist Party, were perhaps the best-known cases. However Europe's current traumas do not flow from a sense of alienation from the factors of production, but from an alienation from a humanly-craved sense of continuity and belonging. It is not difficult to see why it is the national populist movements which generate courageous dissidents able to transcend the narrow and often covertly racist narratives of their colleagues, to see Islam as a repository of timeless wisdom that enables them to lead lives that are genuinely in line with tradition, but which as an important bonus allows them to accept Jesus, the historic moral and spiritual patriarch of Europe, now wonderfully accessible as prophet rather than as Pantocrator. No alternative thought-system can offer them such a combination, and *in hoc signo vinces*.[59]

---

59 The Fearful cannot grasp that feuding Europe may be marching to a new

Fifteen years after *Platform* Houellebecq considered the question of Islam and European modernity from an altered angle. While the figure of the existentially-wounded, ageing male narrator is retained, as indeed he is in all his novels, we are now given a differently-twisted sense of the ontological presence of France's Maghrébin and Muslim Other. The novel *Submission* begins familiarly, with the protagonist François (the name perhaps chosen because he is in a sense representing the normative *homme français*) repeating standard French Islamophobic tropes: all Muslims are anti-Semitic and look threatening, while a liberal media and an 'oppressive multiculturalism' conspire to conceal their crimes; he praises his local shopkeeper: 'I was grateful to the Chinese for having always kept the neighbourhood free of blacks or Arabs.'[60] A Sorbonne professor, he knows the hollowness of contemporary thought from within, his *ennui* and black-comedic obsession with the meaninglessness of modernity are honest, though cold. He records the spectacle of 'Western civilisation now ending before our very eyes,'[61] it is old (and as George Steiner puts it, 'core-tired'); and he hardly cares. Only *eros* stirs him, and his looming andropause feels like a dismal premonition of death itself.

François' massive doctoral dissertation was entitled 'Joris-Karl Huysmans: Out of the Tunnel', and the novel is conceived as an exploration of various potential exits from modernity's directionless but brilliant mediocrity. Huysmans' 1884 novel *À rebours* had been a classic of decadent literature, a landmark on the road which linked de Sade with Baudelaire and Céline. Unlike the empirical English

---

but spiritual Milvian Bridge, thanks to the power of Ishmaelite monotheism which so often inverts hierarchies and confounds predictions. One reads with amusement this prediction in a 1909 missionary manual: 'Dedicated to the Public Schoolboys of Great Britain, who have a Big Part yet to play in shaping the Future of Islam'. Theodore R.W. Lunt, *The Story of Islam* (London, 1909), v.

60 Michel Houellebecq, tr. Lorin Stein, *Submission* (London, 2015), 58.

61 Houellebecq, *Submission,* 6.

and their pragmatic American children, French thinkers, amputated systemically from theology, were truer to the modern spirit, being willing to experience and even savour an aesthetic rush of vertigo in the honest contemplation of the void left by the retreat of religion. In *À rebours* Huysmans documents the crepuscular pleasures of inactivity, erotic excess and a habit of scathing critique directed against all classes of society. François' thesis focuses on Huysmans' crisis, in which the contemplation of a statue of Christ impels him finally to choose Catholicism over suicide, moved by the idea that the world finds its meaning in pain and suffering. Something similar befell Louis Massignon, a disciple of the later Huysmans, who after his own conversion to Catholicism spent his life creatively experiencing the vertigo of a different nearness: that of Islam. Houellebecq's narrator, a century on, considers whether he should take the same road, and so he visits monasteries; in fact in the author's original plan for the novel François does accept baptism. The climax of the book takes place at the shrine of the Black Virgin of Rocamadour, a historically-freighted location which is also home to the venerated sword once wielded by Roland against the invading Moors. The narrator has fled Paris because of riots between Muslims and skinheads which have left the city paralysed. Here, in the middle of a dreaming rural France he hardly knows, the narrator feels himself connecting with ancestral impulses: this is, after all, the very place where Charles Martel finally defeated the Saracen hordes in a battle redolent today with vast symbolic significance for the New Right across the European continent.

Standing between the magnets of modern physicalism and Catholic faith the narrator records this:

> I went back to the Chapel of Our Lady, which now was deserted. The Virgin waited in the shadows, calm and timeless. She had sovereignty, she had power, but little by little I felt myself losing touch, I felt her moving away from me in space and across the centuries while I sat there in my pew, shrivelled and puny. After an hour, I got up, fully deserted by the

> Spirit, reduced to my damaged, perishable body, and I sadly descended the stairs that led to the car park.[62]

Driving back to Paris the narrator finds that in the crisis of French politics a Muslim Party has entered government, the Socialists having enlisted its support to keep Marine Le Pen from entering the Elysée. (Muslims needed their own political formation, he reflects, since the existing left-right spectrum had effectively disenfranchised them: socially conservative, they were rejected on cultural and national grounds by the Right.) The new party gains the education portfolio, and the new Islamic University of the Sorbonne promotes a cohort of hitherto submariner converts who now break surface, many of them readers of Guénon and of back issues of his storied journal *Études Traditionelles*. A formerly right-wing and nativist colleague is now François' line manager: a convert who worked on Rimbaud (who had arguably also been a Muslim neophyte, and had been important for the Decadent movement a century before). Reflecting on the demographic inevitability of Muslim prevalence the convert Rediger observes: 'liberal individualism triumphed as long as it undermined intermediate structures such as nations, corporations, castes, but when it attacked that ultimate social structure, the family, and thus the birth rate, it signed its own death warrant.'[63] Islam is, in contrast to Huysmans' Catholic embrace of tragedy, world-affirming and lyrical, and allows man's sensuality a lawful and even polygamous outlet. And thus Houellebecq changes his plot: the narrator drifts into Islam.

Of the many novels written to explore Europe's fears about Muslim minorities this is certainly the most subtle and ambiguous, and on its publication in 2015 the reviewers struggled to place it. Houellebecq, true to his ostensibly Decadent principles, adores shocking his readers; even in the 21st century *épater les bourgeois* is a familiar but still rewarding game which he plays masterfully; and so having

62 Houellebecq, *Submission*, 139.

63 Houellebecq, *Submission*, 226.

offended blacks, lesbians, Muslims, feminists, Belgians, and assorted human rights activists, he must here be crafting the greatest and most decadent shock of all: a portrait of an Islamic future for the City of Light which is successful, not dystopic; a very *raisonnable* alternative to modern *anomie* and social implosion.

But in fact the novel marks the author's choice for (as one would have put it a century ago) Symbolism over Decadence: François cites Mallarmé, and Baudelaire should be added: this is the choice of an experience of modernity's void which allows the intuition of transcendence. In words, in what we say, as George Steiner puts it, there is a real presence. So Houellebecq, who in some ways is writing the novel as an exploratory and dramatised exercise in literary criticism, is no outsider, but remains strongly and faithfully part of a French literary tradition. The richness of his prose and the miracle of language's containment of fine human subtleties and intersubjectivities—a paradox which he ponders early in the book—point us to what is outside itself. What is new is that Islam now replaces the mystical, Masonic or Hermetic dabblings which seduced nineteenth-century Symbolists, just as it out-narrates a dusty and inaccessible Catholicism: thanks to its fecundity and its Dionysian *jouissance* it is more within his Parisian reach, despite the ambient shouting of Islamophobes and the ironic shrugs of Sorbonne deconstructionists. Although Houellebecq himself has not followed his François he has given us a work which reminds us of the complexity and balance of the current somewhat apocalyptic situation in the world's first secular republic; amidst the wild unhappiness of those who became the *gilets jaunes* this presents an outstanding and rather beautiful sign of vertigo.

The author has evidently shifted his ground: in the 'republic of Islamophobia' Islam as literally a *bête noire* has become in his near-future fantasy an imagined and a moral alternative. He has, following recent difficult events in his personal life, moved on from his former atheism, and now realises that 'there is a real need for God'. On his ongoing pessimism about European civilisation he records in an interview which seems hardly to have been noticed by his reviewers, that

> the despair comes from saying good-bye to a civilization, however ancient. But in the end the Koran turns out to be much better than I thought, now that I've reread it—or rather, read it. The most obvious conclusion is that the jihadists are bad Muslims. Obviously, as with all religious texts, there is room for interpretation, but an honest reading will conclude that a holy war of aggression is not generally sanctioned, prayer alone is valid. So you might say I've changed my opinion. That's why I don't feel that I'm writing out of fear. I feel, rather, that we can make arrangements. The feminists will not be able to, if we're being completely honest. But I and lots of other people will.[64]

Houellebecq goes on to comment that globalised and 'product-addicted' Europe is committing suicide, but that Islam's witness, far from being a cause of decline, is in fact grounds for optimism: 'for people to convert is a sign of hope; it is not a threat. It means they aspire to a new kind of society.'

This recurrent gravitation should allow theologians to remember the true calling of Ishmaelites in Europe. For the populist politicians who become Muslim, whether in fiction or in reality, it seems that it is the universalism of Islam and its Abrahamic recognisability which open hearts. As with Klawun, who converted with the help of Goethe, they experience Islam as a kind of homeward journey, adding an ironic twist to Yeğenoğlu's insight.

The Fearful will find this phenomenon as difficult to understand as the journalists and sociologists do, and will typically treat it as an anomaly,[65] or perhaps as an opportunity to brandish trophy-converts

64 'Scare Tactics: Michel Houellebecq defends his controversial new book,' interview with Sylvain Bourmeau in the *Paris Review*, 2 January 2015.

65 See the memoir of a guard at Guantánamo, where the detainees refused to believe his conversion to Islam, thereby revealing their lack of faith in its power to satisfy the spiritual need of the human heart. Terry C. Holdbrooks

in order to prop up a shattered self-esteem. The reality, however, particularly among thinking people, is that the gravitational field of Islam is felt most strongly on the Right, even on the nativist Right. In France, despite the national rage against Islam, public intellectuals (a breed virtually unknown in England) have always been conscious of Islam not only as an exotic principle, but as an annoying, detestable but acknowledged alternative: consider the place in French culture of Isabelle Eberhardt, Valentine de Saint-Point, Eva de Vitray-Meyerovitch, Roger Garaudy, Maurice Béjart, René Guénon himself and others: in France the supposed Other was within as an indigenous alternative to the Same, long before the migrant Arab appeared *intra portas*.

On careful, unemotive consideration, this philo-Islamic substrate and present-day conversion pattern will not startle us. Islam, despite Orientalism, is not proper to any given culture or the proudly exotic performances staged by facsimile *ṭarīqas* or the race temples: it is universal, and its scripture exercises global appeal and power, having existed at the revered centre of life for thriving and spiritually fecund communities across the enormous and enormously-diverse Islamic world for many centuries. *Tanfīrīs* tend to reduce Islam to a form of diasporic Arab nationalism, since they have little respect for cultural difference or evolutions in Islamic history beyond the first three generations. However Islamic culture's historic reality, shaped by a more careful understanding of Qur'an and Sunna, has been supportive of a vibrant diversity: Muslims in Turkey, for example, can hardly be seen as an Arab diaspora.[66] To engage the *ummat al-daʿwa* in Europe we must re-activate this rule. It imposes the duty, painful for some, of shedding the *ʿurf* and *ʿāda* decorations of foreign lands. Amsterdam Muslims who wear Indonesian apparel, eat Indonesian food and maintain an Indonesian outlook, cannot expect to spread their faith to their neighbours, who naturally will

---

Jr, *Traitor?* (Lexington KY, 2013).

66 See Chapter 3 in this book, also Umar Abd-Allah, 'Islam and the Cultural Imperative', at http://www.artsrn.ualberta.ca/ .

not be enabled to envisage how Islam might be for Dutch people.

The progressive but merciful elimination of overseas *ᶜurf* and *ᶜāda* must therefore become an urgent priority for Muslim organisations, if they accept that the prime Sharia legitimation of their presence is *daᶜwa*. It is also a matter of prudence. Enmity towards Ishmael is often driven by dislike for conspicuous cultural or even culinary superficialities that are not required by Sacred Law. For us to hold such targets over our hearts is foolhardy.

Beyond this inhabiting, European Muslim communities should explore strategies of reactivating their historic patterns of cultural enrichment. When Islam touched the languages of Iran, Central Asia, the Malay archipelago and all the other linguistic worlds which it penetrated, the result was not the decline of those languages but their quick invigoration. The same should be expected for the languages of Europe, in which Muslims should not only read but write expressively. We need to master and live at home in the national tongues of Europe, for it is only in those languages that we will be heard. A principle of vertical integration should encourage Muslims to excavate the local literatures to discover genres and themes which can enrich Muslim sensibilities and which in turn could be enriched by Islam, and which could deepen the appeal and rootedness of Ishmaelite religion in these new semantic homes. *Mawlid* and other literatures are frequently composed in the vernacular, and as they appear in European languages they will ennoble them and give Islam a voice that vindicates it as a universal rather than a foreign faith.[67] When the majesty of Muslim monotheism and the beauty of its narratives appear in worthy English, or French, or Danish verse and prose, the defences of anti-immigrant zealots and 'counter-jihad' protestors will be crucially enfeebled, for as Iris Murdoch observed, beauty has an 'unselfing' power.

Such opportunities have, to date, been very conspicuously missed. Migrant communities which were transported by global

67 For a good English *mawlid* see Noor-un-Nisaa Yusuf, *The Soliloquy of the Full Moon* (Birmingham, 2015).

economic forces to the former colonial metropoli in the 1950s and 1960s to serve in industrial and menial roles came not to spread their religion but to improve their living standards. In almost every case their *hijra* was for *dunyā*. They did not consult the ulema, or the muftis, or the *pīrs*, for guidance on the validity of their choice to leave the *Dār al-Islām*, perhaps because many or most were convinced that their sojourn in unbelieving lands would be temporary. Even when the continuing economic failure of their countries of origin, resulting usually from secular or carceral-Islamist mismanagement, persuaded them to stay, the intention continued to be materialistic and pragmatic, and at no point did these communities engage in a systematic study of their situation from a classical Sharia angle. This defect of intention (*niyya*) is one reason why the second and third generations, to whose spiritual and moral formation the first generation gave no careful thought, now often manifest ugly and growing dysfunctions, including *tanfīrī* recruitment, drug addiction, the predatory grooming of underage girls, and large-scale criminalisation. The older generation threw their babies into the melting-pot, hoping for the best, and failed to give their growing children a theology of belonging, with the result that the youth were not securely established in a consistent cognitive frame or an attendant comprehensive morality. As their misfortune unfolded, the ambient society either ignored them, queried their presence, or treated them according to social science paradigms rooted in the incongruous 'race relations' philosophy. An Islam whose articulation belonged overseas proved only weakly capable of claiming the deep loyalty of a new generation Europeanised by the schools and confused about its identity. In Britain the Dār al-ʿUlūm seminaries, mostly determined to replicate Indic scholarly and cultural forms, tended to produce graduates who are, as the sceptics claim, 'mango trees planted in Lancashire.' When a European Muslim leadership at last emerged that claimed to be religious rather than merely ethnic, it was for years influenced by Movement Islams whose agendas had been devised abroad and which spoke only faintly to Western

Muslims, and which often platformed the segregationist and insulting rhetoric of 'not imitating the *kuffār*', a perennially indicative theme for the Fearful.

The major alternative to their dreary conference-centred ideology-religion with its grievance culture and its often distinctly Pecksniffian cast of characters was the Sufi-themed mosque formations. These, however, seemed to retain no interest in reviving the historic patterns of Islamic mission through inculturation: the seventeenth-century Chishtī saints had learned and sung in local vernaculars to local unbelievers, and hence secured proselytes in many millions; and yet the spiritual heirs of the Qādirīs, Naqshbandīs, Chishtīs and others who settled in the UK turned their assemblies into defensive bunkers of overseas Islam which are notable for a mindset of seeming apathy towards their *daʿwa* responsibilities. The same applies to many Mourides in France and Tijānīs in Italy. The cultural mediators who once generated the most hospitable areas of overlap and cultural hybridisation have thus created in Europe a constellation of spaces which are among the least open to cross-fecundation, Islamic diversity and mutual regard. To read the ethnographic studies of, say, Pnina Werbner on *pīr-murīd* networks in England is to be astounded at the inauthenticity which lies behind the façade of uncompromising and faithful mimesis of subcontinental Sufi life. Indian *taṣawwuf* grew and established its glory through *daʿwa*; when this priority vanishes it finds it difficult to become more than a harmless and exotic amateur dramatic society or an ethnic glee club.[68] The same applies to many communities of converts and others who have studied *taṣawwuf* abroad, and who on their return to Europe insist on defying the deep traditions of the Sufi vision and even the direct instructions of their teachers by creating enclaves of deep cultural difference. Even where they are picturesque such exotic performances are poorly equipped to refute the Lahabists of Generation Identity. Still more troublingly, reli-

68 For a critique of this meaningless formalism see Abū Fayḍān Farīdī (Muhammad Riedinger), *The Broken Kashkol of Sufidom* (Karachi, 2015).

gion's unique ability to abolish our sense of alienation can only be enfeebled by the adoption of forms which are only weakly-related to the realities which participants experience in their more everyday lives and linguistic practice; again, a painful state of cognitive dissidence tends inevitably to ensue. For this reason, converts, who historically have played a key role in the revival and spread of Islam,[69] must shoulder a heavy share of blame: they have in many cases misread Sufism and missed their strategic vocation.[70]

A more authentic, less compromised *taṣawwuf* would confidently return to the classical principle of inculturation for the sake of *daʿwa* and the ready conveyance of *tawḥīd*. The form of this in Europe necessarily varies according to culture and region. In Germany, younger Muslims are already rejecting the moribund culture of the race temples and the facsimile-*ṭarīqas*, and attempting to mine their country's heritage for gold that can be smelted in a Muslim way. 'Wisdom is the believer's lost riding beast; wherever he finds it, he has the most right to it,' as a hadith advises.[71] Goethe's *Mahometsgesang* is a remarkable proof of the convergence of Fearless Islam with many of the concerns of Romanticism, presenting the Man of Praise as a youthful mountain stream bringing life and civilisation to the world; and its impact on one AfD neophyte has already been mentioned.[72] There is an entire literature which displays or hints at this invaluable starting-point for a genuinely German Muslim

---

69 Richard Bulliet, *Islam: the view from the edge* (New York, 1995); Tobias P. Graf, *The Sultan's Renegades: Christian-European Converts to Islam and the Making of the Ottoman Elite 1575-1610* (Oxford, 2017).

70 The point is made by Etsko Schuitema, *The Millennium Discourses* (Johannesburg, 2011), 12.

71 Tirmidhī, ʿIlm, 19; Ibn Māja, Zuhd, 15; for variants see Muḥammad al-Sakhāwī, *al-Maqāṣid al-Ḥasana fī bayān kathīrin min al-aḥādīth al-mushtahira ʿala'l-alsina* (Beirut, 1405/1985), 310-21.

72 Cf. Johann Von Goethe, tr. Eric Ormsby, *West-Eastern Divan, complete, annotated new translation, including Goethe's 'Notes and Essays' and the unpublished poems* (London, 2019).

narrative.[73] In their quest for a vertical integration into a truly great culture Muslims will not accept everything by any means; but no German ever did. The exercise will be a quest for the *fiṭra* and its expressions and approximations, in architecture, literature, and song.

In the United Kingdom a Muslim history already exists in the literature and idiom of Abdullah Quilliam's community in Victorian Liverpool which, unlike most more recent groups, insisted on a recognisably local religious style to attract and retain newcomers.[74] The literature of that community is still available for use.[75] But the integration must find further roots, researching and accessing those dimensions of British moral and sacred style which are compatible with Islamic revelation. These are abundant, although rejected and ignored by the moderns; can we tell, for instance, whether the following text originates in seventeenth-century Herat or in Hertfordshire?

> The Services which the world doth you, are transcendent to all imagination. Did it only sustain your body and preserve your life, and comfort your senses, you were bound to value it as much as those services were worth: but it discovers the being of God unto you, it opens His nature, and shews you His wisdom, goodness and power, it magnifies His love unto you, it serves Angels and men for you, it entertains you with many lovely and glorious objects, it feeds you with joys, and becomes a theme that furnishes you with perpetual praises and thanksgivings, it enflameth you with the love of God, and is the link of your union with Him. It is the temple wherein you are exalted to glory and honour, and the visible

73 Jeffrey Einboden, *Islam and Romanticism: Muslim currents from Goethe to Emerson* (Oxford, 2014).

74 Ron Geaves, *Islam in Victorian Britain: the life and times of Abdullah Quilliam* (Markfield, 2010), 131-65.

75 Abdal Hakim Murad, *Muslim Songs of the British Isles* (London, 2005); Brent D. Singleton, *The Convert's Passion: an anthology of Islamic poetry from late Victorian and Edwardian Britain* (Rockville MD, 2009).

> porch or gate of Eternity: a sure pledge of Eternal joys, to all them that walk before God and are perfect in it.[76]

Of George Herbert's poem 'Love bade me welcome', Clifford Longley writes that it has 'some affinity with medieval Islamic metaphysical poetry,'[77] a judgement which may be an understatement; and cases of such convergences in sensibility could readily be multiplied. Xenophobes on both sides will bridle at this, their fearfulness insisting on clear dichotomies and oppositions; but the reality is that just as many aspects of Islamic architecture, music and literature are valued in England, venerated in its museums, and welcomed into educated homes, there are traditional English and European religious styles worthy of Muslim respect, offering a subsoil where Muslim roots may discerningly penetrate, thereby enabling the project of vertical integration. Fearful Islamists, *tanfīrīs*, Eurabia paranoics and social scientists may be incredulous, but England's past is not another country.[78] Our roots may sit uncomfortably in the shallow surface of materialist Britain, but once they sink deeper they will find much to remind them that this earth, like every earth, belongs to God.

Lahabism or Islamophobia, then, is a case of mistaken identity. Ishmael is not validly Europe's paradigm of the Dark Other, the 'newer Semite', the barbarian who will invade, proliferate and conquer civilisation in the name of an utterly different and savage god. As we will see in the next chapter, an authentic Islam which rises above Fearful complexes and insecurities is able to see that European Muslims and Bible believers, *ahl al-kitāb,* evidently converge on key Abrahamic ideals, though never perfectly. Neirynck's apocalypse would be the outcome not of any intrinsic instability of Abrahamic neighbourliness, but of the neglect of Abrahamic love and hospitality, of curiosity and the ability to find value in others and

76 Thomas Traherne, *Centuries of Meditation* (London, 1960), 57.

77 Clifford Longley, column in *The Tablet*, 2 April 1999.

78 T.J. Winter, *British Muslim Identity: past, problems, prospects,* 2nd edition (London, 2013).

in their cultural forms. In 2020, Britain was astounded to learn that the first doctors to die of the Corona virus were all Muslims; these martyrs witnessed with their lives to Islam's culture of sacrifice and service, driving a stake through the heart of the nation's Lahabists. And so Muslims face a choice between fundamentalism and authenticity which is not simply a choice between Fearful and classical interpretations of scripture, but entails a major decision about the future of *daʿwa* and the flourishing of Ishmael in the European context, at once so dangerous and promising.

CHAPTER 3

British Muslims and the rhetoric of indigenisation

SINCE THE 1960S, the screenwriter Alan Bennett has kept his thumb unerringly close to the British national pulse. He began with the comedic revue *Beyond the Fringe* with Peter Cook and Dudley Moore, and then moved through *Talking Heads* and the *Madness of King George*, to his 2009 hit *The Habit of Art*, which played to packed houses at the National Theatre. A North Country man who once thought he would be a vicar, formed in the now unimaginable England of the Forties and Fifties, his humour and determinedly humane scrutiny of the national character make him, perhaps, the nearest thing England has to Matt Groening, creator of *The Simpsons*. He remembers the Christian values of close-knit Yorkshire towns of the 1940s, but unfailingly observes the comedy of the new Britain of the iPod, the iPad, and the metrosexual generation.

Bennett recently emerged from a bout of writer's block to deliver up a short story.[1] His head had been full of ideas, apparently, but they were 'too bleak to visit on the public'. The story that finally appeared, 'The Laying On of Hands,' is, he says, 'as dark as I could let myself be publicly without being rejected altogether.' At first blush it is not clear what he means. The story is written with a light touch, and is in places riotously funny. But it does have a sharp point.

The chief character is a young and moderately high-church vicar and the action takes place entirely in his church, as he conducts a

1 Alan Bennett, 'The Laying On of Hands', in *Four Stories* (London, 2014), 1-78.

memorial service for Clive, a masseur and rent boy whose services he had himself enjoyed. The congregation, made up largely of the Cool Britannia elite, includes many of the discreet masseur's other clients. Chat-show hosts and academics are disproportionately represented, of course, but there is also a bishop, a senior Treasury official, and an architect. Some are men, but there are grieving women also, since Clive, like Bennett himself, had been of ambiguous preferences. (In a postmodern world that resents fixed essences of any kind, even the idea of a gay identity seems to have become *passé*.)

The liturgy cannot, of course, presume any religious commitment on the part of the bereaved. Readings and prayers are generic, and the life hereafter goes unmentioned. Yet the spirit of judgment is in the air. This takes its most immediate form in the shape of a diocesan inspector, Archdeacon Treacher, who sits at the back to make notes on the incumbent's performance. Of course, he is interested only in his liturgical propriety; in the Noughties it is not the vicar's homosexuality which is the object of judgment. As Treacher reflects,

> Once upon a time homosexuals had made excellent priests and still could so long as they were sensible. The homosexuals Treacher preferred were dry, acerbic and, of course, unavowed; A.E. Housman the type that he approved of, minus the poetry, of course, and (though this was less important) minus the atheism.[2]

The other judgment that hangs in the air is that of HIV/AIDS. The congregation, free of any concern for their friend's fate in an afterlife, are pondering their own mortality. Towards the end of an embarrassing and very un-English addition to the liturgy, when the congregants stand up one after another to reminisce about the deceased, it becomes clear that Clive had been killed not by the modern plague, but by a poisonous caterpillar while holidaying in Peru. As this revelation dawns on the congregation, the church seems

2 Bennett, 28.

filled with light, and the burden is lifted. The priest, too, feels that he has been saved.

The dismayed diocesan inspector, formed in a very different age, slips out. 'He is not entirely to be deplored,' says Bennett, 'standing in this tale for dignity, formality, and self-restraint.'

> Less feeling was what Treacher wanted, the services of the church, as he saw it, a refuge from the prevailing sloppiness. As opportunities multiplied for the display of sentiment in public and on television—confessing, grieving, and giving way to anger, and always with a ready access to tears—so it seemed to Treacher that there was needed a place for dryness and self-control and this was the church. It was not a popular view and he sometimes felt that he had much in common with a Jesuit priest on the run in Elizabethan England—clandestine, subversive and holding to the old faith, even though the tenets of that faith, discretion, understatement and respect for tradition, might seem more suited to tailoring than they did to religion.
>
> Once out of the churchyard the Archdeacon lit up, his smoking further evidence that there was more to this man than has been told in this tale. There had briefly been a Mrs Treacher, a nice woman, but she had died. He would die soon, too, and the Bishop at least would be relieved.[3]

Of course Bennett seeks neither to edify nor to warn us with this yarn. He merely invites us to reflect on the ironies implicit in a national life in which a state church, whose superb buildings and ceremonies offer an image of dignity and restraint to an age in which those principles are strange, still tries to accommodate the diversity of godless Britain. The price, however, is its commitment to *kerygma*. Preaching, conversion, truth itself, can hardly be appropriate features of such settings.

The 'tarnished throng' in Bennett's church might, he says, 'be taken as a version of England,' and a battalion of sociologists will

3 Bennett, 61-2.

agree. The Church today can resemble an eggshell, a membrane of propriety and dignified forms, behind which throbs the secular drumbeat of the modern Mardi Gras: the aspirational yuppie culture cultivated by Thatcher, the feelgood spin of a Labour without socialism, the National Lottery, pole-dancing clubs, Facebook and Myspace.

British Muslim communities have been studied in many ways; but the surely obvious backdrop of the decline of the nation's religious life has not always been sufficiently noted. Perhaps this is symptomatic of the training of many researchers in the older paradigms of the study of that vague thing, 'race relations': it was understood that the default normalcy in Britain, a kind of generic whiteness, was permanent. Shift the focus from race to religion, however, and it is not clear that there *is* an unchanging British default. Understanding the journey British Muslims have made from the 1950s and earlier, to the current decade, cannot properly be attempted unless we recall that British religiosity and the value system it supported have changed almost beyond recognition. At the beginning of this period Muslims found themselves in a largely churchgoing society ruled by Mrs Miniver, where queers were in the closet and nice girls said no. Now, in the words of the Anglican essayist Michael Hampson:

> Christianity today occupies the same space on the fringes of mainstream culture as any other major or minor religious cult or claim from any continent—spiritualism, astrology, reincarnation—perhaps more respectable than Wicca or clairvoyance but less respectable than reiki or domestic feng shui.[4]

The statistics need only brief citation. In a 2004 poll, only forty-four percent of British citizens responded positively when asked whether they believed in God. A 2007 Tearfund survey found that sixty-six percent of British subjects, that is to say, 32.2 million people, had no contact with the Church or with any other religion.

---

4 Michael Hampson, *Last Rites: the End of the Church of England* (Cambridge, 2006), 14.

Half of these were once religious, but are now lapsed; the other half (16.1 million) had never experienced membership of any religion.[5] A British Social Attitudes survey suggests that the percentage of those who claim membership of the established church has fallen from forty percent in 1983 to only seventeen percent in 2014. Only three percent of British adults under the age of twenty-four describe themselves as Anglican.[6]

The decline of the national church has been so precipitous that in 2007 a survey by Christian Research indicated that for the first time since the Reformation, more people in this country were attending Catholic than Anglican services. The average attendance at the Roman mass was 861,000 people, compared with 852,000 who appeared at a Church of England Sunday service. The decline in Anglican worshippers reached a vertiginous twenty percent between 2000 and 2006; the decline in Catholic attendance was somewhat less, at thirteen percent, thanks in part to immigration from Catholic countries, notably Poland. Religious illiteracy also appears to be widespread: a recent report commented that the 1979 Monty Python film *The Life of Brian* could not be made today because a modern audience would not understand the religious references.[7]

A contest is underway among sociologists of religion who ponder these data. An older school maintains that Britain's faith has seen a steady decline since the Industrial Revolution and the Enlightenment. What we are now seeing is simply the endgame of a very slow process. Steve Bruce, in his book *God is Dead*, is one exponent of this view.[8] Others, however, have suggested that the evidence simply does not support this image of a slow and steady decline. Callum Brown, for instance, claims that as late as the mid-twentieth cen-

5 Jacinta Ashworth and Ian Farthing, *Churchgoing in the UK* (Teddington, 2007).

6 Damian Thompson, '2067: The end of British Christianity', *The Spectator,* 13 June 2015.

7 Elizabeth Butler-Sloss (chair), *Living with Difference: community, diversity and the common good* (Cambridge, 2015), 26.

8 Steve Bruce, *God is Dead: Secularization in the West* (New York, 2002).

tury Christianity was moderately thriving and that its current weakness is the result of a very recent and precipitate collapse.[9] Compare the figures for religiously-solemnized marriages. In 1962, seventy percent of the population was married in a religious ceremony, a figure commensurate with nineteenth-century norms. Only eight years later it had fallen to sixty percent, slumping to thirty-nine percent in 1997. By 2012 it had declined further to thirty percent.[10]

The figures for Anglican baptism tell a similar story. In 1900, for every thousand live births, 609 baptisms took place. In 1927 the number had actually risen to 668, dropping back to 602 in 1956. And then the same slump can be observed: down to 466 in 1970, 365 in 1981, and 228 in 1997. The de-baptism movement is a particularly striking sign of this: according to the National Secular Society, by the year 2009 a hundred thousand people had felt strongly enough to pay three pounds to download forms and officially register their rejection of their baptism.

Brown shows that church membership, too, indicates that the older model of a gently secularising Britain needs to be replaced by a model of robust religiosity which endured well into the mid-twentieth century, followed by a sudden decline. Church membership rose in the nineteenth century, reaching a peak in England and Wales in 1904, and in 1905 in Scotland. The figures decline until the Second World War, when they pick up again, rising to a second climax in 1959. Then the sudden descent begins, and it is continuing apace. On current trends the Church of Scotland calculates that by the year 2030 it will have ceased to exist. Former Archbishop of Canterbury George Carey claims that the Church of England is 'one generation away from extinction'.[11]

---

9 Callum Brown, *The Death of Christian Britain: Understanding Secularisation 1800-2000* (London, 2000).

10 John Haskey, in Joanna Miles, Perveez Mody and Rebecca Probert (eds.), *Marriage Rites and Rights* (London, 2015), 28.

11 Thompson, '2067'.

In the context of this chapter we need not spend time considering the various explanations of this trend, or the odd, and to many analysts still confounding, contrast with the continued (though sometimes exaggerated) buoyancy of religious faith in America.[12] But it helps to remember that integration today, whatever it means, must signify something radically distinct from what it was thought to require in the Britain which Muslim migrants reached before, say, the Wolfenden Report, the Chatterley Trial, and the Beatles' first LP. Integration signifies not the deepening engagement of an essential Muslimness with a recognisable Britishness, which was supported by a national church rooted in perennial truths. It looks more like an eternally renegotiated process whereby a religious minority is expected permanently to keep in step with values of markedly utilitarian and secular provenance, values which are not anchored to a Rock of Ages but drift in tides of ceaseless emendation and change. In other words, the current Government or academic agenda on integration and social cohesion is always highly provisional, since the social beliefs to which citizens are invited to comply are themselves permanently mobile. 'Ideas of justice are as timeless as fashions in hats,' as an atheist philosopher observes.[13] Perhaps Muslims should be encouraged by this: a Britain that required accession to values conceived as true or absolute would be theologically far harder for believers, who believe that theirs are the true absolutes, to engage with. The elites should not insist on compliance with their social beliefs too absolutely, since they must appreciate that they will almost certainly drift and change.

Having begun by sketching the unexpected situation of British Muslims, who find that they migrated to a strongly religious culture just before its substantial collapse and replacement by an ever-shifting claimed consensus on 'values', we will now change the

12 Churchgoing is in decline in the US also; see Pew Research, 2015, at pewforum.org: 'Christians Decline Sharply as Share of Population'.

13 John Gray, *Straw Dogs: thoughts on humans and other animals* (London, 2002), 103.

subject rather precipitately, and offer some reflections on the nature of the Islam which is being invited to experience integration, as seen from a pre-1960s British perspective. We will do this by enlisting two neglected and underestimated observers, both popular writers and Catholic apologists: G.K. Chesterton (1874-1936) and Hilaire Belloc (1870-1953).

Chesterton first. As a revanchist English Catholic he had no difficulty with the old preconciliar formula of *extra ecclesiam nulla salus* (no salvation outside the Church). His view of Islam was remote from the ecumenical and interfaith mood of Vatican II, and he would have frowned in amazement upon the John Paul who kissed the Qur'an and addressed Muslims as brothers. But like some other brilliant Catholic conservatives such as Louis Massignon and Louis Gardet, his own life of faith and his deep intelligence allowed him insights into Islam as a religious force that, in our age of Interfaith (so often a superficial *ballo in maschera*), are now seldom to be encountered. His view of the clash of Christendom with Islam as a struggle of truth against falsehood is clear enough, evinced, for instance, in his best-known poem, which is nothing less than a celebration of the Battle of Lepanto. But his take on Islam turns out to be a perceptive one.

Chesterton was uninterested in abstractions. He was a popular applied theologian, a realist who enjoyed pointing up the dangerous if farcical agendas of utopian reformers. He clearly savoured the writing of his novel *The Flying Inn*, first published in 1914, and in which, like Neirynck and Houellebecq, he looks to a fictional future. In its pages we discover that following a revival in Ottoman military fortunes, England is in the grip of profound Islamic influence. Throughout British society, old beliefs and values are giving way to an inexorable tide from the East. On the seafront of coastal resorts, Muslim soap-box preachers are boldly holding forth. We meet one of these:

> A little owlish man in a red fez, weakly waving a green gamp umbrella. His face was brown and wrinkled like a walnut, his

> nose was of the sort we associate with Judea, his beard was the sort of black wedge we associate rather with Persia.[14]

The ridiculous missionary is explaining how England is only superficially Christian. At root, he says, everything thought to be characteristically English turns out to be of Islamic origin. The evidence he uses is striking.

> 'Loo-ook', he said, wagging a curled brown finger, 'loo-ook at your own inns ... Your inns of which you write in your boo-ooks! These inns were not poo-oot up in the beginning to sell ze alcoholic Christian drink. They were put up to sell ze non-alcoholic Islamic drinks.'[15]

The preacher then offers a list of pub names which indicate a distant Islamic etiology, beginning with the Bull, which was once the 'Bulbul'. The 'Admiral Benbow' is in fact the great Moslem warrior Amir Ali Ben Bhoze. The 'Saracen's Head' is a corruption of 'The Saracen is Ahead'. Even the word 'alcohol' is of Islamic origin, and so, claims the preacher, we may claim for Islam everything that begins with the Arabic definite article, including Alsop's Beer, and even the Albert Memorial. The Islamic influence in London is plain for all to see: some deluded souls may point to King's Cross and Charing Cross, but wickedly fail to mention Denmark Crescent, Grosvenor Crescent, or Mornington Crescent.

> 'Everywhere, I say, homage paid to the holy symbol of the religion of the Prophet! Compare with this network and pattern of crescents, this city almost consisting of crescents, the meagre array of crosses, which remain to attest the ephemeral superstition to which you were, for one weak moment, inclined.'[16]

---

14 G.K. Chesterton, *The Flying Inn* (London, 1914), 2. For a discussion see John Coates, 'Symbol and Structure in *The Flying Inn*', *Chesterton Review* 4 (1978), 246-59.

15 Chesterton, 3.

16 Chesterton, 6.

In this new Britain, Government and the busybodies of Whitehall, inspired by such messaging, and also, more pragmatically, driven by the need to cooperate with a reinvigorated Turkish empire, incline to an acceptance of Islam, and thus Prohibition comes to England. The remainder of the novel follows two fugitives who travel around the land with the country's last barrel of rum, encouraging the habitués of now dry pubs to sing and be merry.

This is a romp; but Chesterton does have a point to make. He is not predicting our current secularity, he is warning about alienation. In particular he is taking aim at the Edwardian middle-class fad for Eastern religions, adopted by a vapid generation simply on the grounds of their exotic and unconventional surface. More seriously, however, *The Flying Inn* seems to be a parable about the ideology of the Temperance movement. True religion, for Chesterton, involves a kind of acceptance of traditional British normalcy, a Tory scepticism about radical projects of any kind, and a repudiation of a Puritanism which is foreign to Merrie England. Islam, for him, is where reformed Christianity may finally lead us, if wiser heads don't look out.

It is not clear whether Chesterton had actual Muslim missionaries in mind. He might have heard of Abdullah Quilliam (1856-1932), many of whose first converts were picked up in temperance halls, and there is certainly a strongly Nonconformist feel to Quilliam's writings and hymns. One imagines that another celebrity convert, Lord Headley (1855-1935), might also have furnished a target. For Chesterton it would have been unsurprising to learn that British Islam, as a contiguous movement, emerged not as a radical xenotransplant from a foreign place, but as a continuation of the world of Congregationalism, Pledges, and Temperance Hotels.

This convergence between nonconformity and the Muslim way of doing business with God is dealt with by Chesterton only here, in the pages of an essentially frivolous novel. But it is developed much more carefully by his contemporary and fellow Catholic writer Hilaire Belloc, as we learn in Chapter Four of Belloc's polemical work *The Great Heresies*, entitled 'The Great and Enduring Heresy of Mohammed.'[17]

Belloc was close to Chesterton; so close, in fact, that Bernard Shaw referred to them collectively as 'Chesterbelloc'. Like Chesterton he knew his history (in which he had gained a First at Oxford), and regarded Islam as a historic enemy, regretting bitterly the failure of the Crusades to destroy it. That failure, he wrote 'is the major tragedy in the history of our struggle against Islam, that is, against Asia'.[18] We don't know if he feared an Islamic future emerging from chapel Christianity; but he would surely have sympathised with the moral of the *Flying Inn*.

Yet his account of Islam deserves respect, and cannot be dismissed as simple prejudice. His explanation of the mass conversions of Christians to Islam in the wake of the early conquests is indicative: he has no time for theories of the bloody scimitar; instead, he writes that Islam 'zealously preached and throve on the paramount claims of justice, social and economic [...] Wherever Islam conquered there was a new spirit of freedom and relaxation.'[19] Not only did it offer a more just social order, it was easy to understand, evincing 'an extreme simplicity which pleased the unintelligent masses who were perplexed by the mysteries inseparable from the profound intellectual life of Catholicism, and from its radical doctrine of the Incarnation.'

For Belloc, the success and persistence of Islam are to be explained by its combination of Christian truths, such as the Virgin Birth, the messiahhood of Christ, the second coming, and a staunch life of prayer and fasting, with a kind of social gospel which medieval Christianity, in its feudal and ecclesial rigidity, could not accommodate. This is why, like John of Damascus centuries before, he treats Islam not as a new religion but as a Christian heresy. It is 'not a denial,' he writes, 'but an adaptation and a misuse, of the

17 Hilaire Belloc, *The Great Heresies* (London, 1938), 71-140.

18 Belloc, 102.

19 Belloc, 82.

Christian thing.' Muhammad 'preached and insisted upon a whole group of ideas which were peculiar to the Catholic Church'.[20]

Like Chesterton, Belloc lived in an English Catholic world of converts and recusants eternally pinched between an Englishness usually associated with the established Church, and the universal but foreign church of Rome. The Protestant triumph in his adoptive land was eternally on his brain. Hence, just as Chesterton imputes to Nonconformity the capacity to turn Britons into Mussulmans, Belloc ends by defining Islam as a kind of Reformation.

Belloc was not the first to classify the rise of Islam in such terms. Carlyle, in his *Heroes and Hero-worship,* had implicitly made this connection years previously. So had Oswald Spengler (the 'Magian Reformation'). And a specifically Catholic polemic against Islam as a precursor to Protestant error dates back to Counter-Reformation polemicists such as Ludovico Marracci (d.1700), who, according to Robert Irwin, viewed Protestantism as 'essentially a variant form of Islam'.[21]

But Belloc makes the link explicit. The most lethal threat to the Roman Church comes from a direction which may be very generally described as Arian, Islamic, and Calvinist. All these heresies denied the ordained priesthood and the communion of saints, downgraded or abolished the sacraments, and insisted on a programmatic return to an imagined apostolic age before Chalcedonian strictures turned the God worshipped by Jesus into a Greek conundrum. It was heresy in the name of *sancta simplicitas.*

Belloc writes this:

> There is thus a very great deal in common between the enthusiasm with which Mohammed's teaching attacked the

---

20 Belloc, 73.

21 Robert Irwin, *For Lust of Knowing: the orientalists and their enemies* (London, 2007), 106. See for Protestant anger at this suggestion, Alastair Hamilton, 'After Marracci: The Reception of Ludovico Marracci's Edition of the Qur'an in Northern Europe from the Late Seventeenth to the Early Nineteenth Centuries,' 175-92 of *Journal of Qur'anic Studies* 20 iii (2018), p.180.

> priesthood, the Mass and the sacraments, and the enthusiasm with which Calvinism, the central motive force of the Reformation, did the same. [...] It insisted upon the equality of men, and it necessarily had that further factor in which it resembled Calvinism—the sense of predestination, the sense of fate; of what the followers of John Knox were always calling 'the immutable decrees of God'.[22]

He goes on to repeat the longstanding theme of an *alliance satanisée* between Islam and the rise of Lutheranism: 'One of the reasons that the breakdown of Christendom at the Reformation took place was the fact that Mohammedan pressure against the German Emperor gave the German Princes and towns the opportunity to rebel and start Protestant Churches in their dominions.' It is true that both Luther and Calvin had railed passionately against the Turk, but this does no more than disguise a real sibling rivalry or even envy. In the end, all were against the fond superstition of the Mass, against images, against the ordained and celibate clergy, and against the Petrine principle without which there is no salvation.

In contrast to a widespread Orientalist trope of his day, Belloc does not, then, see Islam as *sui generis*, an eternally dissimilar Levantine Other. Muhammad is simply an Arab Calvin, and Madina is Geneva in a hot climate. But he claims that Islam's reformation is stronger, having succeeded permanently, while Protestantism is failing. He points to the ongoing possibility of a great Islamic awakening:

> In Islam there has been no such dissolution of ancestral doctrine or, at any rate, nothing corresponding to the universal breakup of religion in Europe. The whole spiritual strength of Islam is still present in the masses of Syria and Anatolia, of the East Asian mountains, of Arabia, Egypt and North Africa. The final fruit of this tenacity, the second period of Islamic power, may be delayed: but I doubt whether it can be permanently postponed.

---

22 Belloc, 80.

> That culture happens to have fallen back in material applications; there is no reason whatever why it should not learn its new lesson and become our equal in all those temporal things which now alone give us our superiority over it whereas in Faith we have fallen inferior to it.[23]

Here we are back with Chesterton: ordinary Nonconformity, a milksop affair, can never win England, but Islam (Protestantism's strongest strain) just might. Protestantism, as Weber thought, led to fragmentation and secularity; but the more successful and enduring Reformation, that of the Prophet, has proved better than Christianity at resisting this. And in contrast to Hegel, who voiced the usual assumption that Islam's energy was spent, following which it 'has retreated into oriental ease and repose',[24] Belloc warned that 'the power of Islam may at any moment re-arise.'[25]

The subsuming of Islam into the general category of Protestant heresy, as here suggested by Belloc and Chesterton, will not find a consensus. 'Traditionalists' of the school of René Guénon will see Protestantism as a decadent fundamentalism, a superficiality, and contrast it absolutely with Islam, the very essence of authentic 'traditional' religion. It might also be claimed that the Protestant-Islamic equation represents a misprision of the centre of Islam as scripturalist and unmediated, upholding an older Orientalism and ignoring Massignon's paradigm shift towards finding a devotional fertility in the Qur'an which implies a Catholic contiguity with Islam as a religion of miracles, saints, relics, rosaries and local pilgrimage.

Who is correct? At root, we might perhaps say that the contest is over Abraham. Derrida's well-known treatment of Massignon proceeds from the perception that the category of 'Abrahamic religion' is itself Islamic, which although revived aberrantly by Kierkegaard in emphatically Protestant mode, is properly appropriated by

---

23 Belloc, 132-3.

24 Muhammed Khair, 'Hegel and Islam', *The Philosopher*, Volume LXXXX No. 2 (Autumn 2002) at www.the-philosopher.co.uk

25 Belloc, 76.

Massignon, who constructs Abraham as a sign of *sacramental* origins and purpose. Derrida calls the Abrahamic a 'volcanic' principle, which purports and can indeed supply hospitality, but which also is a figure of iconic difference and alienation. Abraham, as seen particularly in Gil Anidjar's meditations on Derrida's reception of Massignon, figures as the contested archetype for essentialised oppositions: 'Europe and the Jew', 'Islam and the West', Letter and Spirit, Isaac and Ishmael. As Anidjar writes: 'The Abrahamic confronts us as a divisive and repetitive machine, and an explosive ghost that interrogates hermetic histories and their dividing modes of operation.'[26] But Derrida has missed a further antinomy: Abraham is not only the *vorlage* of the supposed three-way schism of the Jewish, the Christian, and the Islamic. Massignon's sacramental reading of the binding of Abraham's son makes the patriarch a contested theme for Protestant and Catholic belonging, and therefore, using our link between the Reformation and Islam, for Islam's engagement with the two major branches of Western Christianity.

Abraham's sacrifice, later claimed as the anticipation of the Paschal mystery, is received in Islam's self-image as the Ishmaelite cast out but vindicated at the Hajj. Hence Azraqī's report that the horns of the ram were once hung from the veil of the Kaᶜba.[27] In his life of relationship with Muslims, Massignon stressed the vicarious and substitutionary: Ḥallāj as a *Christ manqué*, the *Badaliyya* sodality, *le deuil de Fatima*, joint Marian shrines. But this need not be taken as proof of an inbuilt Roman instinct in Islam. In all this we find Massignon emphasising Islam as mere aspirant to Catholic fullness, as a proleptic, indeed *the* proleptic, Semitism, showing Arabs (and also Jews) the way to experience Christ through sacraments only dimly intuited in the Qur'anic data. Massignon's disciples (including those who joined Islam, like Vincent Monteil) have generally not taken this proleptic theory further; Monteil, indeed, frankly retreated

26 Gil Anidjar, *Acts of Religion* (London, 2002), 7.

27 Muḥammad ibn ᶜAbdallāh al-Azraqī, ed. Rushdī al-Ṣāliḥ Malḥas, *Akhbār Makka wa-ma jā'a fihā min al-āthār* (Madrid, 197?), I, 64; II, 66.

from it. The notion of Islam as a 'sign to Semites' pointing to the fullness of the Incarnation and of the Petrine succession has generally lapsed; one would be hard put to find advocates for it today.

So Massignon's project may finally be read as a support, rather than a challenge, to Belloc's assumption that Islam was the first and greater Reformation. Just as Ishmael and Isaac are, in the West's story, signs of a failed fraternity, so that Derrida's hope for a reconciling category of 'Arab Jew' has turned out to be without a resolution, so too Ishmael will always signify the non-sacramental, since Isaac was the one redeemed. Speculations about a 'first binding', which have Ishmael as the first sacrificial victim in his banishment to the desert and presumptively certain death, are marginal in the West, and in any case do not end with *fidā'*, with a ransom. Isaac appears as the forerunner of the eucharistic, sacerdotal and mediative; Ishmael of the suffering servant who is to generate no priesthood.

The Abrahamic volcano, then, includes this outcome: the recurrent internal schism in the Western Church yields non-sacramental, non-conformist, non-confessing sects, whose etiology is more likely to conflate with Ishmael than with the churches of the priests. Belloc and Chesterton would surely have agreed.

To turn the clock back again: how did this apparent congruity find expression in the moment of Reformation itself? The actual history of the role of Islam in the Reformation has yet to be adequately attempted, beyond historiographies of the theme of the Turkish scourge. In Germany Islam was a positive theme not of Reformation but of Enlightenment—witness Goethe's *Mahometsgesang* and Lessing's *Nathan the Wise*. As a non-mediative relation with God it is implicit also in Rilke, where he startlingly writes:

> Muhammad was immediate, like a river bursting through a mountain range; he breaks through to the One God with whom you can talk so wonderfully, every morning, without the telephone called 'Christ' into which people constantly shout, 'Hallo, is anyone there,' and no-one replies.[28]

28 Cited in Minou Reeves, *Muhammad in Europe* (Reading, 2000), 275.

In France, too, a sympathy for the Man of Praise accompanies some dimensions of the anticlerical early Enlightenment: the Comte de Boulainvilliers (d.1722) held that 'there is no more plausible system than his, more agreeable to the light of reason';[29] but his concerns here are those of the *lumières*: it is the simplicity and purity of the desert, not Ishmael specifically, that have allowed Islam to avoid the superstitions of the Catholic Church. For such French writers, institutions such as *wuḍū'*, circumcision, and the prohibition on pork, are primarily worthwhile because they are reasonable and hygienic, not because they enact a submission to a personal God.

The English evolution, however, here as on other matters, was decidedly different.

This has been dealt with elsewhere, where an enduringly Pelagian streak in the national religious style is identified, reinforced in complex ways by the rediscovery of Plato during the Reformation period and subsequently.[30] Figures like Henry Stubbe, physician and mathematician, and author of the first appreciative biography of the Prophet ever written by a Christian, indicate the real convergence which his contemporaries noticed between Islam and a certain kind of Puritanism. He writes:

> This is the sum of Mahometan Religion, on the one hand not clogging Men's Faith with the necessity of believing a number of abstruse Notions which they cannot comprehend, and which are often contrary to the dictates of Reason and common Sense; nor on the other hand loading them with the performance of many troublesome, expensive and superstitious Ceremonies, yet enjoyning a due observance of Religious Worship, as the surest Method to keep Men in the bounds of their duty both to God and Man.[31]

---

29 Cited in Reeves, 147.

30 Winter, *British Muslim Identity*, *op. cit.*

31 Henry Stubbe (ed. Hafiz Mahmud Khan Shairani), *An Account of the Rise and Progress of Mahometanism, and a Vindication of him and his Religion from the Calumnies of the Christians* (Second edition Lahore, 1954), 177.

The history of reformed Christianity in England is extremely intricate, and it is important to recall that the established Church represents a settlement substantially less protestant than was normal on the Continent. In her *Reason and Religion in the English Revolution*, Sarah Mortimer documents the role of Socinianism as the trigger for an Arminian reaction which led ultimately to the settlement of the 1650s, which to this day defines the relations between church and state in the United Kingdom.[32] In other words, on Mortimer's view, the Socinian and, by implication, the so-called 'Mahometan controversies' in England were an antithesis that fed only weakly into the final Anglican synthesis; the role of Unitarianism and crypto-Islamic currents at the time of the Civil War was only to goad the bishops into the definition of a reaction which was firmly Trinitarian and also sacramental.

Yet whatever the official line, the deeper Protestant scepticism about the mysteries continued among the populace. La Rochefoucauld, during a year's stay in Bury St Edmunds, wrote as follows:

> As for the beliefs of the English, what are they? I have heard much talk on the subject since I have been here. Many have argued and I have not perceived any conclusion. The only thing on which the majority are agreed is that all English people hold different beliefs, all believe things peculiar to themselves; some of them, and nearly all the women, decline to believe in the Trinity and shut their books when it is mentioned during their service.[33]

A few have claimed even the settled Anglican will to synthesis and compromise as indicative of an Islamic convergence. Most notable here is the former Bosnian president Alija Izetbegović, whose book

---

32 Sarah Mortimer, *Reason and Religion in the English Revolution* (Cambridge, 2010); Justin Champion, *The Pillars of Priestcraft Shaken: The Church of England and its Enemies, 1660–1730* (Cambridge, 1992).

33 La Rochefoucauld, 64-5.

Islam between East and West concludes with an unexpected eulogy to Anglo-Saxon religion as a middle or a third way.[34]

Because neither Muslims nor Anglicans have felt very flattered by this the debate over Izetbegović's claim has been subdued, with many treating it as eccentric. However our point here is not dependent on its outcome. We need only to signal the continued implicit hospitality to Islam, at the energetic margins of British religion in the early modern period, of forms of radical dissent which were descended organically from the Socinian disputes which produced the likes of Henry Stubbe, or John Toland's Mahometan Christianity, indicated for instance in his 1718 attempt to repristinate the Christian religion 'before the Papal corruptions and Usurpations',[35] and to show that Islam was in fact a branch of Christian religion.

One might, then, make this claim for 'British Islam'. It originates as a community in the temperance halls of Liverpool: Quilliam's mosque cleverly replicated core dimensions of their form and function, to the extent of adding a pedal-operated chapel organ to the adjacent meeting room. This matrix is unsurprising and the continuity persuasive. Further, the Reformation itself had been a kind of (in Belloc's language) second Islam, revisiting the old errors of the Arabian reform and bringing them to the north of Europe where Berber and Turkish incursion had never penetrated. Chapel Christianity, in particular, would be seen from this perspective as an implicit victory for the Ishmaelite error. Hence the growth of Islam here is not so much the transplantation of a quintessentially foreign essence; instead, from the viewpoint of Chesterton and Belloc, it can be seen as a belated incorporation into the country's religious

34 Alija Izetbegović, *Islam between East and West* (3rd edition, Indianapolis, 1993), 271-280.

35 Champion, 125-9; see also John Toland, ed. Justin Champion, *Nazarenus* (Oxford, 1999), p.135: 'There is a sense, wherin the Mahometans may not improperly be reckon'd and call'd a sort or sect of Christians, as Christianity was at first esteem'd a branch of Judaism [...] they might with as much reason and safety be tolerated at London and Amsterdam, as the Christians of every kind are so at Constantinople and throughout all Turkey'.

life of a principle which is superficially exotic, but whose deep logic is already partly indigenous as one of the themes of the Reformation and of some of the most characteristically English forms of chapel-going Dissent. If the Protestant settlement in this country envisaged the existence of marginal groups—Quakers, Congregationalists, Ranters, Unitarians and others, many of which may be seen as partaking in this convergence we have noted between Islamic and Reformation principles—then British Muslims might potentially be seen as best incorporated in the nation's religious life by expanding the principle of the settlement. This organically English move might prove more helpful than to treat them in an *ad hoc* fashion as a diasporic community of emphatically foreign roots which upsets Whitehall by seeking recognition in confessional rather than conventionally ethnic terms. Such a model does seem to have potential. On this view, mosques might be seen by unbelievers not as exotic temples to an unknown Eastern God, but as Socinian meeting houses of a particularly successful kind.

The parallel and the continuity, it must be constantly stressed, will not be at all exact. For instance, the model of community life in the dissenting sects is substantively different from the Islamic notion of the *umma*. The *jamāʿa*, the mosque congregation, might seem, in its obedience to an elder or presbyter rather than a priest ordained by a bishop, to set Muslims well within the familiar Protestant order; however the larger community is defined not as *ecclesia*, but as the Ishmaelite ecumenical world, the *umma*. One boundary marker of this is the dietary and purity laws, which are all but unknown to Protestantism. Of course they are not, as with some 'Old Testament' religion, understood as defining solidarity and identity against a hostile Other. Still, Islamic and Reformed notions of sociality will be considerably different. The Reformation proposed an often charismatic spirituality, but one linked to an individualism which, in its idea of the equality of every believer's reading of scripture, sometimes seemed to reduce the spiritual value of human community. This is the alleged but widely-admired Reformation root of modern individualism; in an Islamic context, where bodies are collectivised and made intersubjective through purity laws, and where a principle of *ijmāʿ* controls scriptural reading, the more fissiparous tendencies of the Reformation moment are avoided. It is noteworthy that it is Shi'ism, a more hierarchical, mediative form of religion, which in Islam has generated the larger number of sects; while the Sunni, apparently 'Protestant' mainstream, has usually managed to remain more integrated.[36]

This chapter has ranged rather widely, from an account of the state of local Christianity to an assessment of the claim that Islam could meaningfully be seen by outsiders as a kind of Reformation, thereby confounding xenophobic talk of a categoric Islamic foreignness, and facilitating the project of vertical integration. The conclusion is perhaps already evident. Chesterton and Belloc, looking forwards a hundred years ago, expected Britain to move in one of three general directions. Firstly, it might board the Tractarian conveyer-belt until it accepted full communion with Rome, heralding a new era of faith when England would be rededicated to the Virgin. Secondly, it could mechanise until Merrie England was no more and the churches were turned over to secular use. Thirdly, it could continue with the Whiggish instincts of the nonconformist Reformation, as revived in Wesleyan and other anti-alcoholic movements, a trajectory which Chesterton warns us is a sort of Mahometan Christianity. In this scheme, only Catholicism, the deep stratum of English religion, will allow us to be indigenous: the Church of Rome is the true Church of England. Anglicanism, following the rupture of the Henrician and Elizabethan inquisitions, is a kind of alienation from the indigenous, although still, in its prayer book and vestments, nostalgic for the forms and habits of the old Sarum Rite. Chapel Christianity comprises the furthest point of the alienation.

---

36 This is particularly evident if we follow the widespread contemporary practice of treating Salafism and Wahhabism as non-Sunni movements, cf. Nahouza, *Wahhabism*.

We are likely to be impatient with this anachronism. To define medieval England, 'Mary's dowry', as the ultimate referent of local authenticity, is arbitrary, and such whims may equally open the way to the neo-pagan claim, currently gaining ground, that monotheism itself is inauthentic, a Middle Eastern intrusion into a Celtic Eden. As with all arguments for ultimate identity, this one essentialises a past which was itself always a time of difference, transition and synthesis. What is religiously most authentic in the valleys of Wales, for instance? Rood screens and the Ambrosian chant? The druidical fancies of the Eisteddfod? We are more likely to say Methodist revivals of Handel's *Messiah*. As the Islamic conception of *isnād* and *silsila* makes clear, authenticity hinges on attachment to a tradition that is still alive. All else is a kind of abstracted fundamentalism.

We do not possess a definitive culture, we share in a process which is forever in a state of becoming. Authenticity eludes us as soon as we propose a fully fixed essence. Englishness has no uniform self; neither has Muslimness, although we tend to notice when we are in the presence of either, and the *ijāza* system works to ensure the perpetuation of an Islamic core. English identity, like all social identities, has historically been constructed primarily in relation to a set of differences: not being French, or Catholic, or Republican, for instance; and these have hugely shifted or even vanished. To take one example, the early twentieth-century novelist E.M. Delafield proposed an English Creed, expressed in the following four articles:

> Firstly, God is an Englishman, probably educated at Eton.
> Secondly, all good women are naturally frigid.
> Thirdly, it is better to be dowdy than smart.
> Fourthly, England is going to rack and ruin.[37]

Compare this checklist to the values espoused by the congregation in Alan Bennett's story. Englishness has not only been revised, it has been inverted.

---

37 Jeremy Paxman, *The English: a portrait of a people* (London, 1998), 14.

Islam, as a category familiarly used, can boast more substance; but it still, as Monteil has shown, always passes through a historically-conditioned kaleidoscope of perceptions and practices, united in the Sunni doctrinal and liturgical core, no doubt, but variously interpreted by *madhhabs, mujtahids*, and a non-magisterial consensus, not least when in a minority condition.[38] Part of that kaleidoscope, as we have seen, can helpfully be seen as interlocking with the themes of the English Reformation. In that sense, once we abandon what is superficial (all British people wear duffle coats and like warm beer; all Muslims eat curry and support the Taliban), and recognise that certain deep structures of religious coherence and resemblance lie beneath, it is not hard to see how we may set aside the failed race relations paradigm of integration, and recognise that an integration is already present. But it is not an integration based on shallow and opportunistic liberal claims about 'shared values'. In fact, liberal secularity, on our model, may turn out not to ease integration but to obstruct it. For if Islam's appropriateness to the United Kingdom is to be identified most substantially in the fact of a shared monotheism, then the diminution of the religious will make Islam's difference all the more salient.

38 Vincent-Mansour Monteil, *Aux cinq couleurs de l'Islam* (Paris, 1989).

CHAPTER 4

Islamophobia and the Bosnian War

though there's a brute on your back,
sapping you with blows
(while we observe)
though he'd rip your women apart –
he's *our* brute.

help? If only we could –

it's not your blood, or your deeds
but that we can see
a foreign weed in your heart –

the excuse we won't declare.[1]

AONGHAS MACNEACAIL

ONE OF THE MOST disturbing features of the Lahabist war which devastated Bosnia between 1992 and 1995 was the widespread reluctance of Western politicians, churchmen and newsmen to acknowledge the role which religion was playing in the conflict. It only seemed worth acknowledging during periodic denunciations of the risks of Islamic extremism, a phenomenon that, when pressed, journalists working in Bosnia conceded was rather elusive. The reality, which was frequently one of militant Orthodox extremism, seemed seldom to be frankly discussed. The war was, we were told, a contest between 'ethnic factions' driven by 'ancient hatreds'; and

1 In Ken Smith and Judi Benson (eds), *Klaonica: Poems for Bosnia* (Newcastle, 1993), 44.

the fact that its protagonists were divided primarily by religion, and shared a 'race' and a language, was deemed insignificant. Anti-Muslim prejudice was no doubt at work here: one may assume that had the Serbs and Catholics been Muslims, and their victims Christians, then the Western mind would immediately have characterised the war as a case of violent Muslims murdering secular, integrated, democratic Christians. Since in Bosnia the favoured stereotypes were almost perfectly reversed, the memory has largely been dismissed, censored and forgotten as an annoying and scarcely possible anomaly.

A quarter-century on, that official characterisation, by and large, persists. Generally it is the case that the European and American popular consciousness has consigned Bosnia to oblivion, although fewer than three decades have elapsed since over nine thousand Muslims were tipped into mass graves at Srebrenica, while the local UN commander accepted a glass of champagne from the victorious Serbian general, who then went off to church.[2] And where Bosnia is still remembered, there is a dogged resistance to defining it as what it was: a war which, at least for its Orthodox participants, was an intensely religious experience.

However among European Muslims, and a small but significant non-Muslim public around the world that uneasily recognises that the crime of Srebrenica was far worse than that of 9/11, this comforting amnesia is rejected as an unacceptable whitewashing of crimes whose sectarian foundations must never be ignored. War crimes

2 For an excellent, if chilling, account of the massacre see Sylvie Matton, *Srebrenica: un génocide annoncé* (Paris, 2005); for the Dutch soldiers' assisting the Serbs in separating the women from the men see Lara Nettelfield and Sarah E. Wagner, *Srebrenica in the Aftermath of Genocide* (Cambridge, 2014), 15. Thanks perhaps to the intensifying anti-Muslim atmosphere in Holland, in 2006 it was possible for the Dutch government, massively applauded by neo-Nazi elements, to award medals to the battalion which had failed to protect the Srebrenica 'safe area': see 'Dutch honour soldiers who stood by at Srebrenica massacre', *The Guardian*, 6 December 2006.

investigators have consistently found that the Serbian forces placed religion at the very centre of their hardline national vision, and that many of the most iconic atrocities bore a strongly religious aspect.

> In Bratunac, Imam Mustafa Mujkanović was tortured before thousands of Muslim women, children and old people at the town's soccer stadium. Serb guards also ordered the cleric to cross himself. When he refused, 'they beat him. They stuffed his mouth with sawdust, poured beer in his mouth, and then slit his throat.'[3]
>
> Routinely, Muslims held in concentration camps also told of being forced by their captors to sing Chetnik songs or to make the sign of the cross. Suggestions to Muslims that they convert to Serbian Orthodoxy could be viewed as yet another means to eliminate the Muslim presence.[4]
>
> Almost from the first, the Serb-led war was accompanied by an assault against the Muslim religious and cultural tradition, an assault whose impact has become clear as scholars examine the pattern of destruction. Muslim clergymen have been dispersed, imprisoned or killed, according to a variety of Muslim sources. National libraries and religious seminaries have been destroyed. And Bosnian scholars estimate that well over half of the mosques, historical monuments and libraries that comprise a six-century old religious and cultural heritage have been wiped out.[5]
>
> The film was shown in which the notorious Scorpions were seen killing children, after having first been blessed by Father Gavrilo.[6]

3 Roy Gutman, *A Witness to Genocide: the first inside account of the horrors of 'ethnic cleansing' in Bosnia* (Shaftesbury, 1993), 78.

4 Norman Cigar, *Genocide in Bosnia: the policy of 'ethnic cleansing'* (College Station, 1995), 59.

5 Gutman, 78-80.

6 Mirko Djordjević, 'Scorpions dressed as priests', *Bosnia Report* (London) 49-50 (December 2005-March 2006), 36.

> A Serbian Orthodox bishop, blacklisted by the EU for allegedly supporting war criminals, denied Thursday that he had sheltered top UN court fugitives Radovan Karadžić and Ratko Mladić although he claimed the men were heroes. [...] Bishop Filaret appeared in front of TV cameras with a skull in one hand and a machine-gun in the other during the 1992-95 war.[7]
>
> [Hague War Crimes Tribunal Chief Prosecutor] Carla del Ponte accused the Church of 'involvement in politics and hiding those indicted of war crimes'.[8]
>
> The old Balkan pattern of clerically-inspired political violence has once again emerged in recent years: first come the priests [*popovi*] and then the cannons [*topovi*].[9]
>
> The symbols appeared in the three-fingered hand gestures representing the Christian trinity, in the images of sacred figures of Serbian religious mythology on their uniform insignia, in the songs they memorized and forced their victims to sing, on the priest's ring they kissed before and after their acts of persecution, and in the formal religious ceremonies that marked the purification of a town of its Muslim population. The term 'ethnic' in the expression 'ethnic cleansing', then, is a euphemism for 'religious'.[10]

Over the past quarter-century a succession of studies has meticulously documented the wartime activities of the Islamophobic clergy, and particularly the bishops who proudly sat in the front row of the rebel Serbian 'parliament' whenever it assembled in its pirate capital of Pale. In the West these studies have not usually been the

---

7 Agence France-Press, July 3, 2003. During the war Filaret, appointed Bishop of Mileševo by Pavle, was a close associate of the extremist warlord Vojislav Šešelj, and an unwavering supporter of Slobodan Milošević.

8 www.bosnia.org.uk/news/news_body.cfm?newsid=2067

9 Branislav Radulović, spokesman of the Social Democratic Party of Montenegro (www.rferl.org/reports/southslavic/2005/09/26-080905.asp).

10 Michael Sells, *The Bridge Betrayed: Religion and genocide in Bosnia* (Berkeley, 1996), 15.

work of Muslim scholars.[11] One pioneering example has been the book of Michael Sells: *The Bridge Betrayed: religion and genocide in Bosnia*. Sells is a Quaker, who became professor of Islamic Studies at the University of Chicago. Here is a paragraph from the conclusion of his book:

> The violence in Bosnia was a religious genocide in several senses: the people destroyed were chosen on the basis of their religious identity; those carrying out the killings acted with the blessing and support of Christian church leaders; the violence was grounded in a religious mythology that characterized the targeted people as race traitors and the extermination of them as a sacred act.[12]

Another invaluable breaking of the silence came from G. Scott Davis, a professor of religion and ethics at the University of Richmond. Scott Davis' edited volume is entitled *Religion and Justice in the War over Bosnia*.[13] It documents the attitude of local churches to what happened; and also includes some sustained reflections on the ability of Europe, Mazower's 'dark continent', to protect religious minorities. Further analysis has been provided in many of the papers included in Raju Thomas' *The South Slav Conflict*.[14]

Many have been heartened by these and other studies. For some time it seemed that the religious dimension of the Bosnian war would be buried forever; but now, rather like the victim of an atrocity, it is being disinterred and reluctantly examined. A clear picture has emerged at the hands of such scholars, supported also by the detailed evidence heard by the International Criminal Court

11 One distinguished exception has been the British Muslim legal expert Saba Risaluddin; see Nermin Mulalić and Saba Risaluddin, *From Daytonland to Bosnia Rediviva* (London, 2000); Saba Risaluddin, *Case of the Zvornik Seven: ethnic cleansing of the legal system in Bosnia-Herzegovina* (London, *ca.* 1998).

12 Sells, *Bridge*, 144.

13 London, 1996.

14 Raju G.C. Thomas (ed.), *The South Slav Conflict: History, Religion, Ethnicity, and Nationalism* (London, 2016).

investigations at The Hague,[15] and intellectuals such as Susan Sontag and Juan Goytisolo have been sufficiently thoughtful to see Balkan Islamophobia, and Western apathy, as a sign and warning about growing prejudice everywhere in Europe. Baudrillard even added this:

> The miraculous end will be at hand only when the exterminations come to an end, and when the borders of 'white' Europe have been drawn. It is as if all European nationalities and policies had acted in concert to take out a contract for murder with the Serbs, who have become the agents of the West's dirty jobs—just as the West had taken out a contract with Saddam Hussein against Iran [...] Modern Europe will rise from the eradication of Muslims and Arabs—unless they survive as immigrant slaves.[16]

The individual most regularly cited in connection with the ethnic cleansing process and with Lahabist atrocities, Bosnian Serb leader Radovan Karadžić (finally convicted of genocide in 2016), was widely feted as a hero in Orthodox church circles. 'Not a single important decision was made without the Church,' as he boasted during the war.[17] The bishop closest to him, Vasilije Kačavenda, became a minister in his government and championed the warlord Arkan, author of a campaign of systematic violence against Muslim civilians.[18] Nor was this a parochial Serbian affair: at the height of

---

15 One example from my own reminiscences: in 1995 at the Saraj refugee camp in Macedonia, which held ethnic cleansing survivors from the Drina Valley region, one woman told me that her small children had been killed by being pushed down onto bayonets held by Serb soldiers. The soldiers, pulling down the trousers of the last of her children, a boy, saw that he was uncircumcised. Telling him that he would be a good Serb, they let him live.

16 Jean Baudrillard, 'No Pity for Sarajevo', in Thomas Cushman and Stjepan G. Meštrović (eds.), *This Time We Knew: Western responses to genocide in Bosnia* (New York and London, 1996), 83.

17 Mitja Velikonja, *Religious Separation and Political Intolerance in Bosnia-Herzegovina* (College Station, 2003), 268.

18 In 2013 Kačavenda was forced to resign following the release of numer-

the ethnic cleansing process the Greek Orthodox synod chose to award Karadžić its highest honour, the Order of St Denys of Zante. The Greek bishops who conferred the honour upon him called him 'one of the most prominent sons of our Lord Jesus Christ.'[19]

In Western Europe a few lone voices were raised against what Michael Sells was calling 'the silence of the self-identified Christian leaders in many parts of the world'.[20] Perhaps the most outspoken was Professor Adrian Hastings (d.2001), a Catholic theologian from Leeds, who asked:

> What have the churches done to speak out in defence of Bosnia, of its peace-loving Muslim community and against a revival of the most virulent racism? There appears to have been a most striking silence from all the principal church leaders in Britain. It will go down in history. We pour out our tears at the Holocaust but close our eyes to the Holocaust happening now. 'Only he who shouts for the Jews may sing the Gregorian chant', declared Bonhoeffer fifty years ago. Only he who shouts for the Bosnian Muslims is entitled to do so today.[21]

In a later article Hastings fired a second broadside:

> Why are Christian leaders behaving like this? There is a misguided ecumenism at work here. Anglicans in particular are

---

ous videos showing him performing sexual acts with young men. Evidence against him also included a claim by a Muslim girl that when she was 16 the bishop forcibly converted her before raping her; other charges are legion. 'Serbian Church Removes Sex Scandal Bishop', *Balkan Insight,* 23 April 2013; see also www.rferl.org/a/serbia-orthodox-church-bishop-orgies-rape-scandal/24965214.html

19 Cited in Sells, *Bridge,* 85; Velikonja, 265. Perhaps in divine retribution, several of the bishops who signed this decree were later humiliated in spectacular fashion; see Helena Smith, 'Sex and fraud woe for Greek church', *The Guardian,* 19 February 2005.

20 Sells, *Bridge,* 91.

21 Adrian Hastings, *The Shaping of Prophecy: Passion, Perception and Practicality* (London, 1995).

> anxious to remain on good terms with the Orthodox, and the Serbian Orthodox Church has had closer relations with the Church of England than any other. It is also doing a very great deal to fuel Serb nationalism. To take a strong line against Serb aggression could be to displease one's Orthodox friends. Better to stress instead that this is a complex matter and that there must be wrongs on every side.[22]

In an article published in *Theology* in 1994 Hastings commented on international Protestant reaction to the Bosnian war, which he again found wanting. He discussed the main World Council of Churches resolution on the war in former Yugoslavia, pointing out that 'for ecumenical reasons' Bosnia was not mentioned once in 27 pages, and that its discussion of civilian suffering mentioned only Croats and Serbs, with no discussion whatsoever of Muslims. He went on:

> Reflecting on the response of the churches in Britain and within the Ecumenical Movement to Bosnia once more, I remain appalled by how little they have done at the level of their leadership to recognise without ambiguity what has been happening, to condemn what is evil and above all to offer any significant support to a European nation oppressed in a way unprecedented since 1945. Again and again, church leaders in this country have been urged to visit Sarajevo, to show some really significant degree of human and religious solidarity with the Muslim community of Bosnia in its ordeal. They have entirely failed to do so.[23]

Hastings was probably one of the heroes of the war, appearing at countless rallies and on television, to denounce the apathy of Europe and of its political and spiritual leaders. To make sure of his facts he visited Sarajevo in the darkest days of the siege. Not many retired professors would have consented to be pulled on a trolley through the makeshift tunnel which was Sarajevo's lifeline, and then face the

---

22 Reprinted in Hastings, 149.

23 Hastings, 151.

lurching drive along 'Sniper's Alley' in a car with polythene sheets for windows, to a city where three thousand people and even animals in the city zoo had already been killed by snipers. However he did it. He was the most honourable of exceptions.

Hastings found, as subsequent research uncovered, a European religious war. In Sarajevo itself, it is true, this was not immediately apparent. The Serb cathedral, despite four years of siege by Serbs, was never vandalised by the population. The Muslim president and religious hierarchy continued to sit at the front row of the Catholic cathedral every Christmas Eve. The commandant in charge of Sarajevo's defenders, Jovan Divjak, was himself an ethnic Serb;[24] another Serb, Miro Lazović, was the speaker of Bosnia's parliament. Although the defence of the city had first been mounted by the heroic young Sufis of the Sinanova Qadiri Tekke, for many of the defenders this was never a religious war; except for those who saw the defence of the city's history of tolerance as a sacred task.

In Serb-controlled territory, however, chauvinistic religion was rampant. West of Sarajevo, just over the front line, stood a Serb church where one could hear a list of captured Muslim settlements being read out in triumph by a priest, who then blessed the congregation, which comprised followers of the religious warlord Vojislav Šešelj, now a convicted war criminal, and who once fought an election in Serbia with a promise to remove the eyes of his prisoners with a rusty spoon.[25]

In Trebinje, 'an Orthodox priest led the way in expelling a Muslim family and seizing their home.'[26] In the formerly Muslim-

24 See his *Sarajevo, mon amour: entretiens avec Florence La Bruyère* (Paris, 2004). He has subsequently campaigned for educational charities in undivided Sarajevo, despite ongoing attempts at persecution by the Belgrade government; see Nettelfield and Wagner, 279.

25 In 2018 after a complex set of proceedings he was convicted of crimes against humanity.

26 Sells, *Bridge*, 80.

majority town of Foča a religious ceremony was held to celebrate the city's capture. Senior churchmen at the ceremony heard a Serb professor explain that 'the [Serb] fighters from Foča and the region were worthy defenders of Serbianness and of Orthodoxy.'[27] The city's exquisite Aladža Mosque, built in 1550 by Mimar Sinan, was then pulled down, as the complete ethnic cleansing of the town proceeded.[28] When this event was criticised in a liberal Montenegrin newspaper, the highest Herzegovinan bishop defended it strongly.[29]

Several other militias were no less explicitly religious. The leader of the White Eagles militia, Mirko Jović, called for, as he put it, 'a Christian, Orthodox Serbia with no Muslims and no unbelievers.'[30] His ideological mentor, the Belgrade far-right politician Vuk Drašković, who promised to 'cut off the hands of those Muslims who carried flags other than Serb ones', published his ferociously anti-Muslim writings with the official publishing house of the Serbian church.[31] The Church itself regularly thundered against 'enemies of God' who would not join the struggle for a Greater Serbia, and official Church journals were a leading forum for Drašković and other national populists advocating the dream of a 'Greater Serbia,' and the destruction of the 'disease' of Islam.[32]

---

27 Sells, *Bridge,* 80.

28 The mosque was rebuilt and reopened in 2019. For the destruction see 'Indictment confirmed for Goran Mojović for destruction of Aladža Mosque', *Sarajevo Times*, 30 December 2018.

29 Cited in Sells, *Bridge,* 83.

30 Cited in Velikonja, 267.

31 For Drašković, see Mirko Kovac, 'Vuk Drašković: another hero of our time', *Bosnia Report* 51-52 (April-July 2006), 44: 'He describes himself as a very devout man. Former Communists are fond of stressing their religious feelings, which the ideology to which they once belonged had denied to them; and it is precisely they who have increasingly imposed the Church and the clergy as new authorities.'

32 Cigar, 31. For more on the common image of Islam as an 'Asiatic plague' see Cigar, 185.

A further tell-tale sign of the involvement of the church was apparent when, in 1994, the Geneva Contact Group tabled its new partition plan for the country. Under this plan, the thirty-two percent of Bosnians who were Orthodox were awarded forty-nine percent of the land, including many formerly Muslim-majority areas which had suffered ethnic cleansing. But the church was unsatisfied even with this: Metropolitan Nikolaj of Sarajevo demanded that Sarajevo itself should be incorporated into the Serb-held areas.[33] The argument he gave, which was supported by Karadžić himself, was that since the city's majority Muslim population was supposedly descended from Serb converts to Islam, the city naturally belonged to Orthodoxy. This idea of the Bosniaks as 'bad Serbs' who should be guided by Karadžić's 'warriors for Christ' back to the Orthodox fold (or face expulsion, or worse), lay at the ideological core of the debates in the priest-filled Republika Srpska parliament in Pale.

Rather different was the view of the Patriarch in Belgrade, Pavle (d.2009). Like his admirer the militia leader Zeljko Ražnatović[34] he argued throughout that the Serb nationalist claim to Bosnia was based on the fact—as he believed—that the Muslims were interlopers from the East, and were not indigenous to the region. Hence 'I believe that Serbs must fight, now as never before.'[35] This was akin to the widespread argument, advanced by the nationalist Dragoš Kalajić, which held that Bosnian Muslim culture was alien, or what he called a 'semi-Arabic subculture', caused by a 'genetic predetermination' which the Bosniaks had inherited from the Ottomans and which in fact originated in North Africa.[36] Another intellectual, former Sarajevo University dean Biljana Plavšić, who became Karadžić's successor as premier of the rebel Bosnian Serb parastate, insisted that 'it was genetically damaged Serb material which passed

33 Sells, *Bridge,* 83.

34 This is the indicted war criminal known as Arkan (d.2000). For the connection see Velikonja, 265.

35 Cigar, 68.

36 Cigar, 26.

over to Islam',[37] lending pseudo-scientific support to a thesis deeply rooted in Islamophobic religio-political mythology.

Although the Patriarch's rancorous dislike of Islam played a major role in guiding the national spirit during the war, he was outspoken in his denial of the war crimes which were increasingly being attributed to Orthodox militias. After Maggie O'Kane and other journalists had flashed around the world pictures of the detention camps in which thousands of Bosnian Muslims, Croats and Gypsies were being tortured and executed, the Episcopal Synod in Belgrade issued the following statement:

> In the name of God's truth, and on the testimony from our brother bishops from Bosnia-Herzegovina and from other trustworthy witnesses, we declare, taking full moral responsibility, that such camps neither have existed nor exist in the Serbian Republic of Bosnia-Herzegovina.[38]

In the eyes of the Church, the pictures on the West's TV screens, and the testimonies collected by Helsinki Watch, the US State Department, the Red Cross, EU observers, and others, were simply falsified. The 'Semi-Arabs' had deceived the world.

Again, when a new peace plan was placed on the table, the Church showed itself more radical even than Milošević. Pavle, Amfilohije and others insisted that the Belgrade strongman was scandalously weak in upholding the Serbian right to territory. Bishop Atanasije of Herzegovina enjoined Serbs, as he said, 'not to capitulate to the world as Milošević has. The vultures from the West will not get our signature.'[39]

Overall, as Norman Cigar recalls:

> The Serbian Orthodox Church, both in Serbia and in Bosnia-Herzegovina, continued to provide its legitimacy to the Bosnian Serb authorities' ethnic policies. It backed the most

37 Cited in Velikonja, 248.

38 In Sells, *Bridge,* 84.

39 Sells, *Bridge,* 85.

> uncompromising options formulated in Bosnia, which had as their goal to create a Greater Serbia, and did not envisage the continued presence of the Muslims.[40]

Examples of this could be multiplied; but the general picture should by now have become clear. Later in this chapter we will try to unpack the reasons why Orthodox churchmen supported the terrorist far right. Before doing so, however, it will be helpful to discuss the rather more complex relationship of nationalism to the other Christian hierarchy in Bosnia: that of the Catholic Church.

Croat nationalism has its immediate roots in the widespread support in Croatia for the Axis powers during the Second World War. Ante Pavelić, the Croat president, had pleaded with Eichmann to allow Croatia to jump the queue for the ethnic cleansing of its Jewish population. As the Irish human rights investigator Hubert Butler, who worked in the Croat archives after the Second World War, recalls:

> When I was in Zagreb I spent several days in the public library looking up the old files of the newspapers that were issued in the occupation period, particularly the Church papers. I wanted to see what resistance, if any, was made by organized Christianity to the ruthless militarism of Pavelitch, the Croat national leader, and his German and Italian patrons; I am afraid the results were disheartening. [...] I was wholly unprepared for the gush of hysterical adulation which was poured forth by almost all of the leading clergy upon Pavelitch, who was probably the vilest of all war criminals. He was their saviour against Bolshevism, their champion against the Eastern barbarian and heretic, the Serb; he was restorer of their nation and the Christian faith, a veritable hero of olden time.[41]

Franjo Tudjman, the Croat president throughout the 1992-5 war, made his own ethnic preoccupations quite clear in his book

40 Cigar, 66.

41 Hubert Butler, *In the Land of Nod* (Dublin, 1996), 106-7.

Wastelands of Historical Reality, published in 1990. In this book he suggests that 'Jews are genocidal by nature', and that their problems are of their own making. Had they heeded what he calls the 'traffic signs', the Holocaust would never have occurred.[42]

Tudjman's main concern, however, as an unreconstructed national populist, was with the Muslim presence in Bosnia, which he spoke of in terms of 'contamination by the Orient.' Claiming to be acting at the behest of Western powers he asserted that 'Croatia accepts the task of Europeanising the Bosnian Muslims.' On the ground this tended to involve rape, the demolition of mosques, forced baptism, and strategies indistinguishable from the radical Serb methods of conquest. Particularly recurrent was the Croat policy of constructing 'blood shrines', which took the form of Christian shrines or crucifixes constructed on the site of demolished mosques.[43] The justification was the need to create a Catholic *cordon sanitaire* against Islam. His defence minister, Gojko Šušak, fantasised to an adoring Israeli audience about '110,000 Bosnian Muslims studying in Cairo', in order to create 'a fundamentalist state in the heart of Europe.'[44]

In Croatia proper, and in Bosnia proper, the Catholic hierarchy was often able to condemn Croat extremism.[45] Archbishop Vinko

---

42 Sells, 95.

43 Michael Sells, 'Crosses of Blood: sacred space, religion, and violence in Bosnia-Herzegovina,' *Sociology of Religion* 64 (2003), 309-331.

44 Cigar, 124; Sells, *Bridge*, 119. For a detailed account of Israeli popular support for Serbia during the genocide, see Daniel Kofman, 'Israel and the War in Bosnia', in Cushman and Meštrović, 90-127. Quoting the *Ma'ariv* editor and columnist Yosef Lapid, who wrote 'We must support the Serbs no matter what they do' (p.100), he adds: 'His views have been not at all unrepresentative of the rest of the Israeli political spectrum' (p.102). 'The *Jerusalem Post* actually distinguished itself throughout the war by running what could only be called straight Belgrade propaganda repeatedly in its op-ed pages, while disallowing responses' (p.108).

45 This may change with the growing influence of the Church on public life: see Vjekoslav Perica, 'The Most Catholic Country in Europe? Church, State and Society in Contemporary Croatia', *Religion, State and Society* 34 (2006), 311-46.

Puljić of Sarajevo, in particular, emerged as a man of stature, consistently opposing the logic of ethnic partition. The main exception was in Herzegovina. Here the Franciscan clergy included a large number of ultra-nationalists. The city of Mostar, capital of Herzegovina, was partitioned between Muslims and Catholics. After the conflict, the European Union, which appointed a mayor for the city, struggled hard to reunite the two halves. However a major opponent of reintegration was the provincial superior of the Franciscan order, Tomislav Pervan.[46] Bishop Ratko Perić was also a known opponent of mosque reconstruction and the return of Muslim refugees;[47] in 2004 he conspicuously refused to attend the ceremony of the reopening of Mostar's famous bridge, destroyed in 1993 by Croat extremists.[48]

Church sympathy for Croat nationalist aims was highlighted in the world media when, in 2005, Carla del Ponte, the chief war crimes prosecutor in The Hague, complained that the leading Croat war crimes suspect, General Ante Gotovina, was being sheltered in a Catholic monastery. 'The Catholic Church is protecting him,' she concluded, adding that 'I have taken this up with the Vatican and the Vatican totally refuses to cooperate with us.'[49] More generally she complained that the Church 'is adding legitimacy to visions of history which are twisted in accordance with nationalist biases'.[50]

Serbian nationalism, however, is a less familiar phenomenon, and we should try to account for what has been, on the face of it, the most striking alliance of men of religion with extreme xenophobic agendas seen in Europe since the collapse of Franco's 'National Catholicism' in 1975. As it happens, 'theo-democratic' Serbia resembles

46 Sells, *Bridge,* 106.

47 See Ivo Banac, 'Games beneath Stolac', *Bosnia Report* 27-28 (Jan-May 2002); Helen Walasek, *Bosnia and the Destruction of Cultural Heritage* (London, 2015), 240, 277-8.

48 http://balkanwitness.glypx.com/sells-reports.htm

49 news.bbc.co.uk/1/hi/world/europe/4263426.stm

50 www.un.org/icty/pressreal/2005/p1001-e.htm

Franco's Spain in certain respects, most notably through the idolising and idealising of a Christian past. It seeks to be authoritarian and traditionalist, but not Nazi or monarchist. In many ways its vision stands very close to that of Franco's favourite theorist, José Maria Pemán:

> The new state must be founded on all the principles of traditionalism to be genuinely national [...] Our fascism, our juridic-Hegelian absolutism, must necessarily sustain itself, as form, in the substance of historic-Catholic tradition. Spanish fascism will be the religion of Religion. [...] German and Italian fascism have invented nothing as far as we are concerned; Spain was fascist four centuries before them. It was one, great and free, and truly Spain, in the sixteenth century when state and nation were identified with the eternal Catholic idea, when Spain was the model nation and alma mater of Western Christian civilisation.[51]

German and Italian Fascism had defied the medieval legacy through a largely pagan *risorgimento*. Spain, however, would solve her identity crisis by remaining in organic continuity with the Catholic past. Her Christianity recognised the church-state marriage as divinely-willed and indissoluble. No doubt the verbal and practical resemblance between Serb 'ethnic cleansing' strategies and the Inquisition's 'blood purity' measures, was more than coincidental, forming in fact a key method in what, in Joseph Pérez's words, became 'the eradication of Semitism', a parallel destruction of ancient Jewish and Muslim populations in which Church and State worked hand-in-hand.[52]

Although there is, therefore, more than a whiff of *francoismo* about Serb national populism, the role of Serbia's very obscurantist

---

51 Cited in Raymond Carr, *The Spanish Tragedy: the civil war in perspective* (London: Weidenfeld, 1977), 209-10.

52 Joseph Pérez, *The Spanish Inquisition: a history* (London, 2004); see chapter on 'The Eradication of Semitism,' pp.26-57 for the Church's policy towards Muslims and Jews; for 'blood purity' see pp.55-7.

church has nonetheless been subtly distinct. Even more than Franco's bishops, the bishops in Pale, Knin, Belgrade and Podgorica were heirs to a tradition of radical affirmation of the political *status quo,* an attitude whose roots lay ultimately in Byzantine readings of scripture. As one human rights observer sees it:

> Orthodoxy, by negating the importance of 'life on earth', can and does sanction and legitimate whatever political regime holds the reins of power. This subordination in turn ensures that the Orthodox Church will survive and retain power. Throughout history the Church has uncritically acquiesced in authoritarian and dictatorial regimes; it has no history of opposition to repression. And in modern times the merger of religion with nationality has reinforced further the Church's defence of the status quo in the name of the *ethnos* and religion.[53]

It is easily forgotten, by Muslims as well as by Orthodox, that the Church has no natural affinity with rebellion. The Orthodox bishops had opposed the Greek revolt against the Sultan which, in 1821, produced an independent Greek state and triggered a wave of violent insurrections throughout the Balkans. The Ecumenical Patriarch of the day, horrified by the violence, insisted that the Ottoman sultanate was the proper instrument of God's order on earth. The Church leaders, led by the Patriarch, formally excommunicated the rebels and called for the return of independent Greece to the Ottoman fold.[54] It is not the case, then, that Orthodox believers can never be loyal citizens of a non-Orthodox state, or faithfully subject to Muslim authority. Why, then, did the Bosnian bishops support the insurgency in 1992 and reject the results of the election? Presumably because their loyalties lay not locally but with

53 Adamantia Pollis, 'Eastern Orthodoxy and Human Rights,' *Human Rights Quarterly* 15 (1993), 351.

54 Charles A. Frazee, *The Orthodox Church and Independent Greece 1821–1852* (Cambridge, 1969), 28; cf. Pollis, 347n.

the hierarchy in Belgrade, and therefore with the map and ideology of 'Greater Serbia'. One might speculate that had the Orthodox in Bosnia been granted autocephalous status during the Ottoman period, with the creation of a Bosnian patriarchate in Sarajevo, the consequent abolition of Belgrade's spiritual influence might have allowed Bosnian Orthodox believers to remain peaceable subjects of their elected government in 1992. But that was not to be.

In Serbia itself the Church not only backed the national populists but was their major inspiration. To find the reasons for Pavle's passionate support for Serb national populism it is helpful to delve into Serbian theology, and in particular into its mobilisation of the ancient trope of a dichotomy between Semitic Letter and Christian Spirit.[55] That this principle is still very much alive is shown by the Church's recent record of fierce anti-Semitism. In 2003 the Serbian bishops appointed as their seventy-seventh saint one of the twentieth century's most voluble anti-Semites: Bishop Nikolaj Velimirović (1880-1956). Velimirović had been famous for his anti-Muslim outbursts, but his anti-Jewish feeling seems to have been even more heartfelt:

> All modern European principles have been made by the Jews, who nailed Christ to the cross: democracy, strikes, socialism, atheism, religious tolerance, pacifism, and universal revolution. These are the inventions of the Jews, or their father, the Devil. All this with the sole aim of humiliating Christ and placing on Christ's throne their Jewish messiah, unaware to this day that he is Satan himself, who is their father and who has bridled them with his bridle and whips them with his whip [...] It is surprising that the Europeans, who are a Christian people, have surrendered themselves completely to the Jews, and now think with a Jewish head, accept Jewish

55 Developed first by Paul in Galatians and Romans; see E.P. Sanders, *Paul* (Oxford, 1991), 84-100; for the bitterness and consistency of the theme see Charlotte Klein, tr. Edward Quinn, *Anti-Judaism in Christian Theology* (London, 1978), 39-66.

> programmes, adopt Jewish hatred of Christ, take Jewish lies as truth, endorse Jewish principles as their own [...][56]
>
> Pursuit of cleanliness has turned into a mania for cleanliness. Unfortunately, here too the Yid (*Čivutin*) is involved [...] Plumbing, plumbing, plumbing! Baths, baths, baths! Cleanliness, cleanliness, cleanliness! And everyone tired out with washing and cleaning themselves externally.[57]
>
> The Jews, and their father the Devil, have succeeded, with their gradual poisoning of the spirit and heart of European humanity, in deflecting the latter from true faith and persuading it to worship the idol of culture [...] smoke, dust, mud, sludge [...] an imbecile nothing.[58]

The bishops' choice of Velimirović was no doubt informed by his central role in the development of Serbian religious nationalism. As an official report from the International Contact Group concluded, 'much of the Church's current thinking derives from the writings of two right-wing anti-Semitic clerics active during the Second World War: Bishop Nikolaj Velimirović, who received a civil decoration from Adolf Hitler, and Archimandrite Justin Popović'.[59] 'The Church, together with the VJ's counter-intelligence service KOS, has been closely linked to the anti-Semitic ultra-right wing nationalist youth group Obraz.'[60] Since the 1995 Dayton Peace Accord, denounced by the bishops for not giving Serbs enough

56 Cited by Slobodan Kostić in *Vreme* (Belgrade), 29 May 2003, translated in *Bosnia Report* 32-4 (December 2002-July 2003), p.43; also Jovan Byford, 'Bishop Nikolaj Velimirović: "Lackey of the Germans" or a "Victim of Fascism"?', in Sabrina P. Ramet and Ola Listhaug (eds.), *Serbia and the Serbs in WW2* (Basingstoke, 2011), 136.
57 Kostić, *op. cit.*
58 *Ibid.*
59 'Serbia After Djindjić', *ICG Balkans Report* No.141, 18 March 2003, cited in *Bosnia Report*, loc. cit. For Church collaboration with the Germans during the Second World War, see Sabrina P. Ramet, *Balkan Babel: The Disintegration of Yugoslavia from the death of Tito to the War for Kosovo* (Boulder, 1999), 253-4.
60 *ICG Balkans Report*, 141.

territory in Bosnia, 'the Serbian Orthodox Church has strengthened its position in society significantly'. As the ICG report adds: 'The Church seems to be increasingly and openly tied to ultra-conservative and nationalist groups.' As a direct result of this enhanced role of the Church, non-Christian minorities suffered from intensifying repression and even a kind of enforced invisibility:

> On the evening television news, one sees exactly how far the government goes to marginalize Serbia's minority populations. The Muslim majority city of Novi Pazar, the largest urban centre in the Sandžak region, with a population of over 100,000, is absent from the national map during the weather report. Rather, the map and announcers refer to 'Ras', a Serbian medieval settlement that once existed in the vicinity of Novi Pazar.[61]

In this emerging 'theodemocracy',[62] where the old Byzantine ideal of a *symphonia* between religion and state is a nationalist axiom,[63] Jews and Muslims, even if they have survived ethnic cleansing, are to be truly invisible. Even non-Orthodox Christians are to be treated with derision. Western Church leaders on well-meaning visits to the Balkans are usually unaware, as they kiss Orthodox cheeks, that the leading Serbian theologian on ecumenism, Justin Popović, regarded them as absurd heretics:

> Ecumenism is the common name for pseudo-Christianities, for Western Europe's pseudochurches. All European humanism, headed by papism, are in it with all their heart. All these

---

61 Kostić, 44.

62 For modern Serbian theories of 'theodemocracy', see Branimir Anzulović, *Heavenly Serbia: from myth to genocide* (London, 1999), 125.

63 For the strength of this *symphonia* in present-day Serbia, see Mirko Djordjević, 'Shadow of the "Third Rome"', *Bosnia Report* 51-2 (April-July 2006), 55: 'In contemporary Serbia we are exposed to daily political tirades that actually use the anachronistic term "symphonia"'.

> pseudo-Christianities, all these pseudo-churches are nothing but one heresy after another. [...] There is no essential difference here between papism, Protestantism, ecumenism, and other sects, whose name is legion.[64]

As the new century began the ubiquitous presence of the Church seemed to be suffocating Serb society. In the words of the Montenegrin dissident Mirko Djordjević:

> For the last ten years Serbia has been living in the black shadow of the Srebrenica crime, the most monstrous since the end of World War II. A great proportion of lay opinion and probably of believers too has been asking the Church to speak up. Then again, the SPC [Serbian Orthodox Church] was not actually silent: no one can say that bishops such as Filaret, Amfilohije and Atanasije have kept their own council. For these bishops, Mladić, Karadžić and Milošević are great heroes and worthy Christian warriors. Their declarations have been riding roughshod over the human and religious rights of millions of citizens who do not think like them. In the current alliance of church and state, few have dared to challenge them.[65]

Again, in seeking to understand the force and spirit of Serbian Islamophobia it is helpful to see it as an analogue to anti-Semitism.

---

64 Cited in Anzulović, 126. As Anzulović reminds us, Popović 'is, besides Bishop Nikolaj Velimirović, the most important twentieth-century Serbian Orthodox theologian. He was the teacher of the aggressively nationalist bishops who are presently playing the dominant role in the Serbian Orthodox Church, and his book on ecumenism is the only major Serbian work on the subject.' Metropolitan Amfilohije, at the time of writing (2019) still the senior churchman in Montenegro, is an ardent disciple; see his eulogy translated at www.orthodoxinfo.com/ecumenism/eulogy.aspx. A certain naiveté shapes Western Christian views of this church: see John Binns, *An Introduction to the Christian Orthodox Churches* (Cambridge, 2002), 198-9, where the crimes of the Church leadership are passed over in silence.

65 Mirko Djordjević, 'Scorpions dressed as priests', 36.

Anti-Semitism in Europe traditionally located at least some of its roots in the Gospel idea that Jews had claimed responsibility for the death of Jesus (Matthew 27:25).[66] Islam, however, as other religiously-minded national populists in Europe have noticed, is not mentioned in the Bible, and did not figure as a hostile Other in the early formation of Christian identity and theology. It is hence not immediately clear how Lahabism could be more than a general attitude of rejection of a post-Christian and therefore false claim to prophecy.

Despite this, in Serbia—but not, it seems, in other Orthodox regions—a mythology emerged which portrayed Muslims as 'Christ-killers', and hence as authentic analogues to Jews. To understand this odd transposition it is necessary to be aware of the great, resonant event of Serbian history, which was the defeat of the Serbian King Lazar by the Ottoman Empire in 1389 at the Battle of Kosovo. According to the Serb chroniclers, an Ottoman sympathizer in the Serbian army, Vuk Branković, betrayed his king's battle plans to the Ottomans, and Serbia is defeated in an apocalyptic battle in the course of which Lazar, and also the Ottoman sultan, both perish. Thus are ushered in five centuries of Ottoman ascendency in Serbia.

This mythology ignores the actual record of very frequent Serbian alliances with the Ottomans against the Byzantines.[67] Even the Serbian revolt of 1802, characterised by modern nationalists as anti-Ottoman, was in fact 'not against the Sultan, but against the janissaries who were themselves defying the Porte.'[68] Overwhelmingly the Serb people and clergy were loyal to their Ottoman rulers, who allowed them extensive rights and privileges, and the church played

66 See Luke T. Johnson, 'The New Testament's Anti-Jewish Slander and the Conventions of Ancient Polemic', *Journal of Biblical Literature*, 108 (1989), 419-41.

67 One of the most notable was the support offered by the Serbian ruler Stefan Lazarević to Bayezid I, who in 1396 was in danger of defeat by the Hungarians (Colin Imber, *The Ottoman Empire 1300-1481* [Istanbul, 1990], 46).

68 Barbara Jelavić, *History of the Balkans: Eighteenth and Nineteenth Centuries* (Cambridge, 1983), 197.

a vital role in facilitating this. It was only in the mid-nineteenth century that the Lazar legend, which had survived in folk tales, was mobilised by nationalist ideologues as the foundation stone of a furiously xenophobic national myth.

In this metaphor King Lazar becomes a kind of reincarnation of Jesus, who is betrayed by the Serbian Judas (Branković) and is killed by the Muslims, who thus parallel the Jews. Just as Christ will only return again on earth as a vengeful judge when the Jews have been made to suffer sufficiently for their treachery, so also the punishment of Muslims will atone mysteriously for the death of Lazar, ushering in a Serb millennium. Hence the recurrent popularity of paintings of Lazar's 'Last Supper', surrounded by his entourage, including the scheming traitor Branković, whose face already seems as Muslim as the face of Judas was, in traditional Christian painting, Jewish. The nose is hooked, the skin brown, the eyes glint with a scheming malevolence.

In this mythic version of Serbia's past the Balkan Muslims become essential symbols of treachery. Like Branković they betrayed Christ; they are hence the devil's seed, whose only just fate must be humiliation or death. They had converted to Islam, thus being treasonable to God Incarnate, only out of cowardice and greed. They were pollutants of the Serbian nation, which is perceived as inherently, irreducibly Christian.[69]

This poisonous nineteenth-century mythmaking was not, as is sometimes thought, a simple evolution of older Serbian epic tradition. During most of the Ottoman centuries Serbs had lived peacefully and loyally under Ottoman rule, conscious, no doubt, that the Ottomans provided an effective bulwark against the crusading warriors of Western Catholicism. (In fact, the Serbian people's survival as a religious community would have been unlikely were it not for the Ottoman security umbrella.) Instead, the authors of this mythology, many of whom were the agents of Russian imperial designs on the Ottoman lands, borrowed from German Romanticism, in particular

69 Anzulović, 11-32.

from mischief-makers such as Herder, who were seeking to create a unifying national myth out of carefully selected rural songs and epics. But if Serbian nationalism is, historically speaking, not very Serbian, the anti-Muslim core, the sublimating anti-Semitism, was nothing new. The poem which is generally recognised as the national epic of Serbdom, and which stands at the beginning of the romantic creation of 'Serb identity', draws on ancient, violently Islamophobic sentiments. This poem is the *Mountain-Wreath* by Bishop Njegoš of Montenegro (d.1851). It is a *chanson de geste*, which celebrates another bishop, Danilo, who in the early 18th century had eliminated Islam from Montenegro: the so-called Christmas Eve Massacre.[70]

The *Mountain Wreath* is interesting in several ways. Not least is the way in which the bishop portrays the Muslims, who plead for coexistence. One of them, for instance, says:

> Small enough is this our land,
> Yet two faiths there still may be
> As in one bowl soups may agree
> Let us still as brothers live.

Repeatedly the Muslims are shown as advocates of coexistence; but in the poem this is simply a satanic temptation, the smile of Judas, which the bishop finally overcomes.

So he replies: 'Our land is foul; it reeks of this false religion'. And, following his command:

> No single seeing eye, no Muslim tongue,
> escaped to tell his tale another day.
> We put them all unto the sword
> All those who would not be baptised.
> But who paid homage to the Holy Child,
> were all baptised with sign of Christian cross.
> And as brother each was hail'd and greeted.
> We put to fire the Muslim houses,

70 Sells, *Bridge*, 41. Some sources estimate the number of casualties at over a hundred thousand, but this is unsure.

That there might be no stick nor trace
Of these true servants of the devil!

When news of the massacre reaches the Serbian leaders, one of the abbots starts weeping. Out of shock at the idea that he might be expressing sorrow for the victims he is reproached, but he replies that he is weeping for joy. The poem ends with an ecstatic recital by the Serb warriors returning from the massacre, and observes that they have no need to go to confession before taking communion.[71]

Njegoš is the Serbian Shakespeare; his poem was required reading in all schools in prewar Yugoslavia. Even the reformist maverick Milovan Djilas praised this 'poet of massacres'; and the militant saint Nikolaj Velimirović honoured him with a book-length eulogy.[72] One of his most committed readers was Radovan Karadžić himself, who although not a priest, loved to wear large crosses, and still strongly identifies himself with the heroic bishop of the story. His favourite self-image is that of an itinerant bard, fiddling at a *gusle* (a traditional Bosnian instrument) and singing with his soldiers. These sessions, regularly broadcast on Republika Srpska TV during the war, begin with the passing round of an alcoholic drink, and all the soldiers make the sign of the cross before beginning with the words:

Serb brothers, wherever you are,
with the help of Almighty God,
For the sake of the Cross and the Christian faith,
I call you to join the battle of Kosovo.[73]

Karadžić's favourite folk song, he tells us, is called 'The Last Supper', which as he says: 'has something to do with Jesus Christ, symbolising Serbian faith after that lost battle.'[74] Karadžić, after all, claims kinship to the same Vuk Karadžić who collected the *Moun-*

71 Anzulović, 52–3; Sells, *Bridge,* 43.
72 Byford, 131.
73 Sells, *Bridge,* 50.
74 Sells, *Bridge,* 50.

tain Wreath and other poems and fashioned them into the matter of Serb romantic nationalism.

Karadžić, and the national populism he represents, can be seen as a product of local Balkan particularities. His 'christoslavism', with its mutant concept that Muslims are Christ-killers and betrayers of Orthodoxy who are thereby expelled from the category of normal humanity, differs substantially from Greek, Romanian, or Russian images of Muslims (although these are not usually more sympathetic). In fact, a characteristic feature of Serbian Orthodox nationalism is a paradoxical portrayal of Muslims as hospitable and eirenic, as evidenced by the *Mountain Wreath*. But this is no more than the devil's subterfuge, and the true Orthodox warrior must not be tempted by it to show mercy. Velimirović, the recently-sainted theologian, is quite clear: 'they are evil, and the evil has to be crushed until it is eradicated. In a row of dried-up heads, Njegoš did not see human heads but only the heads of the enemies of justice. These rows of heads served as trophies of avenged justice.'[75] In 2014, Amfilohije, still Montenegro's senior churchman, preached on the poem, noting that although the killings were unfortunate, 'more terrible is the spiritual death spread by false human beings with false beliefs [...] Bishop Danilo saved Montenegro'.[76]

To conclude. The lurid prophecy of Baudrillard need not be fulfilled, but Muslims should be watching with care. For as long as the Letter-Spirit dichotomy endures in European minds, the commandment of *yezkor*, Remembrance, will stand. Today it is not only Serbian believers who condemn 'the madmen infected with the Asiatic plague, who hold a knife at our backs,'[77] and who oblige Muslims to wear crescent armbands, just as Jews once wore yellow badges.[78] Lahabist nationalism is on the rise throughout the

75 Anzulović, 64-5.

76 Sabina Pačariz, 'Montenegro', in Oliver Scharbrodt et al., *Yearbook of Muslims in Europe,* 7 (2015), 409.

77 Gojko Djogo, president of the Union of Bosnia-Herzegovina Serbs in Serbia, quoted in Cigar, 185.

78 James Gow, *Triumph of the Lack of Will: International Diplomacy and the Yugo-*

Orthodox world, is politically empowered in the United States, and is gaining ground in the secular societies of the European Union. Anders Breivik claimed to find his inspiration in Bosnia's Serbs,[79] while the New Zealand mosque murderer sang Chetnik songs during his assault.[80] Today, Muslims are endlessly instructed to integrate into 'European values'. How can this be, however, when Europe, the 'Dark Continent' of Mark Mazower's grim narrative, clings to its shadow side, populated by ghosts of its violent xenophobic past, so that an MEP is able to call for a new *Endlosung?*[81] How can it be if, as Pope Benedict seemed to imply at Regensburg, Christianity, and hence the apocalyptic contest with 'Semitic legalism', is Europe's true faith? Perhaps, instead of surrendering to demands for assimilation, Muslims on this troubled continent should take on the role of exorcists, seeking to cast out the continent's myriad unclean spirits. That would be, presumably, the more religious response.

slav War (London, 1997), 33.

79 Bangstad, 75.

80 'Christchurch shootings: Serb song in gunman's video opens old wounds in the Balkans'. *Straits Times,* 18 March 2019.

81 'Estonian MEP calls for "final solution" to Syrian refugee crisis', *Daily Telegraph*, 2 August 2019.

CHAPTER 5

The Venomous *Bidᶜa* of *Tanfīr*

Were the truth to be in accordance with their own desires, the heavens and the earth would surely have fallen into ruin, and all that is therein.

QUR'AN 23:71

THE MUSLIM ACCUMULATION in Western minority contexts has not yet been matched by a growth in theological and Sharia reflection or by the appearance of an appropriately credible leadership which might promote it. Many migrant-origin Muslims have roots in weakly-educated cultures, their imams and community leaders having little acquaintance with the higher discourse of classical Islamic scholarship; they suffer likewise from a poor understanding of the European environment and the immensely complex promises and threats which it presents. Many opportunities for entrenchment and growth have been lost as a result of this twofold incapacity, and many gates have been opened unnecessarily for the community's discursive and political enemies.

An intellectual vacuum on this scale has predictably sucked in playful dilettantes and Sharia amateurs, some of them voluble clowns who have afforded much delight to television producers, having found in the bruised resentments of inner-city youth, angered by stop-and-search routines, job discrimination and a growing media repugnance towards the visible signs of Muslimness, a readily dissident audience for their firebrand manipulations of Islam's heritage. The wild lands of the Internet and the diminishing attention span enabled by modern culture combine to short-circuit Muslim interest away from the considered and compassionate language of the classically-trained scholars, towards the lure of endorphin-hit religion, which takes from the heritage only that which can deliver a polarised and simple view of a threatening world in which the foreign policy of Western nations is seen as cruel and outrageous and their domestic policy as lacking in sincere respect. In this way much Muslim discourse ironically mirrors the selective and ignorant exploitation of national and cultural capital deployed by the new national populist movements across Europe and the wider world. The manipulators of identity are similar as well as symbiotic.

Unlike most national populists, however, whose roots stretch down no deeper than the ego and its fears, Muslim communities are heirs to an immensely rich heritage whose purpose is not to confer a reassuring identity but to orientate human beings towards their Creator. It is therefore clear that in the current trap of mutual reinforcement between the identity-obsessed on both sides, it is Ishmael who must take the initiative to break the cycle of mutual disgust. Government certainly cannot, since its instruments are always too blunt: it can slowly transform a country into a panopticon, a Surveillance State which conscripts teachers, doctors and social workers into a kind of Territorial Army for the security services, but it remains unhappily aware that these expensive corruptions of the ideals of liberalism may be more apt to tighten polarities than to unravel them. The real knots lie in the heart, a place where laws and policemen cannot venture, but which is home territory to a religion ready for a 'greater Jihad,' for which it is fully armed with powerful spiritual technologies.[1]

The Muslim is never just a citizen; he or she is a *metacitizen*; unlike the secular reductionist the believer is ethical for a strong and high reason, and is able to endure hate and hardship 'in God's path', *fī sabīli'Llāh*, expecting no earthly recompense. To the extent that

1 'Of all types of mysticism, that of Islam is the richest perhaps in quantity and certainly in the quality of its literature.' Christopher Dawson, *Enquiries into Religion and Culture* (New edition Washington DC, 2009), 131.

Muslims fear God they have no fear of misfortune or its authors; 'no fear is upon them, neither do they grieve,' (2:38) for 'We suffice you against the ridiculers.' (15:95) The only dread, *makhāfa*, is of a failure to harmonise with the Divine reality, and this is treated by means of the calm return to *sunna* and *fiṭra*. It was the hypocrites (*munāfiqūn*) of Madina who panicked during the pagan siege: 'those to whom the people said: "They have gathered against you, so fear them!" yet this increased their faith and they said: "Allah is enough for us, and the best Guardian".' (3:173) The weak or absent convictions of the hypocrites, as they whimper under the Islamophobe's lash in modern as in ancient times, cannot protect them from fear and stress; by contrast, the believers find their faith (*īmān*) paradoxically growing under this pressure, as they recognise more clearly in the midst of misfortune that this world is not comfortable but that everything is still in the Creator's hands. Hence the Bosnian rape victims who rediscovered God and Islam as a result of their traumas.[2] The outcome, as at Madina, is that 'they returned with grace and favour from Allah, and harm did not touch them; they followed Allah's good pleasure, and Allah is of immense grace. It is only Satan who makes men fear his followers, but fear them not: fear Me, if you be believers.' (3:174-5)

The world (*dunyā*), and in some respects our age in particular, is driven and divided by what we have called Fear, awarding an emphatic capital letter to the commonplace word. The material plane of clashing forms, of supernovas and earthquakes, of war and pestilence and human treachery, confronts us with an unbearable series of threats and disappointments, and in our smallness and weakness we feel afraid of them, shuddering like an uncomprehending cat when it hears a firework. Only a mature understanding, a knowledge of the One and Just Source of these phenomena, the Causer of causes (*musabbib al-asbāb*), can protect us from such fears; 'by the remembering of God do hearts find peace.' (13:28) *Īmān*, which we carelessly translate as 'faith', more correctly denotes a state of

2 Takševa, *op. cit.*

knowledgeable trust. When *tawḥīd* sits deep within the heart and guides every human reaction, however immediate, the *mu'min*, the one with *īmān*, will 'follow Allah's good pleasure', and will not fear proximate causes (*asbāb*). 'Fear them not, but fear Me.' (2:150) Such a believer finds himself instinctively crying out '*al-ḥamdu li'Llāh*', praise is for God, even as misfortune strikes.[3] Those who have lived among fully traditional believers will not fail to have observed this seeming paradox.

Hence an Islam rooted in *tawḥīd* rejects any view of society which is merely sociological, since 'social sciences', with their attempts to predict outcomes through a merely material measuring of human beings, are always strictly biased against any acknowledgement of divine intervention. The Qur'anic narratives defy sociology by presenting episodes of unforeseen redemption: Moses trusts in God where Pharaoh trusts the *asbāb*; Joseph endures exile and imprisonment; the Blessed Virgin silently shows her child to the outraged crowd; Noah is patient beneath the mockery of the anti-religious of his day; Abraham accepts an evident tribulation (*balā' mubīn*) which Nimrod would have found outrageous; and all are unexpectedly saved. These insistently recurrent narratives bear the most immediate relevance to ourselves, and serve as a timely reminder that Fearfulness, as trust in the *asbāb*, is a defining pagan quality, a paradigm of *nifāq* and the *ḥamiyyat al-jāhiliyya*, the panic-ridden passion of the Age of Ignorance.

One consequence of this understanding is that when theologising their response to a modern world which seems to bring nothing but disaster and oppression to Ishmael, believers in *tawḥīd* will categorically avoid ideology. The word 'ideology' was invented by Antoine Destutt de Tracy (d.1836) to indicate a purely materialistic view of human society that would replace monotheism with a 'version of zoology' that sought to understand ideas and create a structure of thought that would exclude any reference to the supernatural. Marx picked up the coinage and used it to refer to

3 Schuitema, 121.

the false intellectual systems which justified capitalism; and since that time the word has had negative connotations in the English language, so that today ideology is 'generally a disparaging term used to describe someone else's political views which one regards as unsound.'[4] Ideology, which attributes ultimate agency to the *asbāb*, is the essence of *kufr*, disbelief, and readily engenders totalitarian systems of thought, which seek to impose a single paradigm of human behaviour on society through the agencies of an 'enlightened' scientific state. This may be one reason why some twentieth-century Muslim reformists proposed that Islam itself is an 'ideology'.[5] Presumably not having caught the unsavoury aroma of the word, they chose it because of its connotations of state coercion and, perhaps, because it made Islam sound more 'modern' and relevant to those who suffered from an inferiority complex as the result of a colonial education.

What Traditional Islam requires, however, is the precise opposite of ideology. But that opposite is not 'religion' in anything like a conventional sense. 'Religion', too, is a difficult term because of its Occidental resonances: many contemporary thinkers deplore the essentialising and, as it were, 'ideologising' implications of defining all of the world's multiform sacred traditions as 'religions': 'Hinduism', for instance, is properly not a religion the way Christianity is, for it is far too diverse and polycentric; many historians consider it little more than an invention by British colonial scholars who assumed that Indic traditions functioned like Christianity.[6] Islam to some extent is analogous: while many Orientalists and many of Islam's English-speaking representatives use the word 'religion' as

4 Robert Audi (ed.), *Cambridge Dictionary of Philosophy* (Cambridge, 1995), 360.

5 See for instance Jan-Peter Hartung, *A System of Life: Mawdudi and the Ideologisation of Islam* (New York, 2014).

6 'Hinduism was born in the nineteenth century, a notoriously illegitimate child. The father was middle-class and British, the mother of course was India.' John Hawley, 'Naming Hinduism,' *Wilson Quarterly* 15 (1991), 20–34, p.20; see also Romila Thapar, 'Ancient History and the Search for a Hindu Identity', *Modern Asian Studies* 23 (1989), 209-231.

a convenient translation of *dīn*, it lacks many of the characteristic features of historic Christianity, notably its idea of a unifying ecclesiastical discipline, and of formal structures of church-state integration. What God requires, it therefore seems, is neither ideology nor religion, but simply *dīn*.

This *dīn*, signifying an all-embracing transaction or relationship between humanity and its Creator, maximizes the ability of the former to love the latter (God's love for humanity is already a given). According to the first hadith studied in traditional curricula, 'those who show mercy shall be shown mercy by the Merciful. Have mercy upon those who are on earth, and He that is in heaven shall have mercy upon you.'[7] The believer's horizontal relations are shaped and made selfless by his vertical loyalty to his Maker, Whose paradigmatic name is *al-Raḥmān*, the All-Compassionate. By reconnecting lost and stressed humanity to the Compassionate, the Man of Praise is 'nothing but a mercy to the worlds' (*raḥmatan li'l-ᶜālamīn*). (21:107) Whereas de Tracy and Marx saw society as a regulated structure of essentially hedonistic and self-serving minds bound together for material benefit, revelation invites us to bow the head before pure Compassion, to see the world as luminously phanic, and in consequence to be moral agents and to serve others irrespective of personal gain. 'And they give food in charity out of love for Him, saying: "We seek neither recompense nor thanks from you".' (76:8-9) Duty and service therefore comprise a pilgrimage towards the Kaᶜba of the soul, where we re-experience the calm of God's compassion. Ideology, in sharp contrast, is locked outside the door of the sanctuary, within which only the sincerely merciful may tread.

As metacitizens we are called to *al-Raḥmān*, facing not each other but the collective *qibla*, and therefore we are to be fountainheads of mercy; and in this way we call others to our way. This is *daᶜwa*, which is the work of the Messengers, and of every noble human soul since the earliest age of man. While it is an inflexible and constant duty for every Muslim everywhere, it is a calling and

7 Abū Dāūd, Adab, 58; Tirmidhī, Birr, 16.

a privilege which rests with particular firmness upon the shoulders of Muslims who live in the spiritually-eroded and morally-unfixed Occident. Most Muslims in France migrated in order to eat more *tagine* or to seek a EU passport, but this, in Sharia terms, did not usually comprise a good reason for *hijra*. 'Whoever's migration is for some worldly thing, or to marry a woman, then his migration is accordingly for that.'[8] As we have already observed, those who were led by such an intention are likely to find themselves watching their children being ensnared and stressed even more intensely than they themselves are by possessions and desires. Their intention must now be consciously and decisively changed to embrace what is usually the only real Sharia legitimation for leaving their ancestral hearth: the summons to *al-Raḥmān*. The history of Islam in Europe, as opposed to the history of Muslims in Europe, begins not with migration but with the deliberate adoption of this intention. From this turning-point onwards, *dīn* may be said to have arrived, and the possibility of Divine *riḍwān*, 'good-pleasure'—and therefore success—is opened before the community.

Authentic Muslims are unavoidably people of beauty, for 'God loves the beautiful.'[9] This refers to beauty in its widest sense: moral, physical, and spiritual: the full spectrum of *iḥsān*, of 'doing the beautiful'. Beauty reflects the Divine presence and attracts the heart, thus opening the doors of truth to those who sit in shadows. *Daʿwa* is the pointing-out of what is beautiful. It is therefore a disclosure and confirmation of the state of the refined believing soul. Yet if the soul has been misshaped by the ideologies of the Fearful it will disclose only ugliness: the disorder of a self wracked by stress, disharmony and ill-controlled desires (*ahwā'*). Muslims who are Fearful do not only repel others from themselves, but from the *dīn* which they claim. Nothing is more subversive and obstructive of God's cause than offering an ugly manifestation of the self and claiming it to be Islamic.

8 Bukhārī, Īmān, 41; Muslim, Imāra, 155.

9 Tirmidhī, Birr, 61.

This is what is called *tanfīr*: repelling souls instead of attracting them. The *jāhilī* Arabs were under the authority of ego and Fearfulness; thus their way of existence and their personal presence were ugly and disturbing; the Man of Praise then showed beauty, and hearts melted. This is why *tanfīr* is so absolutely condemned in the Sunna: the sound hadith instructs us to 'bring ease and not hardship, good tidings and not repulsion' (*yassirū wa-lā tuʿassirū, bashshirū wa-la tunaffirū*).[10] As the commentator observes: 'The hadith commands us to give people the good news of God's grace and wide mercy, and forbids us to repel them.'[11] One who drives human souls away from *tawḥīd* is a *tanfīrī*, and is accursed, since he or she is directly undoing the work of the Prophets.

Secure awareness that the Source is the author of all events opens up the seeking of the divine *riḍwān* and brings calm to the soul, which then manifests naturally as the cardinal virtue of mildness (*ḥilm*).

> The Qur'an as a whole is dominated by the very spirit of *ḥilm*. The constant exhortation to kindness [*iḥsān*] in human relations, the emphasis laid on justice [*ʿadl*], the forbidding of wrongful violence [*ẓulm*], the bidding of abstinence and control of passions, the criticism of groundless pride and arrogance—are all concrete manifestations of this spirit of *ḥilm*.[12]
>
> [In the Qur'an's worldview] he who is always willing to help the poor, is slow to anger, forbears from retaliating, and forgives offences—this is the very embodiment of the virtue of *ḥilm*.[13]

10 Bukhārī, ʿIlm, 11; Muslim, Jihād, 5.

11 Shams al-Dīn Muḥammad al-Kirmānī, *al-Kawākib al-Darārī fī sharḥ Ṣaḥīḥ al-Bukhārī* (Beirut, 1401/1981), II, 34.

12 Toshihiko Izutsu, *God and Man in the Qur'an: semantics of the Qur'anic weltanschauung* (Tokyo, 1964), 236.

13 Toshihiko Izutsu, *Ethico-Religious Concepts in the Qur'ān* (Montreal, 2002), 225.

This mildness characterizes the sermons of the Holy Prophet, and bears little resemblance to the cant and rant preaching often heard today on the pulpits of the Fearful. Lack of *ḥilm* is from the following of passion, but 'do not follow passion [*hawā*], for it will mislead you from God's path.' (38:26) It can even lead to the psychological state generally referred to in the present age as extremism, a word which corresponds accurately enough to the Islamic and indeed Qur'anic term *ghuluww*. The Fearful tend to two different reactions to their precarious situation, both of them extreme. Some may respond by lowering their heads in submission, abandoning whichever principles of the religion the dominant culture dislikes, and then calling the result Progressive Islam.[14] This is one type of extremism: a homeopathic view of religion that believes that the more one waters it down, the stronger it will become. It is one consequence of the impact of modernity. However the more common *ghuluww* in our times is for the rage and frustration of the poorly-schooled Muslim to find gratification in ferocious interpretations and vengeful politics. Because it boils up from the ego rather than from the *rūḥ* this is a dire manifestation of the *tanfīr* principle, and does even more harm to the Umma and to Islam's honour.

Ghuluww, defined by Imām al-Shāṭibī as 'exaggeration' and 'harshness' (*mubālagha wa-tashdīd*),[15] is a human frailty repeatedly warned against in the heritage of the Man of Praise. 'O people, beware of *ghuluww* in your religion, because the religious communities that came before you were destroyed by it.'[16] It is the state of the believer who is agitated by Fearfulness and unavowed envy, and who on the basis of that agitation throws himself into religion with the assumption that narrowness is a synonym for piety, and a sign of sincerity and refusal to compromise with falsehood. In some cases this can grow so outrageous in its psychic power that the real essence of *dīn* withers catastrophically, until all that substantively remains is

14 Gilis, *Intégrité*, 49-51.

15 Ibrāhīm ibn Mūsā al-Shāṭibī, *al-Iʿtiṣām* (Cairo, 1332AH), III, 304.

16 Nasā'ī, Manāsik, 5.

the fiery condition of rage and rejection. The Man of Praise observed that some people charge into *dīn* so hard that they come out the other side, like an arrow passing right through its target (*yamruqu min al-dīn kamā yamruqu'l-sahmu min al-ramiyya*),[17] and as Imām al-Nawawī comments, *dīn* then becomes 'like a hunted animal through which the arrow passes, carrying nothing with it.'[18] The same image of passing right through religion occurs in another Prophetic warning: 'Two people will be excluded from my Intercession on the Day of Arising: an unjust, arbitrary, treacherous leader, and an extremist in religion, who departs through it [*ghālin fi'd-dīni māriqun minh*]'.[19] This prophetic rejection of the temptation of *ghuluww* is not only rooted in a practical awareness that extreme religion is self-defeating, but in a concern for the state of those egos which tend to practice with extravagant intensity. 'No-one shall practice *dīn* harshly without being overpowered by it'.[20] For Ibn Ḥajar the meaning of this statement is that 'no-one plunges deep into religious actions while abandoning gentleness without failing and being cut off, and thus ending up in defeat'; he cites Ibn al-Munīr: 'this hadith contains one of the cardinal indications of prophethood. We have witnessed, and our predecessors witnessed, that every religious fanatic [*mutanaṭṭiᶜ fi'l-dīn*] is cut off.'[21] This termination, this extinction of the zealot's mad hope, is the meaning of the Prophetic warning that 'fanatics shall perish' (*halaka'l-mutanaṭṭiᶜūn*).[22]

In the majoritarian Islamic world the cumulation of anger against regime cruelty and disastrous Western interference has exploded into terroristic manifestations which have almost made ours the

17 Bukhārī, Anbiyā', 6; Muslim, Zakāt, 142; Abū Dāūd, Sunna, 28.

18 Muḥyī al-Dīn al-Nawawī, *al-Minhāj fī sharḥ Ṣaḥīḥ Muslim ibn al-Ḥajjāj* (Cairo, 1347AH), VII, 159.

19 Sulaymān ibn Aḥmad al-Ṭabarānī, *al-Muᶜjam al-Kabīr* (Beirut, 1984), XX, 214.

20 Bukhārī, Īmān, 29.

21 Ibn Ḥajar al-ᶜAsqalānī, *Fatḥ al-Bārī sharḥ Ṣaḥīḥ al-Bukhārī* (Riyadh and Damascus, 3rd ed. 1421/2000), I, 126-7.

22 Muslim, ᶜIlm, 7.

Age of *Tanfīr*. But *tanfīr* defeats its own purposes: every outrage, even when intended to anger and distress Islam's enemies, in fact pleases them, for these actions seem to confirm the darkest Islamophobic stereotypes. Hence the realisation now belatedly gaining traction among Palestinians that 'suicide bombing', as a response to an oppressive and ethnocentric military occupation, has in fact considerably benefited the Israeli right and the Zionist lobbies, damaging only the Palestinian cause. In Algeria the regime defeated the GIA and the Salafist Group for Preaching and Combat because of popular revulsion at the rebellion's cruelty.[23] The wave of unbelief (*mawjat al-ilḥād*) currently moving across the Arab world has been triggered, according to its own victims, by the spectacle of extreme violence by *tanfīrī* Salafists in Iraq, Syria, Libya and elsewhere.[24] *Tanfīrīs* primarily kill other Muslims, and their assumption that narrowness equates to authenticity ensures that they also spectacularly fight among themselves.[25] The use of extreme savagery to intimidate populations into unhappy submission turns into a gift for the religion's enemies, and enables, ultimately, a reinforcement of the weakness and American control which generated the *tanfīrī* impulses in the first place.[26]

Where *tanfīr* becomes most lethal to Muslim faith is in situations where it has become empowered. Here believers watch with dismay the ugliness of the state, and feel their faith draining away, because the angry and vengeful authorities have coercively self-identified with Islam.

---

23 Mohammed M. Hafez, *Why Muslims Rebel: repression and resistance in the Islamic world* (New York, 2004), 170, 172.

24 Azadeh Moaveni, *Guest House for Young Widows among the women of ISIS* (Melbourne and London, 2019), 180.

25 Tore Refslund Hamming, *Polemical and Fratricidal Jihadists: A Historical Examination of Debates, Contestation and Infighting within the Sunni Jihadi Movement* (London, 2019).

26 Max Blumenthal, *The Management of Savagery: How America's national security state fuelled the rise of Al Qaeda, ISIS, and Donald Trump* (London, 2019), 152.

> I had heard fewer calls to prayer in Tehran than in any other Muslim city I had visited. During set prayer times, several of the mosques were nearly empty, and some were being converted for other uses. Indeed, one of the mosques in Tehran is now used as a political party's election headquarters. My Iranian colleagues explained, and the rituals demonstrated, that the overwhelming majority of young Iranians (two-thirds of the population is under age 30) neither fast during Ramadan nor pray at the daily required times. It might not be practical to collect mosque-attendance statistics or conduct public-opinion polls, but there is strong evidence that the power of religion over the people of Iran seems to be attenuating.[27]

Several decades after its revolution, Iran, where religion is determined by the state, is becoming a Riddastan, ruled by a carceral ideology which to a growing number of its citizens feels oppressive and irksome. As Imam ʿAlī once remarked: 'Give ease to human hearts, for when they are forced into something, they go blind.'[28] At fault is *shirk al-iḥtisāb*: 'the polytheism of compulsion', forcing citizens to obey God and thereby subverting the purity of their intentions. This, again, is a frequent entailment of the transformation of *dīn* into ideology. Classical Sharia agrees that the ruler has virtually no control over legislation: God's law is found, interpreted and actualized by the Muslim populace through their expert representatives, who are the ulema, who must as a matter of necessity be independent of the ruler.[29] For Wael Hallaq, 'the Sharia has ceased to be even an approximate reincarnation of its historical self'[30] in

27 Amitai Etzioni, 'Flirting and Flag-Waving: The Revealing Study of Holidays and Rituals', *Chronicle of Higher Education* 49/16 (December 13, 2002), 16.

28 Ghazālī, *Iḥyā'*, IV, 321.

29 In Ḥanafī law the ruler has only four powers: establishing Friday and Eid prayers, applying the *ḥudūd*, collecting *zakāt*, and collecting the *khums* land-tax. However even the rules for these four facilities are determined by the scholars, not the ruler.

30 Wael Hallaq, *Sharīʿa: theory, practice, transformations* (Cambridge, 2009), 550.

the modern Muslim world: it has mutated into state law, with elected, dictatorial or clerical regimes choosing which fatwa options to legislate as statutes. In the classical Sharia local communities were expected to be largely self-regulating, almost anticipating anarcho-syndicalist ideas of a transcendentalist self-reliance by small social modules preserving a high degree of sociality and a moral purpose which would be corrupted by state intervention and homogenisation. By contrast, following the British Raj's decision in the nineteenth century to turn personal status elements of Sharia into statutory laws, Western-educated Muslims slowly adopted the idea of religious law as something to be interpreted and enacted by the legislature of a nation state. The result has been systemic failure everywhere, together with the substantial loss of the Sharia's diversity, the *madhhab* system, and the independence and hence the moral authority of many ulema. Every Muslim polity which has attempted to Westernise Islam's ethico-legal vision by reinventing Sharia as statutory law has created a totalitarian, ideological state which, by turning Islam into a Procrustean bed, in the longer term becomes a tragic Riddastan and a global energizer of *tanfīr*. A thousand years ago the Abbasid caliph al-Ma'mūn abused his authority by attempting to impose a Muʿtazilite doctrine on an unwilling population, with the result that within a generation that doctrine had been discredited forever. In our time of all-regulating carceral states, 'protest atheism' is a concerningly common result of this misguided rejection of the basic logic and integrity of God's law.[31] Ideology will inexorably turn souls towards secularity and secularism, and several vocal Islamophobes now are 'dry drunks', their fanatical atheism resulting from the spiritual damage done by regime-imposed Islam reduced to the status of an ideology, a captive eagle with feathers clipped by peasants familiar only with chickens. In this strange new Islamist world, the older, more authentic and uncompromising Islam has been all but forgotten, although a few

---

31 For this concept see Kevin J. Vanhoozer, *Nothing Greater, Nothing Better: theological essays on the love of God* (Grand Rapids, 2001), 10.

elderly Mohicans remain, quietly shaking their heads in the remoter forests.

A further indicative quality of Fearful Islam is its enthusiasm for hurling anathemas and excommunications: the assassin's blade of *takfīr*. The Kharijites in early Islam had failed to sustain themselves because their violent *takfīr* of other Muslims and of each other was deeply alienating to a Muslim public opinion which was steeped in the Prophetic ethos of brotherhood and of 'finding excuses' (*iltimās al-ᶜudhr*) for other Muslims. The Muᶜtazilites (necessarily Fearful given their fantasies about causation) were likewise prone to *takfīr* and fierce internal wrangles: it is said that the Baghdad and Basran Muᶜtazila were divided by a thousand issues, and ceaselessly made *takfīr* of each other.[32] For classical Sunnis, by contrast, the formal declaration of *takfīr* was understood to be immensely complex and difficult,[33] while suspicion (*sū' al-ẓann*) and failure to give others the benefit of the doubt comprised 'the worst of sins';[34] but among modern *tanfīrī* groups mutual *takfīr* has reached epidemic proportions.[35] Again this triggers a revulsion against Islam in the countries concerned; and in the West, too, such extreme divisive behaviour has demoralized Muslims and significantly inhibited the *daᶜwa* process.[36]

---

32 Eric Ormsby, *Theodicy in Islamic Thought: the dispute over al-Ghazālī's Best of All Possible Worlds* (Princeton, 1984), 21.

33 Nawawī, *Minhāj*, VII, 160, citing Imām al-Ḥaramayn al-Juwaynī.

34 ᶜAbd al-Ghanī al-Nāblusī, *al-Ḥadīqat al-Nadiyya sharḥ al-Ṭarīqa al-Muḥammadiyya* (Lahore, n.d.), I, 241.

35 E. Alshech, 'The Doctrinal Crisis within the Salafi-Jihadi Ranks and the Emergence of Neo-Takfīrism,' *Islamic Law and Society* 21 (2014), 419–52; Hayat Alvi, 'Diffusion of Intra-Islamic Violence: the Proliferation of Salafi-Wahhabi Ideologies,' *Middle East Review of International Affairs* 18 (2014), 38-50.

36 Umar Lee, *The Rise and Fall of the Salafi Da'wa in America: a memoir* (St Louis, 2014). The frequent Salafist rush to *takfīr* is to be contrasted with the position of traditional Islam. For Abū Ḥanīfa, 'the status of a Muslim in the territory of polytheism who affirms Islam as a whole but does not know or affirm the Koran or any of the religious duties of Islam' is still a believer. Wilferd Madelung, 'The Spread of Māturīdism and the Turks,' 109-68 of

However *tanfīr* is not only a consequence of frustration and of failure to master emotion. It represents also an ignorance of *uṣūl*, the jurisprudential and ethical methods by which appropriate Muslim behaviour is discovered in revelation. Ideologues may circumvent the ulema by looking for answers that serve their emotional needs, thus abolishing the foundational rule of our jurisprudence, which is that emotion (*hawā*) must never sway exegetic choices. The Internet and social media have greatly facilitated this epistemic bypassing. However it is also the case that classically-trained ulema are less accessible to ordinary Muslims than they were in former ages, partly because of the decline or closure of the *awqāf*-funded colleges which once sustained them,[37] partly because of the imposition of state fatwa agencies established by regimes which have supplanted the tradition of freely associating scholars seeking the objective entailments of revelation, but partly too because of the sheer decadence of the times; and this, too, seems to have been forecast, for the vanishing of the true *mujtahid* is believed to be one of the 'signs of the Hour'.

> God does not remove knowledge by snatching it at once from mankind's hearts, but takes it away by taking the scholars away; and when no scholar remains, people take ignorant leaders; they ask them questions, and they give fatwas without knowledge; they go astray and lead astray.[38]

The knowledge of which this hadith speaks is in the first instance an *uṣūlī* knowledge, in the sense of the heart's wisdom and intuitive understanding of the purposes of the law, which requires spiritual insight. For al-Ḥasan al-Baṣrī:

Actas do IV Congresso de Estudos Árabes e Islâmicos, Coimbra – Lisboa 1968 (Leiden, 1971), pp.122-3.

37 'The decline of this institution [the *waqf*] in the nineteenth century led to the general material impoverishment of Islam that is witnessed today.' John Robert Barnes, *An Introduction to Religious Foundations in the Ottoman Empire* (Leiden, 1987), ix.

38 Bukhārī, ʿIlm, 34; Muslim, ʿIlm, 13.

> There are two forms of knowledge: formal knowledge, and the heart's knowledge, and the first form of knowledge to be removed will be the latter of the two, which is 'useful knowledge', the inner knowledge (*al-ᶜilm al-bāṭin*) which enters and repairs hearts. Then outward knowledge will disappear, then the Qur'an itself, until the end of time when nothing at all remains either in the copies of the Qur'an or in human hearts. Then the Hour will come.[39]

In the European context it is evident that the struggling and generally embryonic madrasa infrastructure has not generated enough scholars who are deeply schooled in the classical jurisprudence and who also have the 'inner knowledge' to which al-Ḥasan al-Baṣrī refers. The shift over the past century in the Dār al-ᶜUlūm curriculum—to take an example relevant to the British case—has been away from *uṣūl* and towards *ḥadīth* and positive law (*furūᶜ*), with the result that much madrasa learning takes the form of the defensive maintenance of inherited fatwa anthologies whose original context was a radically different place and age. The Sufi infrastructure which 'polished hearts' has also been downgraded and in some cases neglected by the ulema, whose concerns have become more formalistic. The result is that the newly-graduated and very erudite madrasa alumnus may be pityingly dismissed by Western-educated youth as a type of idiot-savant, an ambulant database of Moghul, Moroccan or Indonesian opinions who offers only an anachronistic blueprint for community compliance, and struggles to justify the vision of the Man of Praise to those who live the contemporary Ishmaelite reality. One reason for this scholarly fossilization and externalization is that the madrasas are often in competition with one another, an emotive and anxious situation which imposes the duty of a conspicuously strict maintenance of established patterns, and also obedience to moneyed but uninformed patrons who judge authenticity by fidelity to inherited

39 ᶜAbd al-Raḥmān Ibn Rajab, *Jāmiᶜ al-ᶜulūm wa'l-ḥikam fī sharḥ khamsīn ḥadīthan min jawāmiᶜ al-kalim* (Beirut, 1417/1996), II, 191.

curricula, ethnic affiliation, sectarian outlooks and managerial styles. For a scholar to gain a mastery of *uṣūl* and to break out from one of these hyperconformist silos often entails unusual courage and the taking of grave risks.

It hardly needs stating that *ijtihād* for Western-based communities must place the war against *tanfīr* at the centre of its priorities. This does not only refer to political violence. Imams, muftis, race temple managers and *pīrs* who ignore or disregard their Muslim and non-Muslim neighbours are rejecting a cardinal aspect of prophetic loyalty and the divine command which instructs us to 'say to mankind what is beautiful' (2:83) and to honour 'the near neighbour and the far.'[40] (4:36) Consider the spectacle of a *mīlād* procession in Denmark or England, which is often in reality little more than a carnival of *uṣūl*-indifferent exotic display, an unintended challenge to the memory of the Man of Praise who was sent 'to the worlds', but who has been turned into the private hero of a troubled diasporic clan. This is not terrorism, but in its anachronism and geographic ignorance it remains undeniably a form of *tanfīr*.

Ijtihād requires a knowledge of the modality of God's compassionate legislating for humankind, and the Māturīdī tradition of seeking to determine the socio-ethical heuristics of the law, which flourished at the hands of thinkers such as Shāh Walī Allāh al-Dahlawī, has to be resuscitated.[41] At the very heart of its morality is the principle of service to human flourishing. *Maṣlaḥa,* public interest, is not only a 'secondary source' of the Sharia but is its entire purpose, furnishing the indispensable reason for *qiyās* and *istiḥsān*. The Law is not a badge of identity or a barricade of communal defiance, for those are mainly Jāhilī and Fearful constructs. It exists to facilitate a happy human existence in the awareness that this is only complete when the soul is free from ego and at rest in

40 The 'near' neighbour may be interpreted as the Muslim, and the 'far' as the non-Muslim. Ibn Rajab, I, 261.

41 Admirable and also classical in this context is the work of Muḥammad Muṣṭafā Shalabī, *Taʿlīl al-aḥkām* (Cairo, 1947).

God. Thus the classical manuals of Sharia maxims, *qawāʿid fiqhiyya*, consistently and unmistakeably disclose the purpose of the Law by prioritising ease, the controlling policy which the Man of Praise called *taysīr*. One determining maxim, for instance, states that 'hardship must call forth facilitation' (*al-mashaqqa tajlib al-taysīr*).[42] Moreover the dispositions of the Law frequently permit a choice, to be measured by circumstance, between concessionary (*rukhṣa*) or strict (*ʿazīma*) interpretations in fatwa production and religious practice. *Rukhṣa* is preferred where there exists a good permissive reason in the avoidance of hardship, and in some cases it is even considered obligatory.[43] Nowhere in the libraries do we see a legitimation of the contemporary *tanfīrī* love of difficult or onerous choices made as signs of defiance, an aberration we might label *istiqbāḥ*: a juridical preference for the ugly and the onerous. Instead, the classical norm is *istiḥsān,* based in a consistent philosophy of equitable and empathetic *taysīr* for ordinary Muslims (*al-ʿāmma*) because of their weakness and their susceptibility to being overwhelmed and driven to despair and apathy by burdensome edicts. The same determination to make matters easy for the masses is inspired by the good sense of the Salaf themselves. Here is ʿAbd al-Ghanī al-Nāblusī:

> The early Muslims, may Allah be pleased with them, preferred to follow the strict interpretation [*ʿazīma*] for themselves while giving fatwas according to *rukhṣa* for the ordinary Muslims [*ʿāmma*] […] out of compassion for the people. Qushayrī narrates in his *Risāla* that Ruwaym ibn Aḥmad said: 'a wise man's wisdom is expressed in giving wide scope in rulings [*aḥkām*] for his brothers, and maintaining scrupulousness for himself.' Al-Naṣrābādhī said: 'the basis of Sufism is to hold fast to the Book and Sunna, and to avoid desires and innovations, and to venerate the shaykhs, and

42 Jalāl al-Dīn al-Suyūṭī, *al-Ashbāh wa'l-naẓā'ir* (Beirut, 2002), 76.
43 Abū Ḥāmid al-Ghazālī, *al-Mustaṣfā min ʿilm al-uṣūl* (Cairo, 1353/1937), I, 98-100.

to recognise the excuses of ordinary people [*ru'yat aʿdhār al-khalq*]'.[44]

ʿAbd al-Wahhāb al-Shaʿrānī (d.1565) observed that although the ulema faithfully follow *madhhabs* they will sometimes give easy fatwas to ordinary people which do not find a sanction in any *madhhab* position.[45] Like many of his Sufi contemporaries he saw this as a beautiful and merciful aspect of Sharia diversity, which is to be traced back to the diversity of opinions which prevailed among the Companions themselves, who are 'like stars: by whichsoever you are guided, you are guided.'[46] Shaʿrānī was following al-Suyūṭī (d.1505), who had observed that the Muḥammadan Law is easier and more flexible than the earlier sacred laws because it incorporates the best essence of each of them, and allows a range of interpretations which have antecedents in previous prophetic dispensations, which are then manifested in the many different views and orientations evident in the first generations of Islam.[47] This is readily supported by the historical record. In the Mālikī *madhhab*, determined largely by the Companions' legacy in Madina, the early texts provide a snapshot record of the life of the Salaf in all its dignity and lively human difference. No research into the earliest interpretations of Madina's *fiqh* can neglect the eyewitness reports of juridical diversity preserved in highly-detailed texts such as the *Mudawwana,* the *ʿUtbiyya* and the *Mawwāziyya*. Against the Islamophobic and older Orientalist polemic which portrays early Islam as totalitarian and preoccupied with locating a single interpretation, there remains a 'true Salafism' which, reading the texts without prejudice, sees that the way of the first three generations of Muslims was grounded in

44 Nāblusī, *Sharḥ*, I, 230.

45 ʿAbd al-Wahhāb al-Shaʿrānī, *al-Mīzān al-Kubrā* (Beirut, 1432/2010), 12. For this aspect of Shaʿrānī see Michael Winter, *Society and Religion in Early Ottoman Egypt* (London, 1982), 230-41.

46 Muḥammad ibn Salāma al-Quḍāʿī, *Musnad al-Shihāb* (Beirut, 1985), II, 275.

47 Samer Dajani, 'Ibn 'Arabī and the Theory of a Flexible Sharia', *Journal of the Muhyiddin Ibn Arabi Society* 64 (2018), 78-81.

a generous and sane acknowledgement of jurisprudential difference (*riʿāyat al-khilāf*).[48] The Salaf were a prism through which the authentic Prophetic light in its immense plenitude was directed on to the *madhhabs* of the jurists and the entire scholarly family of Islam. Even an *ijtihād* which resulted in an incorrect opinion would, if determined by a qualified and sincere jurist, be rewarded by God.[49] Islam was *sunna* and also the broad *jamāʿa*, the community; here again *dīn* stands absolutely distinguished from mere ideology.

What is required, then, is a rediscovery of a True Salafism, retrieving the subtle wisdom of an earlier Sunni age before the decline of our scholarly institutions and the rise of Fearfulness sent us on the fool's errand of seeking simple and single solutions in the brilliant complexity of primal Islam. This True Salafism, which respects rather than disdains the classical traditions of theology and jurisprudence, will allow us to reconnect, through continuous chains of narration (*sanad*) and formal teaching authorisation (*ijāza*), to the Islam of the earliest times, rather than falling into the trap of what the hadith scholars call *wijāda*: simply finding a hadith which has been written down somewhere, even in an officially authentic collection. A True Salafism will allow communities to benefit from the inconceivably vast spiritual technologies of the Muslim centuries, rooted in the world-renouncing and spirit-filled aspect of the Man of Praise evident in the hadiths in which he wore wool (*ṣūf*),[50] and in which he shows the classic spiritual virtues of *tawakkul*, *ṣabr* and *riḍā* as signs of a life inwardly as well as outwardly immersed in *tawḥīd*, virtues whose presence is a precondition for any Islamic

48 Umar F. Abd-Allah Wymann-Landgraf, *Mālik and Medina: Islamic legal reasoning in the formative period* (Leiden, 2013), esp. 16-22.

49 Ibn Rajab, II, 247, citing sound hadiths; for the idea that 'every *mujtahid* is correct' (*kullu mujtahidin muṣīb*) see Josef Van Ess, 'Political Ideas in Early Islamic Religious Thought', *British Journal of Middle Eastern Studies* 28 (2001), 151-64, p.156.

50 In his ascetical aspect, turning from *dunyā*, the Man of Praise left us with a number of hadiths in which he wears *ṣūf*; see for instance Bukhārī, Libās, 11; Muslim, Īmān, 268; Ibn Māja, Aṭʿima, 49.

scholarly work or judgement, and which allow the soul to recognise rather than recoil from the diversity of the earliest community. And the knowledge of that diversity allows the authentic jurist to choose what is most amenable and least burdensome, rather than capitulating to the ego's desire for narrowness.

The recent Muslim turn to *tanfīr* out of desperation, ignorance and Fearfulness has yielded a bitter harvest of hyperzealous fatwas and monomaniac cognitive frames. It has resulted in the contemptuous rejection of the older consensus on the meaning of innovation (*bidʿa*) and its replacement with a maximal narrowness on the entirely spurious and emotive claim that this is a sign of authenticity. In the Muslim world this tightening of Islam is yielding a weakening of faith and a strengthening of the regimes. In minority situations it emboldens Islamophobes and empowers politicians, journalists and academics who maintain the ancient tropes and attitudes of enmity towards Ishmael.

Instead of this emotive and reactive narrowness, scholars and the givers of *khuṭbas* must remember the Prophetic love of ordinary people for whom religion must be a thing of ease and tolerance, *al-ḥanīfiyyat al-samḥa*.[51] Knowledge of the age is a precondition for knowing the right religious response to it and the parameters of religious being; for one leading jurist, 'whoever is ignorant of the people of his age, is himself ignorant;'[52] while another emphasised that

> preachers and muftis must know the conditions of the people, and what they are accustomed to accept and reject, and

51 'The Prophet ﷺ said: "I have been sent with the tolerant, clear, Ḥanīfī religion". He meant by "tolerant" [*samḥa*] that which did not have any arduous practices in it, such as the monks had devised. Rather in it (this religion) there would be a special dispensation for every valid excuse, making the action attainable for both the strong and the weak, the working person and the unemployed.' Shāh Walī Allāh al-Dahlawī, tr. Marcia K. Hermansen, *The Conclusive Argument from God* (Islamabad, 2003), 369.

52 Muḥammad Amīn ibn ʿĀbidīn, *Radd al-muḥtār ʿalā al-Durr al-Mukhtār* (Beirut, 1405/1985), V, 359.

> their capacity for diligence or sloth. For it is said: 'In every circumstance there is a right thing to say, and for every context there is an expert.' Whoever does not know the custom of his age is an ignoramus, since rulings can change with the times and the people.[53]

Evidently the present age is one in which ordinary believers are weak, and hence a logically-proportional *taysīr*, facilitation, will be the sign of the authentic scholar. 'You are in an age,' the Man of Praise tells his Companions, 'in which someone who leaves a tenth of what he has been commanded to do will perish; but a time will come upon mankind when a man who does a tenth of what he has been commanded to do, will be saved.'[54] Our time may not be that time, and this prophecy is not a licence for sloth, but it is still unmistakeably a reminder that God's justice and mercy govern His expectations of His servants in every age. Already in the twelfth century the prominent jurist Fakhr al-Dīn Qāḍīkhān was writing that 'ours is not the age of scrupulous avoidance of doubtful things; it is incumbent upon the believer just to avoid what is manifestly forbidden;' quoting this three centuries later the Ottoman scholar Birgivī (d.1573) added: 'In our times it is impossible, I say, impossible, to adopt the more precautionary [*aḥwaṭ*] fatwa rulings.'[55]

In our own age, whether or not we inhabit Western lands, the difficulties and challenges are evidently far greater than those which confronted the Muslims served by Qāḍīkhān and Birgivī. Muslim life in a modern French city is more demanding than was the life of a believer in the 'well-protected domains' of Sulaymān the Magnificent; and hence to find lighter and more compassionate

---

53 Muḥammad ibn Muṣṭafā al-Khādimī, *al-Burayqa al-Maḥmūdiyya sharḥ al-Ṭarīqa al-Muḥammadiyya wa'l-sharīʿa al-nabawiyya fi'l-sīrat al-Aḥmadiyya* (Istanbul, 1287AH), III, 126.

54 Tirmidhī, Fitan, 79.

55 Muḥammad ibn Pīr ʿAlī Birgivī (ed. Muḥammad Ḥusnī Muṣṭafā), *al-Ṭarīqa al-Muḥammadiyya wa's-sīra al-Aḥmadiyya* (Aleppo, 1423/2002), 419.

rulings becomes a juridical principle infinitely more authentic and loyal than any angry and Fearful determination to cling to the comforting delights of narrowness and the sense of superiority which it brings. *Tanfīr* is a great sin, a fundamental and systematic innovation in the essence of the religion of the Man of Praise, a violation of the wisdom of the Salaf and a source of division and weakness for an Umma which is in need of unity and mildness in our difficult times. The retrieval of mercy and balance will only be possible, however, when we examine ourselves by turning within, to rediscover the luminosity of the *fiṭra*, the natural way of *dīn*, which is the compassionate way of the heart which is the only stable foundation for *daʿwa* and for honouring Abraham's prayer for Ishmael and his descendents: 'make the hearts of mankind incline towards them'. (14:37)

CHAPTER 6

Good anger, bad anger, and *Shirk al-Asbāb*

Woe to those whose hearts are hard against God's remembrance.

QUR'AN 39:22

THE PROCESS OF entropic degeneration which seems to be foretold by all world religions is marked both by realities that anger us, and by the ready abuse of anger as an emotion.[1] When Babylon the Great appears, mother of harlots and abominations of the earth, how shall the righteous fail to be wrathful against her? Surely the end times, and the times which resemble and seem to foreshadow them, will necessarily be times of outrage? True religion must always, even at that extreme point of history, allow anger at the defiance of Heaven and the rule of hubris, which will both intensify as the age wears on. Yet it must also be vigilant against the anger that is born of the despair and sense of siege which are so common under extreme social and political conditions, and which comprise a poorly-disguised anger against God and His arrangement of history. Success in 'times of abandonment' comes from endurance and self-discipline, driven by the certain knowledge that 'verily with hardship comes ease' (94:6), and that after the Day of Anger itself all wrongs will be entirely righted and their victims healed. To achieve this awareness the alienation from the times must not be divorced

1 The prediction of increasing and final degeneracy is almost universal; see, for instance, the texts assembled in Whitall N. Perry, *A Treasury of Traditional Wisdom* (Cambridge, 1991), 464-474.

from the alienation from worldliness; on the contrary, the latter must be its urgently-needed support, lest we become merely another sign of the times. There will never be an age in which the bulk of Muslim anger should be directed against others, rather than against our own inner demons. The faults of others are conjectural in various ways; our own faults are certain.

So under modern conditions, when Ishmaelites are confronted both by the cruelty of Eastern regimes and by Western calamity-making in Palestine, Iraq and Libya, the discernment between decent and demonic anger is a particularly pressing task for Muslim self-preservation and inner equanimity; but it is not simple. The traditional believer may rightly be wrathful, but this will be for God, never for himself, since the self is a misunderstanding wrapped in a misunderstanding, and selflessness is an aspect of Sunna emulation. Prophetically-conformed individuals must respond passionately to the misery caused by human error, and therefore, *a fortiori*, to the error itself, but they must also remain serenely confident in God's omnipotence. A discernment between right and wrongful wrath, between a cold and a panicked anger, is hence a consequence and corollary of faith, a spiritual discipline of irreplaceable importance in our age of turbulence.

The Man of Praise offers a timeless model of this balance. As witness and sharer in the suffering of his people and in the agony of the weak and orphaned against the complacency of the Qurayshite oligarchs, he could be rightly angry. Here he was hardly an 'innovator among the Messengers'. Moses is furious when the Israelites turn to the Golden Calf (Qur'an 20:86). The Gospels' Jesus is angry with the Pharisees as he forbids the remarriage of divorcees (Mark 10, 5-12), and he calls them 'a brood of vipers' (Matthew 12:34) and 'hypocrites' (Matthew 15:7). His anger causes him to act in true Zealot fashion, driving the moneychangers out of the Temple with a whip (John 2:15-17). The Seal of the Prophets, crying out against the cruelty of the elites and Lahabists of his day, stands faithfully in the same tradition of exemplars who are fully human, and are therefore emotional. 'I am only a human being,' he says, 'I am pleased as humans are; and grow angry as they do.'[2] Anger is certainly and necessarily a dimension of prophethood. His conforming to God, however, also ensured that *ḥilm*, mild forbearance, was his governing trait. Classical treatments of anger cite instances of his righteous wrath but overwhelmingly focus on his mercy and patience, which are unmistakeably and repeatedly more central to the *sunna*. This explains why although anger can be a sign of conformity to God, the overwhelming bulk of hadith on the subject strongly denounce it. When asked how to avert God's anger he replied, 'Abandon your own anger.'[3] And again:

> Anger is a red-hot coal in the heart of Adam's children. Have you not beheld his bloodshot eyes, and his swollen veins? Whoever senses any part of that should lie down on the ground.[4]
>
> Anger is from Satan, and Satan was created of fire. Since fire is only put out by water, let each of you carry out *wuḍū'* if he is angry.[5]

Despite the large number of such hadiths the Prophetic counsel is not to become a Stoic, an emotionally frigid, impassible Vulcan; but rather to use the emotions as God wishes and not in vengeful obedience to the self. Imām al-Nawawī, commenting on the Prophetic commandment, 'Be not angry' (*lā taghḍab*), explains that the meaning is 'do not act in accordance with your anger. The prohibition does not refer to anger itself, for that is part of human nature.'[6]

---

2 Muslim, Birr, 95.

3 ᶜAlī ibn Abī Bakr al-Haythamī, *Majmaᶜ al-zawā'id wa-manbaᶜ al-fawā'īd* (Cairo, 1352AH), VIII, 69.

4 Tirmidhī, 26; Ibn Ḥanbal, *al-Musnad* (Cairo, 1313AH), IV, 19.

5 Ibn Ḥanbal, *Musnad*, IV, 226. Muᶜāwiya once descended from the *minbar*, went away to perform the major ablution, and then returned to complete his sermon, citing this hadith (Abū Nuᶜaym, *Ḥilyat al-awliyā' wa-ṭabaqāt al-aṣfiyā'* [Cairo, 1932-8], II, 130).

6 Muḥyī al-Dīn al-Nawawī, *Sharḥ al-Arbaᶜīn*, presented by Louis Pouzet as *Une Herméneutique de la tradition islamique: Le Commentaire des Arba'ūn*

In the midst of one's valid anger one acts within the boundaries of the Law and maintains good *akhlāq*. Anger may remind us of the need to act, but it is never the motivation or justification of any righteous act. It must not rival the revealed will; God must judge, not the human nervous system.

Here we may locate one reason why the Qur'an praises 'those who, when angered, are forgiving' (42:37) and 'those who suppress their rage and forgive people; and God loves the workers of good.' (3:134) The last expression is *muḥsinīn*, the people who 'do the beautiful', who are, in the famous Hadith of Supererogatory Devotions (*ḥadīth al-nawāfil*), in a love-relationship with their Lord, Who says:

> and when I love him I become the ear with which he hears, the eye with which he sees, the hand with which he strikes, and the foot on which he walks. If he seeks My protection, I shall surely grant it him; and if he seeks victory from Me, I shall surely grant it him.[7]

This is the degree of the individual the hadith calls the *walī*, the 'friend' of God. He is the true *khalīfa*, His 'representative', and it is he who 'has been taught all the names' (2:31). This 'Adamic' archetype is not the one who ignores the relevance of the divine wrath, but is the one who properly discerns true from false anger. As *khalīfa* he manifests qualities whose ontic root lies in the divine perfection; and anger is compatible with these. Prophetic scriptures from time to time use the language of divine anger; and those who are close to God by definition share this. As Niffarī's God tells the saint: 'If I appoint thee My *khalīfa*, I will make thy wrath to be from My wrath.'[8] By contrast, the anger of the self, the *nafs*, is the mark of the non-caliphal rebel soul.

---

al-Nawawiya de Muḥyī al-Dīn Yaḥyā al-Nawawī (m. 676/1277) (Beirut, 1982), 36.

7 Bukhārī, Riqāq, 38, See the translation and commentary in Abdal Hakim Murad (tr.), *Selections from the Fatḥ al-Bārī* (Bartlow, 1421/2000), 17-23.

8 Muḥammad al-Niffarī, *al-Mawāqif*, ed. A.J. Arberry (London and Cairo, 1934/5), 8 (Arabic).

Ḥilm, however, is the divine and prophetic norm; anger is a supervenient exception. It is interesting to reflect that when compared with the Biblical deity, the Qur'anic God is not frequently angry, perhaps because the later scripture's voice is less concrete in its apparent anthropomorphisms than were many of the Bible authors. The Old Testament contains almost four hundred explicit references to God's wrath (*qaṣap*), with another thirty appearing in the New Testament. By contrast the Qur'an uses the cognate word *ghaḍab* only eighteen times (fewer, if we exclude rhetorical reiterations), contrasting with two hundred and thirty-three references to mercy (*raḥma*). It contains no sustained passages on God's anger comparable to the thirty-five psalms consecrated to the subject, or to St Paul's evocation of God's wrath against those who refuse to recognise the atonement.[9] There are punishment stories, but they are not accompanied, as they frequently are in the Bible, by long reflections on the divine anger; instead, they emerge as reminders of the consequence of defying the merciful teachings of God's messengers. Qur'anically speaking, then, an emphasis of the last divine dispensation on earth is that the true *walī* is theomorphically moved to exhibit forbearance and mercy, which are the basis of the saint's actions, despite the entire validity of a mature and periodic 'indignation for the Lord'. Moreover, when he or she is required to uphold God's anger, the divine precedent is never capricious or extravagant. One of the most indicative disparities between the biblical and Qur'anic lives of the Hebrew prophets seems to be that the *ḥerem*, the sacred exterminations of non-Hebrew peoples ordered by God in the Bible, are absent completely from the Qur'anic text.[10]

Al-Ghaḍbān, the Angry, does not, therefore, appear in any list of the divine Names. Neither is it among the hundreds of titles ascribed by tradition to the Blessed Prophet. As liberators the Man

9 Romans, 9:19-29. See Johnson, *op. cit.*

10 For the Sacred Exterminations see Gerd Lüdemann, *The Unholy in Holy Scripture* (London, 1998), 36-55; cf. Matthias Beier, *A Violent God-Image* (London, 2003).

of Praise and his disciples in all ages share God's anger against inward and outward cruelty and injustice, against the ego, and against disobedience to His law; yet in the new dispensation, alert to the weakness of humanity in the latter age, anger seems to be in a minor key throughout. The Seal of Prophecy is described, preeminently, as 'a mercy to the worlds'. (21:107)

Hence human anger is either theomorphic and Prophetic, conforming to God's judgement of human acts; or it is demonic and fiery; it is Mosaic or it is Pharaonic. The latter is what it is because it betrays frustration with God's purposes. As Ibrāhīm Ḥaqqī writes:

Choose you what the True God's chosen,
Know He'll not do otherwise.
Watch His acts until you know Him.
Let us see what God shall do,
For what He does is good and true.

On the True God place reliance
Peace of mind lies in assent.
With His acts be thou well-pleased.
Let us see what God shall do,
For what He does is good and true.

Question not: Why was this so?
Why was that not in its place?
Persevere and see its outcome!
Let us see what God shall do,
For what He does is good and true.[11]

This is what Mir Valiuddin calls 'retrocession of trust'.[12] Anger is sinful, indeed a deadly sin, when it is an implicit challenge to God and His decree. If we claim to believe that the proximate causes (*asbāb*) have a divine author, then one of the most dangerous forms

11 Erzurumlu İbrahim Hakkı (ed. Numan Külekçi), *Dîvân* (Erzurum, 1997), 123.

12 Mir Valiuddin, 'The way to control anger – the Qur'anic approach', *Islamic Culture* 46 (1972), 63-73, p.68.

of idolatry must be *shirk al-asbāb*, to attribute real agency to created things that, in the absolute monotheistic vision of Islam, are in fact directly and utterly subject to His command. So *tawakkul*, trust in Providence, is central to our revealed ethics, for it is the virtue that proceeds most surely from *tawḥīd*.

The figure of Ayyūb seems to body forth the difference between the two visions. Instead of contending with God, wishing that he had never been born, the Muslim retrieval portrays the very type of dignified surrender and acceptance. He acknowledges his suffering, but as a *walī* he does not question God: 'And Job, when he called to his Lord: "Truly distress has touched me; and You are the most merciful of those that show mercy."' (21:83) This *islām* yields unimaginable fruits: the miraculous ability to bring healing water from the earth, and a great following, the signs of Divine acceptance: 'Truly We found him to be patient; how fine a slave, ever turning in penitence.' (38:44)

İsra Yazıcıoğlu finds in this short account the essence of Islam's explanation of the 'problem of evil.' She cites Said Nursi's image of a tailor's poor servant who complains when one beautiful set of clothes is removed from him to make way for the next. As Nursi comments:

> in order to display the impresses of His Most Beautiful Names, the All-Glorious Maker, the Peerless Creator, *alters within numerous circumstances the garment of existence He clothes on living creatures, bejewelled with senses and subtle faculties like eyes, ears, the reason, and the heart*. He changes it within very many situations. *Among these are circumstances in the form of suffering and calamity* which show the meanings of some of His Names, and the rays of mercy within flashes of wisdom, and the subtle instances of beauty within those rays of mercy.

Yazıcıoğlu concludes: 'Thus, whatever befalls humankind, including calamities, serves a great purpose of making Divine art known.'[13]

13 İsra Ümeyye Yazıcıoğlu, 'Affliction, Patience and Prayer: Reading Job (P) in the Qur'an,' *Journal of Scriptural Reasoning*, 4/I (July 2004); etext.lib.Virgin-

Ayyūb can 'complain' to God, for otherwise there could be no petitionary prayer, and hence no sacred humanity; but as a perfected sage he cannot question Him or be angry at His decree. His simple but subtle language recalls the prayer of Moses as he stands destitute at the gates of Midian: 'My Lord, I am without the good things which You have sent down to me' (28:24), a courteously indirect supplication which seems to be the prelude to the unexpected shelter in a prophetic tent and a blessed marriage. The Man of Praise, who combines real and tearful human distress with absolute trust and hope for God's good decree, continues this prophetic method. Having been rejected and stoned by the people of Ṭā'if, and finding refuge alone beneath a wayside tree, he offers these Job-like words:

> O God, unto Thee do I complain of my weakness, of my helplessness, and of my lowliness before men. O Most Merciful of the Merciful, Thou art lord of the weak. And Thou art my Lord. Into whose hands wilt Thou entrust me? Unto some far-off stranger who will ill-treat me? Or unto a foe whom Thou hast empowered against me? I care not, so long as Thou be not wroth with me. But Thy favouring help—that were for me the broader way and the wider scope![14]

The trust of the Man of Praise does not bring a diminution of his humanity. He is far from dispassionate and cold; on the contrary, this prayer is infinitely human. Suffering is real, and its logic is often veiled from us; yet it is God's will, and the faithful monotheist prays only for God's *riḍā*, His 'good pleasure', and hopes that this will be accompanied by an easing of the way. Only under such theological conditions can our valid anger against oppressors be made just, and our egotistic anger against Providence be annihilated.[15]

Personal pain is bitter, but to witness the pain of a loved one is, for the *walī*, far more bitter, and here we enter the realm of what

---

ia.edu/journals/ssr/issues/volume4/number1/ssr04-01-e01.html

14 Lings, *Muhammad*, 98-9.

15 See also ʿAbd al-Qādir al-Jīlānī, *Futūḥ al-Ghayb* (Cairo, 1330), 128. If you are tried, then first deploy *taṣabbur*, then *ṣabr*, then *riḍā* and *muwāfaqa*.

is, barring atheism, the sharpest inner pain of all. In the Qur'anic account of Ibrāhīm the prophet is 'tested clearly' (*balā' mubīn*), not by the prospect of his own death but by that of the death of his son, which is certainly a far more grievous trial. By accepting the test, through his absolute confidence in God's wisdom, a new and unsuspected door is opened for him, as in God's time the child becomes the patriarch of a numberless host. In the Muḥammadan age there is a parallel in the suffering of the Final Prophet, when his own son, symmetrically named Ibrāhīm, dies in infancy. Deeply distressed, holding the dead child, he speaks again:

> We are stricken indeed with sorrow for thee, O Ibrāhīm. The eye weepeth, and the heart grieveth, nor say we aught that would offend the Lord.[16]

'Those who suffer most grievously are the prophets, then those who are near them in degree,' says a hadith.[17] The Blessed Prophet suffered almost unimaginably, for his obedient mission and migration brought the mortal endangering not only of himself, but of his loved ones as well. Despite the final triumph which God gave him, he appears, pre-eminently, as a poor, endangered, suffering servant.

Suffering, therefore, is prophetically understood as an opportunity for waiting patiently at the door of God's generosity and demonstrating resignation in the face of His omnipotence. 'We flourish,' as Anṣārī says, 'in the plunder of Your tribulations.'[18] These may occasion complaint at the surface level, but at the same time are profoundly to be accepted, for 'if chicory is bitter, it is still of the garden.'[19] This spiritual virtue forms proof that the real Muslim has internalised the implications of the acceptance of *qaḍā'*,

---

16 Lings, 327, translating Ibn Saʿd.

17 Bukhārī, Marḍā, 3.

18 Khwāja ʿAbdullāh Anṣārī, *Munājāt*, in *Ibn Ata'Illah, The Book of Wisdom, Khwaja Abdullah Ansari, Intimate Conversations*, introduction, translation and notes of the *Book of Wisdom* by Victor Danner, and of *Intimate Conversations* by Wheeler M. Thackston (Mahweh, 1979), 195.

19 *Ibid.*, 207.

God's decree, 'the bitter and the sweet of it.'[20] Every sickness comes from the Physician; and the only possible grounds for deep anger hence lie in the spectacle of human egotism, which is the devil's fire which brings tyranny into the world and into our own souls. Even the contemplation of the Blessed Prophet's suffering and his renunciatory life allows us to move forwards to a self-emptying which purifies us. In the word of Hacı Bayram Veli:

> Poverty is my pride! Poverty is my pride!
> Did he not speak thus, of all the worlds the pride?
> His poverty recall! His poverty recall!
> Nothing and nought in this soul of mine reside![21]

Shaykh ʿAbd al-Qādir al-Jīlānī writes with passion on the need to repent of any anger against God's decree. Instead of imagining that we have the power to alter His command, we should find in deprivation an opportunity for courtesy, silence, patience, contentment, and conformity to His edicts. 'Repent of accusing Him,' he tells us, 'for He does not sin, nor is there a flaw in His nature as in the case of His creatures when they deal with one another. He alone is pre-existent; He has already created all things, and appointed their benefits and their harm, their beginning and their end; He is wise in His acts, perfect in His deeds; He does nothing idly.' We are to maintain this *islām* to Him, like a trusting baby in its nurse's arms, or the ball which submits to the polo-player, in the knowledge that in His good time He will cause night to end with a new sunrise, and the winter to end with spring.[22] For 'verily with hardship comes ease.' (94:6)

At the origins of British Islam the experience of rejection and scorn, and of physical violence by those who could not tolerate the sight of Ishmael, was dealt with in faithful compliance with this

---

20 This standard doxological formula originates in a hadith (Ibn Māja, Muqaddima, 10).

21 Fuat Bayramoğlu, *Hacı Bayram-ı Veli: Yaşamı, Soyu, Vakfı. Cilt II: Belgeler* (Ankara, 1983), 228.

22 Jīlānī, *Futūḥ,* 78-82 (*maqāla* 34).

wisdom. Stones and garbage were thrown at members of Quilliam's community as they walked to their Liverpool mosque, windows were broken, and glass powder was rubbed into the mosque carpet; on more than one occasion Fatima Cates had horse dung rubbed onto her face.[23] In the face of this Quilliam's community responded with infinite forbearance: the following is emblematic of his philosophy of *riḍā*:

ISLAMIC RESIGNATION.

Thou only Allah giv'st me light,
'Tis Thee who makes the future bright,
Dispels the gloom of doubt away,
And heareth when to Thee I pray.

Though sore the trials of the day,
Thou hast decreed, so I obey,
And murm'ring not at Thy decree,
Allah, my all I yield to Thee.

I know this weary, anxious breast
With Thee will find eternal rest;
And knowing this, I do resign
My Will, O Allah! unto Thine.

My earthly friends though few they be,
And chill the looks that fall on me,
I rest content, full well I know,
Who trusts in Thee need fear no foe.

I work, I wait, while here I live,
For the reward 'tis Thine to give,
Content to leave my future fate
With Thee, Allah, Compassionate![24]

* * *

23 Geaves, *Islam in Victorian Britain*, 63–5.

24 *The Crescent*, XIV (23 August 1899), 123.

The upshot of Prophetic patience is the confirmation of *wilāya*, which the *ḥadīth al-nawāfil* understands as the vindication of love. Yet with all of today's humanity seeming to carry Job's burdens, and with our capacity to bear misfortune drastically reduced by our upbringing in an impatient and pleasure-seeking 'post-cultural' culture, it is inevitable that this degree will not be reached as often as it once was. The mutual perception of madness in the regard of modern and traditional people is a suffering which most cannot carry for long; and the result can be the pathological anger which builds Auschwitz, or 'ethnically cleanses' Bosnia, or flies airliners into office buildings. As our machines grow stronger we seem to diminish; as relationships are publicly defined in terms of the framing of material success and the enjoyment of rights, we grow dissatisfied; as the increasing fundamentalist resignification of religions leaves behind any resourcing of methods of sacred interrelationship, we panic. Our online lives surround us with anxiety-heightening messages from chan culture, fake news, Project Fear, and social media funded by dark money. Technology itself adds to our stress levels.[25] Anger is the condition of the age, with the truly modern represented by the destructive and resentful mindset depicted fifty years ago by John Osborne, although the entertainment industry works hard to sublimate it into a profitable hatred of screen villains or of rival football teams: the *Panem et circenses* ruse which was a cornerstone of the stability of ancient Rome, the monoculture's truest ancestor. For many, the catharsis achieved before the credits roll persists; for others, however, it offers merely a false glimpse of a resolution that in the world seems painfully lacking. Teenage dysfunction, the gulping of Prozac, and religious panic are only three of the more recalcitrant symptoms of this essentially single disorder. And hence the saving virtue for our unhappy time, so rife with psychosomatic pain, must be *riḍā*, satisfaction with what God has decreed. This is why the religion of the Last Prophet is

25 Neil Postman, *Technopoly: the surrender of culture to technology* (New York, 1993).

so emphatic about resignation and the acknowledgement of the unobstructed divine power. 'If you do not have this attitude in this age, you will go mad. There is so much *kufr* around us, so much mayhem and destruction, that it is not possible to stay sane without this attitude.'[26]

To follow prophetic religion is to be challenged to heal one's anger, not by abolishing it but by mastering it by restoring it to its origin in God. This, however, is not a matter of fatalism, the 'Oriental repose' of old Orientalist typecasting, but is a blending of the knowledge of God's agency with an acceptance of His command to act to heal the world. Take (to return again to the British Muslim heritage) that pungent critic of urban *anomie*, Yahya Parkinson (d.1918):

Pale-faced men and sickly women
On the seething river drifting,
At the mercy of its waters;
Now engulfed within the vortex,
Now upborne upon the billows;
Ever striving, ever struggling,
To evade the fate before them;
Prostitution stalking shameless;
Womanhood in tattered garments,
Stranded wrecks upon the pavement;
In the gutter prone and sodden;
In a tawdry, drunken stupor,
Face and form no longer human.
While with heedless eyes averted,
Fellow-men are by them passing;
Scarce an arm is raised in helping,
For to stay them in their falling;
Not a word of fellow-feeling,
Voice unheard of mercy pleading;
While in thousands men are dying,
Sinking in the social vortex,

26 Schuitema, 57-8.

In a hell of lust and passion.
Why this misery and anguish,
That the people they are bearing;
Why this crying, this despairing;
Are not Nature's bounties spreading
Wide along the earth so spacious;
With a lavish hand she's casting
Food in plenty for the gleaning;
Why should people grind their brothers,
Trample them like armies marching
O'er a field of mangled foemen?[27]

Here resounds a properly-aroused prophetic anger, consonant with God's wrath against injustice. The poem goes on to urge a resolution for our alienation in nature. At peace with our bodies and the majesty and beauty of God's making, we find a healing from the dissonant condition of modernity and its concomitant anger, for we realise that amidst the rigour, there is always beauty; and that true anger, which is God's anger, is always resolved successfully in forgiveness or justice in either world. Hence the love of God is identical with an activism shaped by the acceptance of His omnipotence. A true engagement with our enfleshed and political selves yields this mark of true *khilāfa*:

Only they alone are righteous
Who have love for all their brethren,
In this sphere of pain and labour;
And for every moving creature
Living on the world's wide body.[28]

Parkinson implies that true anger is accompanied by love, because it is of Him, 'Who has prescribed compassion upon Himself'. (6:12) It is because of love for the right that humans feel valid wrath. He also suggests that it is only through complete engagement with creation that we can rise above ego. The condition of the partially-detached,

27 Yahya Parkinson, 'Woodnotes Wild,' *The Crescent,* XVI, 229.
28 *idem.*

Parnassian individual, neither floating free in space nor fully engaged with nature, has been the crucible of post-religious European anger. Its satisfaction has been sought in projects to reconnect with land, or with national myth, or, more recently, for that story of libertinism inaugurated by the Enlightenment which can only be fully understood as an existential protest, in a sexuality without restraint. Houellebecq's *Platform*, reporting on the listlessness of technically-advanced French society in the 1990s, in a series of emblematic confrontations proclaims the superiority of a radical promiscuity over Islam, its rival alternative to mediocrity.[29] The Islam that the novel rejects, however, is the Islam of the westernised believer who does not see that he is westernised, with its anger, its belief in the *asbāb*, its lack of real love and its environmental indifference. The Islam of tradition, by contrast, which Parkinson upholds, fully (and against what he takes to be Christianity) engages with *eros* and heroism, but in the name of an acceptance of God's decree, not a revolt against it. What *Platform* cannot see is the great gulf which separates classical *futuwwa* from the reflexes of the damaged modern believer.

Erich Fromm perhaps gets close to this distinction when he speaks of 'benign' versus 'malignant' aggression.[30] 'Benign aggression' he defines as a sometimes violent assertiveness which is the natural response to the deprivation of rights. It is rooted in instinct, although it is by no means enslaved to it, and its purpose is the promotion of life. Malignant aggression, by contrast, is unjust, it is 'necrophiliac', an urge to vengeance and destruction for its own sake, even if a formal ideology be used as a mask. It is the unnatural anger of Achilles, who vaunts his victory over Hector by dragging his corpse after his chariot; the polar opposite of the Prophetic model following its victory:

---

29 Michel Houellebecq, *Platform* (London, 2002).

30 Erich Fromm, *The Anatomy of Human Destructiveness* (Harmondsworth, 1977), 24, 251–4.

No blood he sheds, no fine exacts,
  No prince to prison sends;
Forgives, forgets all injuries past,
  Treats enemies as friends.[31]

Malignant aggression 'is not phylogenetically programmed and not biologically adaptive; it has no purpose, and its satisfaction is lustful.'[32] It is, as we would say, from the fire made possible by the devil's first disobedience, and in all the orders of nature only man is subject to it. While it has manifested itself in past ages, Fromm sees it as a particular hazard of our times, since it is the fruit of a comfortable but threatened boredom and the alienation and marginalisation of humanity by technology: 'The Falangist motto "Long Live Death" threatens to become the secret principle of a society in which the conquest of nature by the machine constitutes the very meaning of progress, and where the living person becomes an appendix to the machine.'[33]

This differentiation allows us to see more clearly the metabolic gulf that separates *futuwwa* from the death cult of the new *tanfīrī* ultras (or their no less dreadful and enraged homologues in, say, the Bible Belt or militant Hindutva). *Futuwwa* is the principle of a positive conflict which is fought to preserve the Five Objects of society recognised by our jurisprudence, and whose goal is the upliftment and celebration of human life; indeed, without such aggressiveness, and the anger which fuels it, the prophetic vocation to oppose injustice would be thwarted. It was this anger which fought against the Crusades and the Inquisition. It is a true anger, and certainly an 'aggressive' one, in Fromm's language; and without it the justice of the world could not endure. However it is entirely subject to the spirit, the *rūḥ*.

---

31 A.D. Tyssen, 'Hymn on the Capture of Mecca', *The Crescent*, XIV (18 October 1899), 250.

32 Fromm, 24.

33 Fromm, 32-3.

In contrast, a reliable sign of the presence of 'malignant aggression' in modern *tanfīrī* religion is the resort to symbolic, brutal acts of revenge. Balked of an easy victory against security forces, many Algerian rebels in the 1990s, such as the Salafist Combat Group, quickly turned their ire against soft targets. In 1992, only ten percent of *tanfīrī* targets in Algeria were civilians; six years later this is said to have risen to ninety percent,[34] and the methods of slaying those who were considered apostates for not joining their supposed *jihād* became more severe. More recently, ISIS issued a text entitled *The Management of Savagery (Idārat al-Tawaḥḥush)* to provide a justification for their deliberately spectacular displays of cruelty.[35] In Fromm's terms, this mindset can resemble 'a permanent idolatry of the god of destruction.'[36] When manipulated online it has proved highly infectious, and the spiritual overload caused by repetitive violent images and hypnotic invocations of an emotive sense of threat and dishonour can overwhelm viewers who are not rooted in the *fiqh* and a degree of spiritual control. Because the most successful propaganda mobilises the art of manipulating fear, such messaging is the mortal enemy of *tawakkul* and of *riḍā*.

The alternative is to return to Holy War, that is to say, the twin-bladed struggle against evil that is driven by conformity to God's anger, as an expression of the love which, according to the hadith, exists between God and the *walī*. The inner *jihād* which makes this possible seems far from the concerns of the new deracinated radical; in fact, malignant aggression is made possible only by the adoption of a pacifism in the war against the ego. The rough

34 Hafez, *Why Muslims Rebel*, 164. The figures seek to exclude poorly-documented or ambiguous attacks, given that the security forces have carried out massacres of villagers in an attempt to increase popular revulsion against the extremists. See the GIA's 1993 declaration: '… targeting all the symbols of the infidel regime from the head of state through the military, and ending with the last hypocrite working for the regime.'

35 Robert Manne, *The Mind of the Islamic State: ISIS and the ideology of the caliphate* (Amherst NY, 2017), 16.

36 Fromm, 369.

Arab is uplifted by love, as Majnūn becomes a model of refined *adab* and subtle diction through his love for Laylā; and, as Ibn al-Dabbāgh tells us, 'if such a lowly person can be so transformed by love, then what must be the potential of those whose natures are already virtuous, and who have completed the processes of self-discipline?'[37]

There is a clue to the healing here. Love cannot exist unless we are fully engaged with God's creation and allow ourselves to be purified by the contemplation of its beauty. This is the message driven home by Parkinson's poem; and it is also clear Qur'anic teaching. 'In the way the heavens and the earth are created, and the succession of night and day, are signs for people of understanding.' (3:190) The consequent cry, 'You have not created this in vain; glory be to You!' indicates the fullness of the knowledge that this contemplation (*tafakkur*) has yielded. The beauty of creation produces love as well as awe, gratitude as well as fear, tenderness as well as rigour; and the scriptural disclosure insists that these must be held in balance. The deprivation of beauty common in modern urban worlds pushes the surviving believers towards the *jalāl*, and, when combined with the decline of classical scholarship and the growth of Fearful religion born of disorienting and rapid change, the result is a Muslim, a Christian or a Jewish self that tends to restrict or even abolish mercy. The world is currently being tortured by this, precisely at a historical juncture in which it needs religion to be at its most healing and compassionate.

Recovering the love of beauty must form part of any Islamic project to defeat ideology and restore the full Sunna. The signlessness of modernised cities both reflects and intensifies the absence of beauty in the hearts of the powerful who commission architects; and those who live in the hideous ghettos which result, even if they be wealthy, find beauty a disturbing or irrelevant prospect. One recalls Christopher Isherwood, in *Goodbye to Berlin*, denouncing the inhuman modernism of the slums where Hitlerism was germinating.

---

37 ʿAbd al-Raḥmān ibn al-Dabbāgh (ed. Helmuth Ritter), *Mashāriq anwār al-qulūb wa-mafātīḥ asrār al-ghuyūb* (Beirut, 1379/1959), 105.

The city-dweller's perception of ubiquitous ugliness hardens the heart, which in turn renders the perception of beauty more difficult, creating a psychological trap or a vicious circle. Beauty is hardly to be found in a laptop or iPhone; it is to be intuited in the heart by confronting it personally, ideally in virgin nature, as the Qur'an recommends. The urbanisation of the world and the desolation even of traditional cities (symbolised in its most extreme form by the Doomsday Clock in Mecca) cuts the soul off from this healing. According to Ibn al-Dabbāgh, 'the human soul finds joy when it beholds flowers and the freshness of verdant gardens, and its worries and anxieties are thereby removed. This is caused solely by the effect of the beauty which their Creator bestowed upon them from His sublime Beauty.'[38] Higher still than the gazing at nature and good architecture and the hearing of harmonies, the supreme object of love in creation is humanity; so that restraining the self from the egotistic and forbidden dimensions of human love is the action of a *mujāhid*, which is why a hadith tells us, astoundingly, that 'whoever loves, and is chaste, and then dies, dies a martyr.'[39] To understand this hadith is to understand something deeply characteristic about the theology of the Final Religion.

There is another famous hadith which reminds us that 'God is beautiful, and He loves beauty'.[40] The *walī* recognises beauty on earth more fully than others, and loves with the love of God. This love of beauty 'has an influence on the human heart, producing subtlety, purity, softness, and all the other qualities which perfect it, and which prepare it to rise.'[41] The religious zealot, in Texas, Kandahar or Zion, who typically manifests qualities of discourtesy and hard-heartedness, thus stands at the opposite pole to the *walī*. Unconscious of beauty, and even suspicious when it is mentioned

---

38 Ibn al-Dabbāgh, 111.

39 Ibn al-Dabbāgh, 120. For the hadith see Sakhāwī, 658, who finds only one sound *isnād* for this widely-reported narration.

40 Muslim, Īmān, 147.

41 Ibn al-Dabbāgh, 105.

in a religious context, he is a nexus of ugliness (*qubḥ*) in the world, and malignant anger comes naturally to him. He and his works may even be the most intense manifestation of *qubḥ*, a prefigurement of Antichrist, whose 'one eye' is the most visible sign of his ugly and misleading nature, incapable of perspective.

What calming alchemical compound could be cast into the modern crucible of anger? Among Muslims, the vanguard might begin by championing the revival of moribund traditional arts, with calligraphy and *tajwīd* having pride of place, as both require and inculcate inward stillness and discipline. No less indispensable would be the upliftment of the aural environment, so frequently grating and cacophonic in modern cities, by means of *samāʿ*. 'By the remembrance of Allah do hearts find peace' (13:28) is a verse whose immense resonances are reduced and downgraded by Fearful zealots alarmed by *iḥsān*. It is ironic that at a time when the ancient Islamic tradition of music therapy is in decay in Arab countries[42] that such therapies should now be enjoying increasing respectability in the West, for the treatment not only of psychological imbalances but of physical disorders as well.[43]

---

42 One of the several reasons for the lack of rage-based radicalism in Turkey might be sought in the continued liveliness of the country's culture of sacred music. In Turkey, more than in any other Muslim country, groups maintain the science of *maqām* in the mosques. Turkey also retains the old tradition of music therapy for the mentally and spiritually ill, using ancient texts such as Shuʿūrī's *Taʿdīl al-Amzija*. Naturally this does not require the use of instrumental varieties of music; what matters is rhythm, tonality and mode, in the context of complete Sharia compliance.

43 Long after Islamic civilisation recognised its value, music therapy is now an accepted procedure in the West. See Andrea Gilroy and Colin Lee (eds.), *Art and Music: therapy and research* (London and New York, 1995); B. Lindsey and J. Hooper, 'Music and the Mentally Handicapped: The Effect of Music on Anxiety,' *Journal of British Music Therapy* 4 (1990), 19-26; Leslie Bunt, *Music therapy: an art beyond words* (London and New York, 1994). For the role of music as a biological mechanism designed to overcome cognitive dissonance see Leonid Perlovsky, 'Cognitive function, origin, and evolution of musical emotions,' *Musicae Scientiae* 16 (2012), 185-99.

The corruption or abolition of a *ḥalāl* auditory culture among radicals is certainly not the only contributing factor in their volatile emotional life, and may even be a minor one.[44] Yet it may be taken as a representative case, for there is something elementally iconic about the replacement of classical Islamic styles of preaching and chanting with the wild, almost insane shrieking of the enraged zealot orator. The destruction of his traditional city and home environment, and their replacement with debased emulations of the worst of European taste (sugary French café paintings, 'Louis Farouk' furniture, mosque chandeliers from the Vegas Strip, the 'Doomsday Clock') is not separate from his abandonment of *taṣawwuf* and classical Sharia in favour of a barren and rancorous *shirk al-asbāb*. His quest for identity and authenticity begins in the urban wasteland, and he cannot help interpreting the scriptures with a mind and soul impoverished and made desperate by that context. His sermon is a cry of hunger.

The ear of the zealot in many Muslim lands has been damaged by the dangerous decibel levels of Third World traffic, exacerbated further by the merciless susurration of air-conditioning. Or in the West it has been hurt by the pulse of house and trance music throbbing through earphones. It has not known quiet even in the mosques. How, then, can it activate Vaughan Williams' advocacy of 'the reaching out towards the utmost realities by means of ordered

44 Diet may sometimes also be a contributing factor. American and Middle Eastern bachelors, and even some married men and women, are increasingly consumers of modern fast-food, processed cheese, and soft drinks, and it would be idle to suggest that this never affects their spiritual and mental equilibrium. See Alexandru Mihai Grumezescu (ed.), *Therapeutic Foods: Volume 8* (Cambridge MA, 2017); anon., 'How Foods and Additives Affect the Brain: Pure Facts' *Newsletter of the Feingold Association, Special Issue on Brain Chemistry* (February, 1995), 12-16. The poor Saudi diet is demonstrated by the very high rate of diabetes in the central province of Saudi Arabia, where a remarkable 16.8% of the population is affected (*IDF Diabetes Atlas*, Sixth Edition http://diabetesatlas.org/atlas/sixth-edition).

sound'?[45] Such a figure is the victim of a modernity which has cut him off from all primordial normalcy.

The atonal quality of the nature-free modern city, polluted by the roar of carbon-belching exhausts and the frenetic assault of popular music, intensifies our alienation from *fiṭra* and hence from responding healthily to the indicative signs present in the natural world, making the quest for authenticity both urgent and difficult. The Sufi orders had always, following the preoccupation with beauty enunciated by the likes of Ibn al-Dabbāgh, sought to reconnect believers with their bodies and the ancient norms of humanity through chants and complex Sharia-compliant musical systems carefully tailored to the spiritual and emotional needs of the constituent ethnic cultures of the Muslim world. The modal system, in particular, showed the sensitivity of Islamic civilisation to the moral and spiritual power of music. Hence, no doubt, the radical's preference for the Najdī style of *tajwīd*, which is crude, nasal and amodal, over Egyptian, Ottoman, Hindustānī and Ḥijāzī styles, which take the listener on a journey through the *maqāms* in a strict order calculated to uplift and also to heal, coming down again through immaculate modulations, typically to the 'base-*maqām*' of *tajwīd, maqām ṣabā*, leaving the audience with a deep sense of peace and resolution. The literalist radical abolishes all such traditions of harmony together with the deep spiritual reintegration which they brought. The *ḥalqa*-circles of *dhikr* are gone, with their wisdom in weaving sacred texts together in ways which restore the heart and connect to the healing Divine presence. In their place he brings a nasal drone and robotic and emotive *nashīds*, followed by the wild cadences of the activist sermon, both perfect mirrors to his cognitive dissonance.[46] Curses abound, despite the Prophetic warning that 'the believer does not frequently criticise or frequently curse;'[47]

45 Robert L. Tusler, *Music: Catalyst for Healing* (Alkmaar, 1991), 10.

46 The Prophet (ṣ) forbade the excessive raising of the voice (Muslim, Dhikr, 43).

47 Tirmidhi, Birr, 48.

and 'I was not sent as a curser'.[48] When he sees other people he does not see them, but finds only an opportunity to confirm his own rightness to his Fearful self.

The hell-like rage (*ghayẓ*) produced by this rasping alienation is easy to distinguish from righteous anger. One litmus test for this is that Prophetic anger reflects the Creator's anger, which is quickly succeeded by forgiveness, and eschews the child's desire for exact and quick redress (God forgives and provides 'without reckoning', *bi-ghayri ḥisāb*). The Fearful ego seeks revenge, to 'get its own back'; the pure soul seeks to right wrongs committed against others. When only the self is the Other's target, the *walī* is pure forgiveness.

This virtue of refusing to be angry for oneself is to be distinguished absolutely from the *jāhilī* quality of *ḥamiyya*, tribal passion. 'It is a violent and terrible passion,' writes Reinhart Dozy, 'the first and most sacred duty of all duties; it is the real religion of the desert.'[49] Fanatical anger and a sensitivity to personal slights are the hallmark of the Arab returning to his pre-Islamic roots, or some other monotheist returning to the rage of paganism (remember the Viking berserkers, or the Malay as he 'ran amok'). This is the inner burning of the soul which sees the immensity of creation and the multitude of apparent immediate threats, and fails to recall the Divine authorship and control.

Responding kindly to hostility was one of the Qur'an's most radical anti-pagan innovations, and requires a strongly non-Fearful mindset. We shall return to this theme in Chapter Seven.

A further healing must come with the Fearless promulgation of the Umma's true narrative. The consensus of ulema holds that for all its waywardness, the mainstream history of our civilisation provided a matrix for the cultivation of real Islamic learning, according to the consensual understanding of the Book and Sunna, allowing the true Sunni of our time to walk through a great Islamic manuscript library with a sense of homecoming. By contrast the False Salafi can

48 Muslim, Birr, 87.

49 Cited in Izutsu, *Ethico-Religious Concepts*, 56.

agree with hardly a single volume on the shelves. The *fiqh* is that of the Four Schools, the doctrine is that of Ashᶜarism or Māturīdism or real Ḥanbalism, the spirituality is that of the mainline *ṭuruq*: and all of these things the zealot has sworn to overturn as treasonable innovations. Of the seventy-odd commentaries which the *Umma* has compiled on *Ṣaḥīḥ al-Bukhārī*, every one is written from a classical Sunni perspective deeply committed to the *madhhabs,* to *kalām* and to *taṣawwuf*. The *tanfīrī* is, therefore, a hostile foreign intruder in all our libraries, and his conclusion that God abandoned the *Umma*, and that the scholars acted criminally for many centuries, can only kindle a great furnace of anger and doubt in his soul. This is 'failurism': the idea that our *dīn* failed, and that only with the rise of the new fundamentalisms in these latter days has it reappeared on earth. God, hence, seems hardly to be trusted: the *Umma* for centuries was abandoned by Providence. Hence *tanfīrī* rage is not only against the consensus of Sunni scholarship, but implicitly against God Himself, for having committed so cruel a dereliction of the Muslim people. Orphaned from his civilisation, unable to trust Heaven, the zealot's soul can only emit a primal scream of agony, fear and hate.

All this confirms the principle that while anger is sometimes valuable, *ḥiqd*, or rancour, is forbidden. *Ḥiqd* has the quality of permanence, and is not open to forgiveness. It is an anger caused by emotional overload, that has solidified to become an obstacle to reconciliation and human continuance, contrasting absolutely with Prophetic anger:

> And when you are angry, it is but an anger
> For Truth's sake, without rancour or contempt.[50]

Such hateful uproar is unusual in our history. The early Khawārij are often cited as a precedent. So are the literalist Ḥashwiyya of tenth-century Baghdad.[51] Later, Shāh Tahmāsp's chief inquisitor,

---

50 Aḥmad Shawqī, *al-Shawqiyyāt* (Cairo, 1939), 23.

51 A.S. Halkin, 'The Ḥashwiyya', *Journal of the American Oriental Society* 54 (1934), 1-28.

the Lebanese al-Karākī (d.1533), made rancour the legitimating emotion of his dynasty with his touring bands of 'pious cursers' (*tabarrā'iyyān-i dīndār*). These men would tour Iranian cities as part of the state campaign to convert Iran's Sunni population to the Shah's Shi'i creed, and would recite long public curses directed against the first three Caliphs. Sunni scholars never developed a reciprocal habit, not only because Sunni Islam originated by definition as an eirenic movement which declined to attack any Companion of the Prophet, but also, presumably, because of their internalisation of *taṣawwuf* and the consequent emphasis on forgiveness and courtesy which made such hatred difficult. It is significant that the furious Karākī was particularly concerned to extirpate *taṣawwuf*.[52]

Times have changed; some suppose that ours are the last times, but classical wisdom seems more urgently required today than ever before. Under conditions of extreme entropy and collapse the Qur'anic retrieval of faith, which stresses patience in the face of the direct omnipotence of God more than any other scripture, seems to provide the perfect armour against the incipient desperation, aimlessness and fear of the modern world, and this is an aspect of its *khatmiyya*. Other religions have commended the virtue of *riḍā,* but Islam is particularly strong in giving us the healing reassurance of the full monotheistic teaching that God is 'over all things Powerful'; and, as the Ottoman proverb had it, 'whoever believes in *qadar*, is protected from *kadar* [misery]:' *man āmana bi'l-qadar, amina mina'l-kadar*.

52 Rula Jurdi Abisaab, *Converting Persia: religion and power in the Safavid empire* (London, 2004), 24-7. For his book refuting Sufism see p.24. The contemporary Ottoman scholarly polemic was not generally against Twelver Shi'ism, still less against Imām ʿAlī and his disciples; but was mainly directed against the extremist Kızılbaş nomads.

CHAPTER 7

'Push Back with Something More Beautiful' (Qur'an 41:34): Minority Muslims from Complainants to Therapists

The villainy you teach me I will execute,
And it shall go hard but I will better the instruction.

THE MERCHANT OF VENICE, ACT III SCENE I

IN OUR ISLAMOPHOBIC age, a popular Muslim response to secular discursive violence has been a tit-for-tat reciprocation: *tha'r*, in the Arabic terminology. Not a few ghetto sermonisers retaliate against the national populists by deploying an angry and bullying agitprop of their own. This, in turn, quickly displays the familiar drawback of a *lex talionis*: it tends to ignite a cycle of feuding until, as Niẓāmud-dīn Awliyā' observed, 'if a man casts a thorn in your path, and you cast another thorn in his, the world will be full of thorns'.[1] Fearful preachers and bloggers, parrying the vitriol of what they experience as a feminist, pansexualist, philo-Zionist establishment media, and goaded by furious anti-Ishmael politicians of the Wilders or Jensen type, often reply in kind, amplifying the faults of Europe and generalising about its violent urges just as effectively as the

1 Nizam Ad-Din Awliya, tr. Bruce B. Lawrence, *Morals for the Heart* (New York and Mahweh, 1992), 13. Perhaps this is the origin of Gandhi's 'an eye for an eye makes the whole world blind.'

chauvinists of the host societies are seeking to do in their typecasting of the Muslim soul. A vicious circle is the certain outcome of this; as so often, chauvinisms become mutually parasitic. But the odds are stacked against the minorities: in the longer term, if matters progress, it is likely that the weaker and smaller side of this zero-sum game will be destroyed.

Of course Islam is certainly not passive or pacifist, any more than is mainline Christianity. Even Buddhism allows a *boddhisatva* to resist someone who is in the act of committing murder.[2] Religion campaigns for justice, and sometimes a *lex talionis*, a *qiṣāṣ*, is needed to instantiate fairness and equilibrium, and to protect the weak. There is an established retributive theory in traditional Islamic jurisprudence no less than in the standard Western accounts that holds that there must be chastisement, and that it must fit the crime. Justice is always, in a certain sense, society's retaliation, its controlled, proportionate use of lawful repression. After learning of David's victory over Goliath we are told that 'had God not pushed back [*dafᶜ*] some men by means of others the earth would have been corrupted' (Qur'an 2:251). In the era of the Man of Praise, the verse authorising the Muslims to fight back against the philistines of Quraysh includes a noticeably similar sequence:

> *And had God not pushed back* [dafᶜ] *some men by means of others, cloisters and churches and oratories and mosques, wherein the name of God is oft-mentioned, would assuredly have been torn down.* (22:40)

As the commentator Rāzī notes:

> God pushes back, by means of some men, others who are intent on riot and stirring up seditions in the world; and those who 'push back' are the Prophets, upon them be peace, and after them the leaders and kings who uphold His laws [...] and this is why there must be rulers [...] for otherwise murder and criminality would prevail in the world.[3]

2 The *Yogacarya-Bhumi Sutra*, cited by D. Keown, *The Nature of Buddhist Ethics* (London, 1992), 152.

3 Fakhr al-Dīn al-Rāzī, *Mafātīḥ al-ghayb* (Beirut, 1985), VI, 206.

Rāzī also confirms that this act is discursive as well as legal. Literally *dafʿ* does mean 'pushing', or 'pushing back', and the reference is therefore to the Prophetic teaching of *amr bi'l-maʿrūf wa-nahy ʿan al-munkar*, 'commanding the good and forbidding the evil', which in the first instance must be verbal; indeed, unless one wields due political sovereignty it can be nothing else. A Muslim theology of just response to European rhetorical assault and the progressive confiscation of civil rights would be well-advised to be intelligent in its 'pushing back', and to avoid the *jāhilī* impulses of panic and outraged pride. Moral excellence, rather than enjoying a succulent dish of revenge served hot or cold, is always the authentic Muslim goal.

A *lex talionis*, a *qiṣāṣ*, provides, as the Qur'an observes (2:179), *ḥayāt*, or 'life'. The social order is protected when authority punishes destructive behaviour by proportionately pushing back against it. Thus were the endless feudings of pagan Arabia brought to an end. The preachers intuit this well enough. Justice is God's requirement, and it is not only their emotions which clamour for it. Yet the Qur'an, as ever, insists not just on a certain instrumental practicality based on God's observed 'customs' on earth, but on a higher, stranger and more radical ideal which announces that what the Ottomans called the 'order of the world', *niẓām al-ʿālam*, is not finally maintained by imposing a dry calculus of benefit and loss, but by sacrificing the ego. This is intrinsic to a real 'theo-sociology'.

Let us, then, explore the possibility of nuancing the discourse of the *lex talionis*, suggesting that justice may be transcended without the consequence being itself unjust. Here we part company not only with the *jāhiliyya* but with a Muʿtazilite ethic which assumes that forgiveness cannot override the strict application of God's justice. Sunnism takes itself to be a form of Islam which champions justice while insisting that it can be consummated, not vitiated, by forgiveness and remission. The Conquest of Mecca represents this as the indicative climax of the *Sīra*. It is represented again by the determination to draw a line under the disputes which arose among the early believers, in the eirenic and medicinal phrase 'the Companions were all upright' (*al-ṣaḥāba kulluhum ᶜudūl*). Eschatologically, too, the entire controversy over the Prophetic intercession is revealing. Beyond strict justice, the Man of Praise intercedes: 'My intercession is for the perpetrators of grave sins in my community' (*shafāᶜatī li-ahl al-kabā'ir min ummatī*).[4] For Muᶜtazilites, God's justice *must* be done; He *must* send the sinner to Hell. For Sunnis, by contrast, God's justice, like human justice, is of a moral nature which admits the possibility that it is not compromised by being transcended in favour of mercy, but is actually reinforced and made characteristically and even mysteriously divine. This is, of course, part of the moral appeal of theism itself: Buddhism can hardly admit of a metaphysical type of forgiveness. Secular jurisprudence, always instrumental, technical and pragmatic, may acknowledge remission, and even a type of mercy—as we see with amnesties, pleas for clemency, or the decisions of parole boards—but this tends to be rooted in ultimately profane considerations of civic utility, and has very limited scope. It struggles even to be Kantian.

So we are faced with this challenge: to speak a Muslim language to an insulting and stigmatising verbal culture, to defend what we experience as the most pure and precious set of virtues and forms of life, but which remains loyal to this anti-Muᶜtazilite style of the affirmation of justice through its transcendence, thus stepping outside the vicious circle whose secular logic seems to promise a world of thorns. There must be a philosophy of 'higher reciprocation' at the heart of what we have called meta-citizenship; but where is it to be found?

To the perplexity of Islam's cultured despisers, such as the theologian who informed readers of *The Times* that Jesus' parable of the Prodigal Son 'neatly marks out his teaching both from Islam and from the cold logic of secularism',[5] the Qur'an, far from presenting a Muᶜtazilite legalism or advocating a God of the type described by

4 Abū Dāūd, Sunna, 21; Tirmidhī, Qiyāma, 11.

5 Tom Wright, letter to *The Times*, 19 February 2019.

Khalid Blankinship as 'a cosmic justice machine',[6] deeply internalises its own theology of the transcendence of strict justice. Indeed, the *lex talionis* has its due place. And indeed that does, in matters of social boundaries, supply *ḥayāt*—life, for the 'made weak', the *mustaḍʿafīn*, in particular. 'Life' is provided for the vulnerable and oppressed: the homeless, the lone mother, the child, the orphan, the pauper, by the egoless wielding of power, where directed by the *qāḍī*. Constraint preserves life; that is its proper legitimation. To that extent we are sociological. But this is only one dimension of the full Qur'anic story; indeed, those Muslim preachers of a *tanfīrī* bent who focus only on a bitter discourse of requital have not adopted even a superficial Qur'anic reading, but have averted their eyes from some key passages which are universally accepted by the exegetes, from the time of the first generation onwards, as defining and axiomatic.

The Sunni principle of a kind of meta-justice, a justice which transgresses the limits of a simple utilitarian logic, is drawn from key scriptural texts. The Qur'an speaks not of virtues, *faḍā'il*, but of an equation between beauty and truth, and hence with conformity to perfections ontologically sourced in the divine nature. The Qur'anic language thus elides concepts of beauty and goodness in one lexical range, that of the root *ḥ.s.n.* Later Sufi theorists took this convergence as the root of a complex aestheticising view of human excellence. However it is not necessary here to propose an esoteric reading of scripture, or some very creative exegesis of a putatively mediocre exoterism. Such manoeuvres are routinely (and often abusively) attempted by assorted reformist or liberalising tendencies, which internalise a letter-spirit dichotomy which is, as Massignon and so many others have seen, simply alien to the tradition, which accepts the *fiqh* as part of the essence of Islam. The texts we will use to explore this Ishmaelite meta-justice will be drawn primarily from the 'exoteric' discourse of ulema who wrote but seldom on esoteric topics.

---

6 Khalid Blankinship, 'The early creed', in Tim Winter (ed.), *The Cambridge Companion to Classical Islamic Theology* (Cambridge, 2008), 50.

The Qur'anic conception of justice, and of the due repulsion of aggression and wrong, emerges in opposition to a culture of tribal honour codes and a *lex talionis* which treated the clan as the legal site of juridical personality.[7] Individual hurts clamoured for emotive 'satisfaction', rather in the stereotypical Mediterranean way.

La vendetta, oh, la vendetta!
È un piacer serbato ai saggi.
L'obliar l'onte e gli oltraggi
è bassezza, è ognor viltà.[8]
(Revenge! Oh, revenge
is a pleasure meant for the wise.
To overlook insult and outrage
is always degrading and base.)

These primitively pagan, Cosa Nostra idioms of feuding had been endemic in Arabia, but were prophetically overturned by the new belief that an enemy's hatred must not lead one into injustice against him or his kin, for the ego is never to be obeyed:

> *O you who believe! Be steadfast witnesses for God in equity, and let not hatred in any people seduce you away from acting justly. Act justly, that is closer to piety. Fear God, truly He is informed of what you do.* (5:8)

Rejoicing at their misfortune is likewise a sign of egotism: the Sunna with its chivalric *futuwwa* ethos rejects entirely the vice of *shamātat al-aᶜdā'*, taking pleasure in the misfortunes of one's enemies.[9] Proportionality and the rejection of emotive responses are to be the Muslim way, in place of the *ḥamiyyat al-jāhiliyya*, the 'feverishness of the Age of Ignorance'. (48:26)

However classical Islam's discourse of *ḥusn*, of moral beauty, went much further than this. While Muᶜtazilites demurred, Ashᶜarite and Māturīdī exegetes were not slow to spot revelation's insistence on a virtue of higher reciprocation which allowed individuals the right to respond not in kind, or simply proportionately, but through, in

7 Ramon Harvey, *The Qur'an and the Just Society* (Edinburgh, 2018), 64-78.
8 Bartolo's aria in Mozart's *Le nozze di Figaro*.
9 Muslim, Dhikr, 54.

the Qur'an's startling phrase, 'repelling'—or 'pushing back'—'with what is more beautiful' (*idfa*ʿ *bi'llatī hiya aḥsan*). This phrase stands at the heart of a sūra which is particularly insistent on ethics as *iḥsān*, in William Chittick's translation, 'doing the beautiful.' The sūra is number 41, entitled *Fuṣṣilat*.

The most compendious accounts here come from Ibn Jarīr al-Ṭabarī (d. 923), al-Qāḍī al-Bayḍāwī (d. 1286), and Fakhr al-Dīn al-Rāzī (d. 1209), exegetes of generally 'exoteric' credentials, whose concerns mainly encompass the grammatical, the moral and the formally doctrinal. Their interpretations of the sūra will comprise the focus of the remainder of this chapter.

The key sequence appears in verses 30 to 36, rendered by Abdel Haleem (with emendations) as follows:

> *As for those who say, 'Our Lord is God', and take the straight path towards Him, the angels come down to them and say, 'Have no fear or grief, but rejoice in the good news of Paradise, which you have been promised. We are your allies in this world and in the world to come, where you will have everything you desire and ask for as a welcoming gift from the Most Forgiving, Most Merciful One.' Who speaks better than someone who calls people to God, does what is right, and says, 'I am one of those devoted to God'? Good and evil cannot be equal. Push back evil with what is better and your enemy will become as close as an old and valued friend, but no-one is granted this save those who show patience, and no-one is granted this save one of great good fortune. Should a prompting from Satan stir you, seek refuge with God: He is the All Hearing and the All Knowing.*

Let us turn to our commentators, beginning with Ṭabarī. The core of his analysis relates to verse 34: 'Push back evil with what is better', which in a more literal rendering might become 'Push against the evil with what is better/more beautiful.' He paraphrases the verse as follows:

> God is saying to His Prophet Muhammad, may God bless him and give him peace: O Muhammad, use your mildness [*ḥilm*] to push back against the ignorance of he who aggresses

> against you [*jahla man jahila ʿalayk*]; apply your forgiveness to those who harm you deliberately; apply your patience [*ṣabr*] to that which you dislike in them and which you suffer at their hands.[10]

Ṭabarī is noted for his encyclopaedic knowledge of the *āthār*, the sayings of the Salaf, and sure enough, we are now given a sequence of these. One representative example is an uneasy tale of the First Caliph:

> Abū Bakr was once in the mosque where someone was insulting him, while the Blessed Prophet was watching the situation unfold [*shatamahu rajulun, wa'n-Nabiyyu (ṣ) shāhid*]. Abū Bakr excused him for a while [*fa-ʿafā ʿanhu sāʿa*]. Then anger overcame Abū Bakr, and he uttered a riposte. At this the Holy Prophet stood and left, to be followed, perplexedly, by Abū Bakr, who asked: 'The man kept insulting me, and I was forgiving and overlooked the actions, while you simply remained seated; but when I started to defend myself [*falammā akhadhtu antaṣiru*] you rose and left!' And the Prophet, may God bless him and grant him peace, replied: 'An angel was replying to him on your behalf [*innahu kāna yaruddu ʿanka malakun min al-malā'ika*]. But when you started to react and defend yourself, the angel left, and the devil came. By God, Abū Bakr, I will never remain in the devil's presence.'[11]

This narrative, which ends with a hint of the next verse: 'Should a prompting from Satan stir you, seek refuge with God', lies at the core of Ṭabarī's understanding of this passage. For him it comprises a masterpiece of religious psychology. He resumes like this: 'The devil may cast into your heart a whispering of the lower self [*waswasa min ḥadīth al-nafs*] because he desires to make you requite the other's wrong with a wrong of your own. He invites you to do him some wrong yourself; but seek refuge in God from the thoughts

---

10 Ibn Jarīr al-Ṭabarī, *Jāmiʿ al-bayān ʿan ta'wīl āy al-Qur'ān* (Cairo: 1388/1968), XXIV, 68, paraphrased.

11 *Ibid.*, paraphrased.

the devil inspires.' The entire passage is rooted in the awareness of God's scrutiny: helpfully, Abū Bakr had the Blessed Prophet to explain what was at stake; but the Qur'an makes this plain: *innahu huwa's-samīʿ al-ʿalīm*: 'He is surely the All Hearing and the All Knowing.'

For Qāḍī Bayḍāwī, the key is the principle of *ṣabr*, patient endurance.

> *No-one is granted this*, i.e. no-one is given this trait of returning good [*iḥsān*] for evil *save those who show patience*, for this holds back the ego from vengeance, and *no-one is granted it save one of great good fortune*, which means goodness, and perfection of soul.[12]

The Moroccan spiritual master Aḥmad Zarrūq (d.1493) explains that to requite harm with another harm would lead to still greater harm, which is why we are obliged to respond with *iḥsān*. As for those who will not accept our gift or our kind word or gesture, the response should not be to return to the exchange of insults, but simply to turn away.[13]

The same Bayḍāwī reflects on a closely-related passage, verse 8 of Sūrat al-Mā'ida, which we noted earlier:

> *O you who believe! Be steadfast witnesses for God in equity, and let not hatred in any people seduce you away from acting justly. Act justly, that is closer to piety. Fear God, truly He is informed of what you do*. Let not the intensity of your hatred for the idolaters cause you to renounce justice towards them, so that you commit forbidden acts, such as mutilating the dead, and cursing, and killing women and children, and breaking pledges, simply in order to heal what is in your hearts.

The repetitions towards the close of the verse exist for emphasis, in order to 'extinguish the fire of rage': the rage which can lead fake

---

12 ʿAbd Allāh al-Bayḍāwī, *Anwār al-tanzīl wa-asrār al-ta'wīl* (Istanbul, 1329AH), 635.

13 Shaykh Aḥmad Zarrūq, *Qawāʿid al-taṣawwuf*, ed. Ibrāhīm al-Yaʿqūbī (Tripoli, n.d.), 97 (qāʿida 181).

warriors to commit war crimes and to target the innocent, all of which reflects 'the dictates of passion [*hawā*].'[14]

Turning now to the interpretation of Fakhr al-Dīn al-Rāzī, we find that the great commentator does not take our sequence in isolation but uses it as a key case to evidence his grand theory of *naẓm,* the miraculous ordering of the divine verses. To grasp his treatment of the virtue of higher reciprocation we need to understand that he sets it in the large context of the entire sūra of *Fuṣṣilat*, which he finds to be a strongly cohesive whole, offering a complex meditation on the nature of justice and of God's protection of human beings from their lower selves. His theory of *naẓm* is rooted in a tradition of Ashʿarite reflection on the Qur'an which derives in part from his predecessor al-Bāqillānī, and which, drawing on the Qur'an's well-known insistence that it is 'guidance to the Godfearing' (*hudan li'l-muttaqīn*), and even a source of misguidance to the hard-hearted (2:26), had been explored by scholars for centuries. For Rāzī, God's speech is not ordered like the words of any other book, and yet it is definitely and wondrously ordered. However this order is one which is discernable only by those who hold the right key to its door, which is a divinely-inspired heart. In his discussion of the *naẓm* of this sūra he develops this teaching, explaining that unbelievers cannot see the coherence of the Qur'an's discourse and its moral vision, and must forever fumble, on the basis of superficial linguistic criteria, for some key to its coherence. However God Himself has said that 'we have placed veils on their hearts, lest they should understand it'. (17:46) The power and narrative art of the Qur'an can only be disclosed by what he calls *al-ʿulūm al-ilāhiyya al-kashfiyya*: sciences of unveiling bestowed by God.[15]

Early in the sūra we hear the following words from religion's cultured despisers: 'Our hearts are veiled from what you call us to' (verse 5), or, as some would nowadays colloquially say: 'This messaging doesn't do anything for me.' Then they say: 'Do not hear

14 Bayḍāwī, *Anwār*, 142-3.
15 Rāzī, XXVII, 125.

this Qur'an, and distort it' (*lā tasmaʿū hādha'l-Qur'āna wa'lghaw fīhi*) (verse 26): the practice of Lahabist misquoters and text-abusers in all ages. This initiates a chain of Qur'anic reasoning which culminates in the key commandment of verse 34.

Rāzī is here proposing a spiritual criterion for understanding the Qur'an, and hence for opening its pages to the human heart. The philologist will spend his life trying to define the text, but has not been gifted with the hermeneutic key. This is no computational Enigma machine, it is *kashf*, divine unveiling—a Sufi term, although, again, Rāzī does not show himself specifically interested in quoting Sufi theories of the Qur'anic phenomenon, despite living in an age in which they had already flowered abundantly. For Rāzī, Sūra Fuṣṣilat expounds the Qur'an's hermeneutic of religious knowing in a way which is not explicitly mystical, but in fact forms part of the text's exoteric and formal logic.

For Rāzī, Sūra Fuṣṣilat provides a grand example of this. God's arguments, which include the divine moral commands, are not heard objectively and in a vacuum. They emerge initially in the polemical cauldron of Meccan debate, a microcosm of the larger cosmic conflict which rages between truth and the ironbound hearts of polytheists. The greatness of a prophet, as opposed to a mere logician, is that he understands the inner life of his adversaries, and constructs arguments that help them to recognise the nature of their own subjectivity. The sūra is, for Rāzī, ultimately about the summons to God in the midst of an incredulous and profane world in which human perception has been damaged. And this is the highest human vocation: as the sūra asks: 'who is more beautiful in speech [*aḥsanu qawlan*] than he who summons to God, and works righteousness, and says, I am among the Muslims?' (41:33) This rises above the duty of the logician: it is not enough to be mentally adept, one must accept a vocation to help the imperfect as well.

It is the Prophets who are summoned to this highest calling, as the sūra says. We cannot aspire to prophecy, when we confront a society mired in mercantile greed, gross inequality, an egotistic *qiṣāṣ* mentality and hostility to faith, including what we now refer to as Islamophobia (a phenomenon which the thought-world of the Qur'an is perfectly familiar with). But we can and must be knowers, *ʿulamāʾ*; and these are of three types. Rāzī tells us that there are *ʿulamāʾ bi-aḥkāmi'Llāh*—scholars of God's rules; *ʿulamāʾ bi-ṣifāti'Llāh*—scholars of His attributes, who are the theologians; and there are *ʿulamāʾ bi'Llāh*—knowers of, or by, God and His wisdom.[16]

Above the jurist, then, there is the theologian; but above the theologian stands the one who knows God in an empirical, experiential sense, 'finding' God as *al-Qarīb*, the Near. Calling others is the *ḥasana* of which the sūra speaks: the beauty and the beautiful act. The highest type of knower is the one who promotes this goodness through, as Rāzī puts it, patience in the face of the disbeliever's harm (*adhā*) and renouncing revenge (*tark al-intiqām*).[17] This is what we have called 'meta-justice.'

So when interpreting the verse that reminds us that the *ḥasana* and the *sayyi'a*, the beautiful and the evil deed, are not 'equal', he insists that its supreme meaning is that the summons to God is not just equal to or balanced by their saying: 'Our hearts are veiled from what you call us to.' It follows an entirely different logic, rooted in truth and the capacity to transcend ego.

The truth of the Real, blazingly manifest to sound minds and hearts, is denied not, finally, by specious though careful arguments, but by arguments perverted by human wilfulness.[18] Modern philosophy refers often to the problem of theory choice: when opting for one good interpretation of a locution rather than another our assessment of the arguments is inescapably weighed by our own needs and self-esteem. Fashionable positions are typically the most favoured, in every age; or indeed, in every faculty. Academic thinkers

16 Rāzī, XXVII, 126.

17 Rāzī, XXVII, 128.

18 *'Those who wrangle concerning God's signs without a warrant having come to them, there is nought else in their breasts save pride which they will never attain. So take refuge in God. He, only He, is the Hearer, the Seer'* (Qur'an 40:56).

cannot afford to be indifferent to Assessment Exercises and the judgement of fellow-members of their guild. Humans are social animals, and are 'created weak'.

Rāzī proceeds to explain how this *aḥsan*, what is best, or most beautiful, can overcome the human wilfulness and egotism that cause human beings to reach for false interpretations, and even for the outright denial of God and His signs. The wrangler, in the Meccan market-square, or in a modern nationalist think-tank, or on the pages of a contemporary philosophy journal, is not a discarnate, passion-free mind; he is likely to occupy a highly-charged affective habitus in which issues of identity, family or tribe, career, and income, are all directly at stake. One thinks here of Malcolm Bradbury's famous send-up of modern French philosophy in his book *Mensonge*, which deconstructs deconstruction itself simply as an option for status and prestige, and not for moral or epistemological seriousness.[19]

Rāzī's discussions of theory choice, in the case, for instance, of the apparently foolproof arguments for both anthropomorphism and its opposite, have been discussed by Ayman Shihadeh, who remarks that Rāzī's final conclusion is that the finest and most convincing argument, when syllogisms are said and done, is the *ṭarīq al-Qur'ān*, the Way of the Qur'an.[20] Rāzī's prophetology and hagiology hold the key to understanding how the conundrums of theological and ethical polemic are finally to be unravelled: through the scripture's deconstruction of the theologian's self, and the establishment of an epistemology grounded in humility and what he calls alienation, *waḥsha*. Here we seem to return interestingly to Ishmael, and his trusting though painful exile.

So how is the Meccan preacher, or the modern follower concerned to overcome contemporary Lahabism, to defeat the *sayyi'a*, the passional, egotistic discourse of identity, nation, race, identity

19 Malcolm Bradbury, *Mensonge: My Strange Quest for Henri Mensonge, Structuralism's Hidden Hero* (Harmondsworth, 1998).

20 Ayman Shihadeh, *The Teleological Ethics of Fakhr al-Dīn Al-Rāzī* (Leiden, 2006), 188.

politics, and job security, of a continent in the tightening grip of populism? Sūra Fuṣṣilat, in what Rāzī takes to be its climax, proposes that 'pushing with what is better' (or 'more beautiful'), *idfaᶜ bi'llatī hiya aḥsan*, by the epistemically-enlightened sage, is the catalyst which is available to break the impasse. This it does not by offering just another, still more reasonable argument, since good and evil acts are not 'equal', but by probing deeper, into the affective realms where arguments begin and are chosen. The *ḥasana*, the goodly summons to God, the healthy argument, is vindicated, in the real world of difficult human egos, by the *aḥsan*, that which is still better.

So Rāzī says this:

> God tells us to push against their ignorance and crudeness in what is the most beautiful of ways [*aḥsan al-ṭuruq*]. For if you endure, and are patient with their ugly manners, again and again, and do not respond to their stupidity with anger, and do not react to the hurt that they do, they will feel ashamed of their ugly manners, and will abandon their evil habits. [...] Then they will move from hostility to affection [*maḥabba*], and from hatred to love [*mawadda*].[21]

This is no textbook diplomatic stratagem or debating trick; God regards it as the highest attitude of all, as 'it is useful for religion, for the harmony of this world, and for our chances in the next.' This is why He calls it *ḥaẓẓ ᶜaẓīm*, a mighty portion or fortune. Rāzī quotes this from the Baghdad grammarian al-Zajjāj (d. 923): 'This beautiful way of behaving is given only to those who patiently endure abuse, and suffer hardship, and suppress their anger, and reject revenge.'[22]

So this capacity to respond to evil with something more beautiful is a divine gift, which is cast upon (*yulaqqā*) those who restrain themselves. Rāzī describes it as the gift of a virtue of the psyche and an exalted degree (*al-faḍā'il al-nafsāniyya wa'l-darajāt al-ᶜaliyya*).

21 Rāzī, XXVII, 128.
22 Ibid.,128.

Ḥaẓẓ ᶜaẓīm means *quwwat al-nafs*, spiritual strength, and a pure inward life (*ṣafā' al-jawhar*); and these are the gifts of God. Such a soul can make choices for 'the most beautiful'.

Rāzī then tells us that the *naẓm* goes on. 'And should a temptation from Satan tempt you [...]' means that the believing human being, emulating Prophecy itself in choosing the *aḥsan*, must seek God's protection from the demonic voices which suggest that the bruised ego must be defended in like kind; for the *nafs*, the lower self, is an expression of the demonic.

The sequence continues still further. Having insisted on the capital importance of the *daᶜwa*, the invitation to God, and explained how to melt obdurate hearts, the next verses startlingly advert to the Qur'an's argument from signs:

> *And of His signs are the night and the day and the sun and the moon. Worship not sun or moon; but worship God Who created them, if it is in truth Him whom you serve.*
>
> *But if they are too proud—still, those who are with thy Lord glorify Him night and day, and tire not.*
>
> *And it is of His signs that you see the earth lowly, but when We send down water thereon it thrills and grows. Verily He Who quickeneth it is the Quickener of the Dead. Truly He is Able to do all things.* (41:37-9)

Thus should our arguments be. Confronted with the rejection of God in damaged and Islamophobic hearts we begin with the *falakiyyāt*, cosmic arguments, appealing to the deepest and most shared human intuition which knows that differentiated and mutable entities must be originated (*muḥdath*). Then come the *āyāt arḍiyya*, the signs on earth, which are usually biological. When softened by the evidence of Muslim good manners and forgiveness, the enemies of faith will give heed to these signs, will make the right choices, and will restore the memory of God to their hearts. Thus the 'pushing back' includes the possibility of enabling the gift of faith.

The above is a brief synopsis of Rāzī's analysis. The important point to note is that the *naẓm*, and Rāzī's ethical view generally, converge on the principle enunciated in verse 34, which is the absolute negation of the old Arabian, *jāhilī*, idea of the ego-driven vendetta. Pushing back against evil with something more beautiful, for Rāzī, was one of the key ethical breakthroughs of the Islamic revolution, and also an epistemological one which provided a key to resolving theological paradoxes and enabling dispassionate theory choices that could envisage a radically new ethical outlook. In defeating evil and ego, we open up hearts to recognising the Divine; and on this basis we can discern the beauty of the higher reciprocation.

Patience and mildness can melt the most stiffly savage breast. Abū Sufyān, arch-enemy to the Man of Praise, a super-rich oligarch puffed up with a thousand angry objections, found faith when he witnessed the Prophet's forgiveness and forbearance when Mecca was finally in his power. His bitterly Lahabist wife Hind bint ʿUtba, who had sworn to kill him, experienced a similar metanoia, so that she finally found that 'no-one was more beloved to her than the Prophet'; and the Man of Praise, hearing this and forgiving her, predicted: 'Your love shall increase.'[23] Thus did Islam capture the wild Arabian hearts: according to the early commentator Mujāhid, the verse *and when they pass by false talk, they pass by nobly* (25:72), means: 'when they are harmed, they forgive.'[24]

As several commentators remark, this is an eternally valid principle, a necessary expression of the Prophetic saying: 'I am sent only to perfect the beauty of character traits.'[25] No such perfection can ever be cancelled out or abrogated, but the *ṣabr* required needs to be buttressed with *tawakkul*, the trust in God, discussed in the previous chapter, which makes all worldly reverses bearable, and

---

23 See Muḥammad al-Wāqidī, ed. Marsden Jones, *al-Maghāzī* (London, 1966), II, 850.

24 *Iḥyā'*, V, 631 (*Kitāb dhamm al-ghaḍab, bayān faḍīlat al-ḥilm*).

25 *Muwaṭṭa'*, Ḥusn al-khuluq, 8.

which knows that trials, *balāyā*, typically but startlingly turn out to be blessings: 'If God wishes to bless someone, He sends against him someone to wrong him.'[26]

Once this counterintuitive and radically strange perspective has been internalised, our conclusion follows quite inescapably. While the *lex talionis*, as a principle of justice, retains its role for the sake of public order, and while ethics must incorporate the possibility of sanction and punishment, the Qur'anic showcasing of a radical principle of 'what is more beautiful still' is clearly so important, in the view of these commentators, and expressed so absolutely in the Qur'anic text, that the Muslim response to Islamophobia, amid the mounting variety of legal disabilities and vexations laid upon Ishmael by an unhappy Europe, needs to transcend the vendetta mentality common in ancient Mecca and the modern inner city, and reach for something less sociologically predicted and more authentically rooted in the virtues and wisdom of the classical age of Muslim moral thought. We see now why highly-trained scholars, unlike self-taught preachers, do not become extremists.[27] The culmination of the Prophet's ministry may validly be identified with the forgiveness of his enemies in Mecca. While the law cannot be set aside, this climax indicates what is deepest and most truly prophetic about Islam. Law is most faithfully served by wisdom and the repudiation of ego, rooted in the awareness that all is in God's hands. And with this virtue, a real integration will become possible: one based on the dignity and moral excellence of a community admired and envied by others, rather than an integration driven by shamefaced compliance with demands to change one's social beliefs.

Of course, Muslim forbearance in the face of chauvinism and misrepresentation is already abundantly present. Most take the

---

26 Ghazālī, *Iḥyā'*, V, 654 (*Kitāb dhamm al-ghaḍab, bayān faḍīlat al-ʿafw*).

27 In the Ottoman world it was the small preachers, *vaizan*, who became zealot Kadızadelis, killing smokers and starting riots, not the scholars (*ulema*). Madeline Zilfi, *The Politics of Piety: The Ottoman Ulema in the Post-Classical Age (1600-1800)* (Minneapolis, 1988), 129-182.

abuse on the chin, silently, and keep their hope in God. *The Economist* heads a report on a survey by describing British Muslims as 'pious and loyal.'[28] It is only the radical *tanfīrī* fringes who take the law into their own hands, or who use hate speech to counter the hate speech of liberal or populist polemicists, and this is because of their inner frailty and a capitulation to an outraged pride. Generally, in Europe, and around the world, one finds that traditional mosque-going Muslims marvellously retain the virtue of *ḥilm*, mildness, which a certain Islamophobic discourse claims to be alien to them. Those who travel in Muslim lands, or know Muslim communities in the West, frequently remark on this.

The task, then, is for the ulema, the truly uncompromising *uṣūlī* scholars of the religion, to challenge those who react destructively and self-destructively to monoculturalist verbal or legal violence. Disciplining the lower self should be preserved as a foundational Muslim act, the basic formation of the believing conscience which may then safely recognise religious options. Zealots should be helped to understand that their abusive language, which one can hear (to cite only one platform) on a sad abundance of Muslim websites, quickly closes Western minds and hearts and makes the spread of the message of *tawḥīd* far more difficult. Sulaymān ibn Tarkhān, disciple of Ibn Masᶜūd, used to say: 'No-one will accept your view if you have made him angry.'

Thorough and successful inner victory alone will qualify us to condemn others. On the matter of *amr bi'l-maᶜrūf wa-nahy ᶜan al-munkar* Imām al-Ghazālī warns us as follows:

> Herein lies a very great danger which must be avoided, as it leads straight to destruction. This appears when a scholar, when drawing attention to someone's fault, beholds the glory of his own erudition and the lowliness of the ignorant person. His criticism may even have the intention of humiliating someone and proving his own superiority. If this is his

28 *The Economist*, 7 May 2009.

> motivation, then this evil [*munkar*] is worse than the evil he is condemning.[29]

And he relates the following of Dawud al-Ṭā'ī:

> Someone asked: 'What is your opinion of a man who visits rulers and commands them to follow the good and avoid the evil?'
> He replied: 'I fear that he will be flogged.'
> 'He is strong enough to endure that.'
> 'Then I fear he will be beheaded.'
> 'He is strong enough to endure that.'
> 'Then for him I fear the hidden disease: pride.'[30]

The elder Ibn Rushd (d.1126) predicted that a day would come when dissension (*fitna*) will be so prevalent that we should occupy ourselves with self-rectification, and avoid commenting on the faults of others, since our comments will only backfire and make matter worse. He ends by wondering whether he may already be living in that time.[31]

Commenting on his *daʿwa* strategy the Qur'an tells the Man of Praise: 'It was by a mercy of God that you were gentle with them. Had you been harsh and hard of heart, they would have scattered from round about you.' (3:159) Mercy is God's gift, and is evidently a foremost precondition for the Muslim political life. Here, in this remarkable verse which takes us to the living heart of this tender Prophetic charism, we discover yet another condemnation of *tanfīr* as a vice entirely inauthentic and anti-Prophetic. So what is required is not some kind of liberalising of Islam, a process which could scarcely be distinguished from dilution; but instead, a courageous retrieval of the authentic Qur'anic discourse, recalling the first Muslims who had been given this divine gift of patience,

29 Ghazālī, *Iḥyā'*, IV, 615 (*Kitāb al-amr bi'l-maʿrūf wa'l-nahy ʿan al-munkar, āfāt al-riyā' ʿinda al-nuṣḥ*).

30 Ghazālī, *Iḥyā'*, IV, 616.

31 Ibn Rushd, *al-Muqaddamāt*, cited by Michael Cook, *Commanding Right and Forbidding Wrong in Islamic Thought* (Cambridge, 2010), 364.

compassion and restraint. Here, as elsewhere, *dīn* slips the bonds of reductionist sociology and of a fundamentalism driven by emotion: the quality of mercy is not strained.

CHAPTER 8

A theology of the *Ahl al-Kidhāb*

> When the Church is no longer regarded, not even opposed,
> and men have forgotten
> All gods, except Usury, Lust, and Power ...
>
> T.S. ELIOT

IN THIS CHAPTER we explore ways in which Ishmaelite religion might develop a sense of its relationship to an ambient British and European culture which no longer self-defines as monotheistic. Those who continue to find comfort in Qur'anic truth while being invited to full membership of a Western community have to live one of the most media-friendly and demanding of claimed antinomies, especially since the argument of those Muslim and non-Muslim populists who claim that the two cannot cohabit and cross-fecundate seems to be strengthened by Europe's general apostasy and by the rise of a remarkable and increasingly widespread prejudice against all religion.[1] Every belief in the 'supernatural' is suspect for this mindset, for which even a 'Christophobia' has become salient. In Spain, for instance, churches have been burned at the hands of atheist extremists, with a bomb exploding in Saragossa Cathedral; elsewhere 'incidents frequently occur in which feminist groups, LGBT activists, pro-abortion groups and others, break into churches, sometimes interrupting the Mass, shouting

1 See for instance Michel De Jaeghere, *Enquête sur la Christianophobie* (Issy-les-Moulineaux, 2006); more angry is the analysis of the (Orthodox Jewish) Joseph H.H. Weiler, *Ein christliches Europa. Erkundungsgänge* (Salzburg, 2004), 71-3.

and staging various provocations (nudity, gay 'kisses', etc.)'.[2] The phenomenon of body-belief terrorism is on the increase and indexes Europe's growing antipathy towards God. In this environment Muslims are especially visible and vulnerable, being seen as the most stubborn and properly-denounced exemplars of a tendency among conservative religious communities to refuse to keep pace with the ever-drifting socio-ethical consensus of what was once Latin Christendom.

In the Muslim case this accusation is often linked to Blairite claims that steadily rising xenophobic tendencies in the majority culture result in large measure from the failure of immigrants to integrate.[3] Muslims respond by observing that such perceptions seem to be rooted in prejudice and a poor access to the facts, and that in fact the UK record is encouraging overall. The best research confirms that Muslims themselves (Blair's most usual suspects) typically show themselves committed to a convivial and integrated existence in their British home, despite its secularity. This is suggested by a number of surveys which have sought to determine their position on various indices of identity and citizenship. In general the results make a nonsense of Blair's 'blame the victim' approach and of many images cherished by the popular press. For instance it emerges that seventy-seven percent of Muslims identify 'very strongly' with the UK, compared to fifty-one percent of the general population. Seventy-six percent of Muslims express confidence in the police, compared to sixty-five percent of the wider public. Only three percent of Muslims feel that other religions are threatening their way of life, compared to a national British figure of twenty-five percent.[4] Muslims are significantly more likely than other communities (67% against 58%) to live in ethnically-mixed areas, and are less willing to

2 Francisco J. Contreras, 'Hostilidad anticristiana en España,' 91-107 of Jaime Mayor Oreja et al., *¿Democracia sin religión? El derecho de los cristianos a influir en la sociedad* (Barcelona, 2014), p.93.

3 https://newspunch.com/tony-blair-we-must-force-migrants-to-integrate-to-combat-rise-of-far-right/

4 'Poll reveals Muslims as model citizens', *The Times*, 17 April 2007.

live in areas largely made up of members of their own group (17% against 33%). Religiosity does not correlate at all with support for violence against civilians; in fact Muslims in London are less likely than the British population at large to support such attacks.[5]

If these surveys are accurate it does seem not only that Muslims in post-Christian Britain want to belong, but that they feel that they do belong. They intuit, presumably, that their heritage allows and even enjoins this rootedness. Yet the exact temper, and the doctrinal and *fiqh* framing, of this Muslim wish to integrate in Britain despite the country's declining awareness of God has not been properly theologised; instead it has been a matter of a practical quotidian assurance by non-Fearful believers living in European contexts that their faith need not be threatened or eroded by conviviality and regular social interaction with secular others. This empirical Muslim wisdom urgently requires a clearer scriptural and conceptual exposition than the community currently receives from academics, Islamist leaderships, or the race temples. There is a discourse of 'minority *fiqh*', mostly of very feeble intellectual rigour,[6] but we miss its underpinnings in a theology, or, as it were, a 'minority *fikr*', something particularly needed in the context of a post-monotheistic society.

We begin with the narrative of a supposedly-lacking 'British Islam', raised with increasing agitation by columnists, social administrators and electorally-sensitive politicians, and which is never going to find a straightforward formulation, as in our complex and mature social landscape there are multiple 'British' and also mul-

---

5 https://news.gallup.com/opinion/queue/173222/british-muslims-feel-british.aspx, see also Tufyal Choudhury, 'British by Dissent: alternatives to jihadi narratives of identity, belonging and violence among Muslims in Britain', 191-215 of Jeevan Deol and Zaheer Kazmi (eds.), *Contextualising Jihadi Thought* (London, 2011), pp. 199, 203.

6 For a good summary of the main debate see H.A. Hellyer, *Muslims of Europe: the 'other' Europeans* (Edinburgh, 2009), 79-99. For Saʿīd Ramaḍān al-Būṭī's rejection of 'minority *fiqh*' see Alan Verskin, *Oppressed in the lands? Fatwas on Muslims living under non-Muslim rule from the middle ages to the present* (Princeton, 2013), 145-8; for a more general refutation see Amjad Mohammed, 38-43.

tiple 'Islamic' identities and normativities which engage a local Umma which represents most of the ethnicities and sects of the larger Muslim world. Patterns of social integration will be highly complex; however it is reasonable to suppose that they will tend to take place on terms with which the communities are comfortable, rather than in compliance with government ideology.

What Blair demands, in tune with the ever-growing bullhorn proclamations of the nativist right, is not an Islamic evolution or version of what is indigenously British, for the substantively post-theistic British themselves, betraying their deepest commitments, have largely forsaken that. The distinctive and moralising world of British churchmanship, together with an affection for Vaughan Williams, briar pipes, and a *Cider with Rosie* romantic memory of the countryside, is recalled only by the very old, who are allowed little or no say in our national discourse. Even among churchgoers, many have converted substantively to the radical new moralities, and hence struggle to empathise not only with Muslims but also with their own ancestral heritage. The entirely secular are even further afield, and it would not be strange to suspect them of treason to the nation's historic narrative and the deepest foundations of its world-view and morality. An intriguing question thus imposes itself: in what sense may British Muslims integrate with deniers of what were until recently the core constituents of Britishness? How are we to understand politicians, journalists and social administrators who call themselves British, but have lost their Christian compass, cannot name their kings and queens, do not know the date of the Armada, are unable to list the Guards regiments, and cannot sing an English song?

In this land flattened and thinned by secularity, instead of a British *patrimony* with which Muslims should engage, we now have British *values*; and these, according to the younger Whitehall apparatchiks, turn out to have nothing to do with our local particularity or heritage, but comprise a raft of globalised liberal beliefs of the latest and most radical kind.

> To the government, integration had come to mean the acceptance of 'British values', full stop. Britain's core national identity was enshrined in gender liberalism, women's physical visibility, an acceptance of homosexuality, and UK foreign policy, especially respect for Israel.[7]

This needs to be seen as an extraordinary evolution for a hitherto self-consciously distinctive island nation. Until very recently the past was allowed a significant vote in our national present; the House of Lords formed a sort of constitutional guarantor of this, together with the Bench of Bishops and the retired blimps and the *noblesse oblige* of the remaining politically-active aristocracy, whose decay is brilliantly portrayed in Ford Madox Ford's *Parade's End*. But this system with its Christian foundations was already in full decline when Thatcher and Blair briskly swept away its mouldering remains and replaced it with a Cool Britannia in which the atomised, pastless individual and her or his rights and success in wealth creation lay at the heart of the determination of values and state approbation. Deregulating the Stock Exchange abolished the public-school chumminess of the stockbroking and banking fraternities. The broadsheet newspapers, forced to compete with the instant response to events enabled by the Internet, tightened their deadlines and coarsened their content. So too did the BBC. Hence the cut-glass tones of the Home Service are replaced fifty years on by the BBC's easy-reading website, packed with clickbait nuggets about one-armed babies and the challenges facing transgendered beauticians in Uruguay. Religious broadcasting has atrophied into near-invisibility. Modesty and reserve, once defining qualities of a people who could understand the Christian values of Lord Longford and Mary Whitehouse, are simply deplored as inhibitions in a culture which mainstreams pornography and is addicted to *Love Island* and *Celebrity Big Brother*. And so in considering the question of integration in Britain we first need to contend with the fact that the national temperament, and British identity, have morphed, globalised, secularised, and been debased into a near absence. Britain is

7 Moaveni, 276.

technically and by definition still home to the British, but in its unprecedented secularity it has become a travelling home, a laboratory for ever more radical beliefs and social practices. We deal not only with the loss of faith within individuals, but with its immense moral and social ramifications.

The point here is not that passport-holders should retreat into a Peter Hitchens sort of dream about a land that was forever England. Nor yet to idealise it: it would be a UKIP fool's errand to attempt giving the kiss of life to the age of empire and of general race prejudice. Instead, any theologically-sensitive response to the current demand that Muslims must integrate needs simply to be alert to the skittish, quicksilver motility of the post-religious culture into which the integration must be done: Bauman's 'liquid modernity', in which all the old metaphysical anchors have been weighed. Britons of migrant heritage are invited to board a train whose next two stops are more or less guessable, but which, following the collapse of religion, and hence of a broader vision of human becoming, never tells its passengers what its destination might be. Take, for instance, the following extract from *The Times* law report, published a few years from now:

> In a landmark judgement, former Tory whip Mark-Anne Nawaz was yesterday convicted at the Old Bailey of three contraventions of the 2042 Equalities Act. In evidence submitted by Stonewall, video footage extracted from a Strangers' Bar phobometer had recorded the disgraced peer making a series of tetraphobic remarks. Summing up, the judge commented: 'Following the Act's abolition of the protected characteristic of religion, in a liberal society an inclusive and tolerant attitude to sexual orientation must always prevail over private religious commitments.' In a statement Ladylord Nawaz's defence counsel claimed: 'My client has never opposed the right of consensual tetrasexual polyamorous circles or mother-son unions to be registered as marriages under English law. We intend to appeal.'

The Ishmaelite feels summoned, and increasingly instructed, to board this train to an unknown terminus, because the next stop is always politically correct and discursively unassailable. If he demurs, or asks too anxiously about the driver's intentions or the purpose of the journey, he may find himself the object of a surprisingly un-British invective. He will be told that he is a chauvinist, a patriarch, that he suffers from a phobia (which is to say, a mental illness). If he is too confident in what he says he risks a Prevent referral, or at least an obscurely-documented entry into what the police now call the 'pre-criminal space'. And perhaps he will find it difficult to run for parliament, or any significant post in local government, or work as a marriage registrar. His social beliefs, once quite respectable in Britain, now seem almost unspeakable; to voice his conscience may make him a pariah.

What, then, is the normative Muslim guidance for a community invited to sink its tent pegs into these shifting sands? The believer's internal library already seems to tell him much about minority status. For centuries the Sharia provided the basis for peaceable co-existence in an almost indefinitely wide range of contexts: witness, for instance, Sachiko Murata's research on Muslims in premodern China, who remained Sharia-faithful and politically useful while living a profoundly Sinicised culture.[8] Sūra Twelve of the Qur'an shows that even a prophet of God like Joseph may become a civil servant under Pharaoh; his career is held back not by his own confessional scruples but by allegations of sexual harassment. Pharaoh was a pagan, but under the *ahl al-kitāb,* People of the Book, matters were even more straightforward, as shown in Dominic Rubin's remarkable book on the history of Islam in Russia.[9] The

8 Sachiko Murata, William C. Chittick and Tu Weiming, *The Sage Learning of Liu Zhi: Islamic Thought in Confucian Terms* (Cambridge MA and London, 2009).

9 Rubin, *Russia's Muslim Heartlands*, which shows that in Tsarist Russia intolerance and opposition to conviviality came almost entirely from the Church, not from Muslims.

host might have been hostile and imposed a thousand sumptuary and other vexations on Ishmael, but the Muslim theological grounds for living as peaceful subjects or citizens were clearly articulated. Traditional sacred jurisprudence possessed resources that enabled the believer loyally to inhabit a minority context,[10] and to permit the Law to adapt to local particularities.[11]

In modern times the Muslim leadership has endorsed platform documents, most notably the *Common Word*, which affirm that Islam's view of other Abrahamic monotheists is respectful and benign.[12] The scriptural and theological basis for this has again proved broad and uncontroversial. Yet one is hard-pressed to find in the Muslim record a systematic guide to the right and moral engagement with the new type of societies which seem to have no higher purpose, and which have deliberately repudiated a religious heritage, with all its immeasurable richness, its contiguities with Ishmael, and its thick reasons for leading a common life.

Modern Britain appears to be no longer a land of the *ahl al-kitāb*, but of the *ahl al-kidhāb*, the People of Denial, who call all faith a falsehood. Statistics firmly show that most of our compatriots now refuse to self-identify as Christians or Jews. Freelance monotheists, or wanderers with some belief in a higher power, bump up the numbers, but it is not clear that these represent much more than the doomed and confused tail-end of a more seriously theistic past. This collapse came quite suddenly: when many migrants arrived in the late 1950s and early 1960s churchgoing in the host society was the stable national norm, and family life was taken to be regulated

10 Amjad M. Mohammed, *op. cit.*; Hellyer, 59-76.

11 For the Sharia's adaptation to regional specificities see for instance Colin Imber, *Ebu's-su'ud: the Islamic legal tradition* (Edinburgh, *ca* 1997), 44; Amjad M. Mohammad, *Muslims in non-Muslim lands*, 107. An instance of current relevance in which theory was able to accommodate diversity, local exigencies and change is the question of gendered sacred spaces; see Marion Holmes-Katz, *Women in the Mosque: a history of legal thought and practice* (New York, 2014).

12 Lejla Demiri (ed.), *A Common Word: a resource for parishes and mosques* (Cambridge, 2011).

by ideals of ultimately Christian justification.[13] National Service recruits were assumed to be C of E unless they protested to the contrary. Now the Social Attitudes Survey tells us that only three percent of young people consider themselves to be Anglican.

From a Sharia perspective this collapse presents interesting challenges. Integration with Christians and Jews is simply easier. Intermarriage and dietary regulations furnish just two indicative examples: we can share bread, and a bed, with fellow scriptuaries, and there can be close neighbourliness and conviviality.[14] But in this new twenty-first century liquidised Britain Muslims often strain to grasp the moods and motivations of many of their compatriots. What might it be like to imagine that at the end of life one faces only an eternal and hopeless absence? That morality should drift with the motions of the current consensus of 'good people'? That the cosmic imaginary has been inverted, so that looking at the miracle of the world brings no breath of transcendence or solace of divine presence? That art is about the interesting vagaries of the self, not about mimesis or truth?

As European Muslims we need to develop an empathetic and compassionate theology of atheism and of the very new type of humanity which it is creating. It is true that globally the percentage of atheists is said to be declining, standing at around 1.8% of the human race.[15] But in the UK and Europe, among our neighbours and friends, the familiar assurance that a deep though complex mutual trust and recognition, a sense of comity, should naturally exist between fellow Abrahamic believers, has become less relevant. Instead we break bread with people who anticipate a bleak and meaningless void, and whose values are potentially in limitless flux. We need an

13 Callum Brown, *op. cit.*

14 Hakan Çoruh, 'Friendship between Muslims and the People of the Book in the Qur'ān with Special Reference to 5:51', *Islam and Christian-Muslim Relations* 23 (2012), 505–13.

15 Center for the Study of Global Christianity, *Christianity in its Global Context 1970–2020*.

account of this, and a programme for convivial and compassionate action.

Classical Islam knew about atheists, usually styling them *dahriyya*, and possessed resources for engaging their underlying beliefs, but the possibility of developing a *fiqh* for Muslims in a *dahrī* polity and society seems never to have been contemplated. The library shelves are bare. If we are to attempt to fill those shelves, the starting-point is likely to be the human subject, and hence the theological doctrine, evident particularly in Māturīdism, of *ʿiṣmat al-ādamiyya*. By virtue of Adamic descent humans possess an inviolability and are the locus of rights. These are not magically conjured out of dumb matter in the manner of the Kantians, but are a radiance conferred on all humans at the moment of ensoulment, *nafkh al-rūḥ*. For the Māturīdīs, the basic entitlements (*ḍarūriyyāt*) of humans are innate and are present even in a person who has no religion.[16] This develops the understanding implicit in the *Sīra*, which, while considering polytheism (*shirk*) the only unforgivable sin, shows that its adherents may still be engaged with positively, if as individuals they are not actively fighting against the Man of Praise.

> Asmā' bint Abī Bakr said: 'My mother came to me when she was still a polytheist, during the truce with Quraysh. I asked God's Messenger (may God bless him and grant him peace) for a ruling [*fatwā*]: "O Messenger of God, my mother has willingly come to me; shall I maintain my duties of kinship to her?" And he said: "Maintain your duties of kinship to your mother."'[17]

In primal Islam's recognition that all humans partake of an inclusive *ʿiṣma* we find the starting-point for the ethic of non-Abrahamic neighbourliness which is now urgently required. But Europe's need for our help is not just economic and civic: to be faithful to their

16 Recep Şentürk, '*Ādamiyya* and *ʿIṣma*: the contested relationship between humanity and human rights in classical Islamic law', *Islâmi Araştırmalar Dergisi* 8 (2002), 39-69.

17 Bukhārī, Adab, 7; Muslim, Zakāt, 50.

calling Ishmaelites should aspire to be the spiritual repairmen of the damaged and dysfunctional continental heart.

> In man there is a love, a pain, an itch, and a desire such that, if a hundred thousand worlds were to become his property, he would still gain no rest or ease. These people occupy themselves thoroughly with every kind of craft, skill, and position; they learn astronomy, medicine, and other things, but they do not find ease, since their goal has not been attained. After all, the Beloved is called 'heart's-ease', since the heart finds ease through Him. So how could it find ease and peace through others?[18]

This assurance that all humans feel the call to Truth underlines our inescapable premise, which is that Godless compatriots are, of course, still sibling humans, *banī Ādam*; they may not sense it clearly but the *ʿiṣma* exists because they have immortal souls, and spiritual cravings which they may misinterpret or suppress. In our eyes their own sense of self-worth is a drastic underestimation. The *imago dei*, so fundamental a concept for the monotheisms, can only be veiled, never lost; and insofar as one perceives beauty, sacrifice, and sweet-heartedness in any human creature, one experiences also the presence of God. Remember the Khalwatī belief that the human face includes all the shapes of the Arabic letters, so that the names of God are all written there. Men and women are theomorphic,[19] heirs to the primordial covenant of *alastu bi-rabbikum* (7:172), and because they affirmed God on that first of days their hearts still beat with the divine name, *Alláh*. Hence while the unbelieving cannot read the meaning in our faces, we read theirs, and are still reminded of God's majesty and goodness. This is the tradition of the *shāhid*, humanity as mutely eloquent of the divine.[20] The related Sufi

18 Rūmī, *Fīhi mā fīhi*, in William Chittick, *The Sufi Path of Love: the spiritual teachings of Rumi* (Albany NY, 1983), 205.

19 To Muslims the absence of a doctrine of a male incarnation seems to make the inclusion of women a more natural and evident truth.

20 Chittick, *Love*, 88-94.

concept of *iltibās* acknowledges the heart's ability to detect the luminous human beneath the garment of flesh, as Schimmel says, 'the concealment of preeternal beauty in created forms', so that Rūzbehān 'sees in love the effort to break once more through the limits of the created world in order to reach the state of true *tawḥīd* as it existed on the Day of the Covenant.'[21] When that *tawḥīd* is grasped, the individual becomes much more than a national subject willing to balance rights and duties in a cold and utilitarian social contract; instead he or she has transcended the state of the Fearful to become, whatever the social context, a light which recognises other lights, pointing all creatures to God and thus becoming the most beloved and most indispensable gift to the community. For Henry Bayman:

> the Law and conscience find their fullest, most mature manifestation in a person who has become pure love. Rote Imitation becomes Realisation. He or she no longer acts out of blind imitation to the letter of the Law but in full knowledge and consciousness of why the Law prescribes or prohibits a certain thing. The clumsy, sometimes mechanical, sometimes jarring and disturbing implementation of the Divine Law gives way to a smooth, harmonious flow—the grace of love. Such people are a guiding light to all beings lucky enough to come within their sphere.[22]

The Fearful cannot see the atheist from such a vantage-point; for them love seems stranger and less natural than suspicion, envy and disquiet, and the world looks Hobbesian; but Muslims who 'do the beautiful', who are people of *iḥsān*, are optimistic and see the best in everyone, since the spirit (*rūḥ*) is active and the ego (*nafs*) is overcome; and whereas the instinct of the ego is to see inferiority and

---

21 Annemarie Schimmel, *Mystical Dimensions of Islam* (Chapel Hill NC, 1975), 299.

22 Henry Bayman, *The Secret of Islam: revealing the compassionate Koran* (Berkeley CA, 2004), 86.

ugliness in others, the spirit craves only beauty and instinctively seeks it out, however partial it may be.[23]

Michael Sugich's masterpiece *Signs on the Horizons* recounts many anecdotes of his experiences with Ishmaelite spiritual masters whose lives, despite personal and physical suffering, were lived in pure delight and love for others.[24] To look at any human being must be to be reminded of God and the compassionate and ineffable work of His hands. A sage, passing through immigration at Heathrow, is not checking his texts, but is composing prayers for the Border Agency officer and for her parents, children, and neighbours; she does not guess it, unless, perhaps, she is taken aback by the hieratic dignity of his face, so unlike the soft and shifting features of the profane. Thus the sage passes his journey in *wajd*, in the ecstasy of finding God in every moment. As Saʿdī says,

> *Be-jehān khurram az ānom, ke jehān khurram az Ūst.*
> *ʿĀsheqam bar hameh ʿālam ke hameh ʿālam az Ūst.*[25]
>
> I am delighted in the world, because the world delights in Him.
> I love every world, for every world is from Him.

Etsko Schuitema reminds us further of the indispensability of a sense of wonder in fostering the believer's dignity and decency.

> To claim to be a Muslim and not to walk around in a world with a sense of wonder like a child, not being able to say Al Hamdulillah, Al Hamdulillah, a smile and kindness bubbling over to everyone you see, is to lie. You are not a Muslim. So

23 Perhaps this is intuited by the activists of Femen, who in their *jihād* against the blind and harassing chauvinism of many males use weapons which chasten their opponents with a reminder of gentleness, vulnerability and nurturing. Even the ostensibly secular cannot fully ignore the *vestigia Dei* in their own selves; the *shāhid* is never adequately veiled.

24 Michael Sugich, *Signs on the Horizons: meetings with men of knowledge and illumination* (n.p., 2013).

25 *Kulleyyāt-e Saʿdī,* ed. Muḥammad ʿAlī Furūghī (Tehran, 1374 solar), 1001.

> these two ways of being, the darkness of *kufr* and the light of Imaan, have a very obvious sign. Their sign is gratitude.[26]

Faith in God is proved when the Muslim sees the world and its inhabitants with grateful wonder, which is the only mature and objective attitude, and when he accepts that the moment and everything in it is a startling and unique creation of God, Who makes the world anew in every fresh instant. This wonder, this amazement, is the underlying state of the real Qur'anic believer which shapes his religious choices and opens his heart to an outlook of positivity towards others. *Kufr*, by contrast, closes our hearts and makes us fear outcomes and hence attribute real power to others: even those who are apparently devout are in fact of the Fearful if this *kufr* infects their reactions to the world and dulls the lens of their spiritual vision, so that their instinct is not to see everything with love and wonder.

What intersubjectivity arises between an Abrahamic man, a *ḥanīf*, boarding the ICE train to Dresden, as he takes his seat beside the post-German hipster nodding to the house music on his stereo, who has never tasted the pleasure of prayer, and who absently scans the slick slogans of the advertising gurus which slide across his iPhone screen? Only the Qur'anic story of the *bezm-i alast,* the Assembly of the Primordial Covenant, seems able to persuade us that they are from the same genus and origin. And yet that story is decisive and sufficient. Whatever biologists may say, all humanity is of a single origin, having been united in fellowship at that *bezm*, and hence we are consanguineous. Everyone is subject to the same summons, for all are human, and are made of the Creator's same gifts.

> Close the crooked eye and open the eye of wisdom!
> The ego is like a donkey, and desire is its nosebag.
>
> Come to the side of the hospital of your own Creator.
> For whoever does not have that physician has only a
> medicine that makes him sick.

26 Schuitema, 46.

> Come, and give thought to Me, Who gave you your thought.
> Buy a whole donkey-load of rubies from My mine!
>
> Come, come forward to the one who gave you your feet,
> Look with your two eyes, on He who gave you sight.
>
> Clap both your hands out of delight in Him, your hand
> is from His sea.
> There is neither grief nor misfortune when compared
> to His delight.[27]

This is a characteristic ode from Rūmī's *Dīvān-i Shams-i Tabrīz*. Perhaps the hipster atheist happens to be listening to Madonna's riff on Rumi. But between the enraptured soul of the lover of God as he waits for his stop, and his neighbour, there seems to be little common ground. As Charles Taylor sees it, the two are divided not so much by 'rival theories' as by 'different kinds of lived experiences involved in understanding your life in one way or another.'[28] What strategy of integration and common citizenhood could bridge such a gulf? Do they have words in common?

Fortunately the language of affect and the wish to be free of anxiety are evidently universal, they are not theories but experiences; and the ecstasy of our literature, however Eastern its origin, retains a strikingly universal appeal. According to the *Christian Science Monitor* Rumi is now America's most popular poet,[29] and even our hipster is listening. The irony is remarkable: here is a devout Sunni from an Afghan town, a famous mosque preacher, whose voice still reaches worldly hearts in Saxony. He is audible even in Trumpistan: the now legally-binding Muslim Ban excludes Afghans from the land of opportunity, but Homeland Security has entirely

27 Reynold A. Nicholson, *Selected Poems from the Divani Shamsi Tabriz* (Cambridge, 1898), 178.

28 Charles Taylor, *A Secular Age* (Cambridge MA, 2007), 5.

29 Franklin D. Lewis, *Rumi Past and Present, East and West* (Oxford, 2000), 1.

failed to exclude their supreme voice. Everyone is *homo religiosus*, with a heart (*lubb*) which, like a seed, longs for and will thrill to the touch of rain.

Here is an asset to be deployed fearlessly by the deplored Ishmaelites as they seek integration from a position of strength and *ṣidq*, on terms that honour *tawḥīd* and are not simply a matter of concession and dilution. As Eric Ormsby has shown, Islam, in the defining vision of Ghazālian revivalism, takes itself to be quintessentially a religion of *maḥabba*, of love for Creator and creature. God loves humanity, and so humanity loves Him, and loves the phenomena which He has made.[30] The Founder's eschatological title is *Ḥabību'Llāh*, God's Beloved;[31] and Muslim literature follows suit, with a cornucopia of love poems to God and to His universe; and particularly to the human *shāhid*, of both genders. Every human, believing or not, is a theophany, a shrine to her or his Source: 'all that is in the heavens and the earth glorifies God.' (57:1) Even the imperfect who lack self-knowledge and cannot name Him glorify Him unconsciously, and carry the sign of the Divine qualities which are latently mirrored in everyone, even if only the perfect can glorify God as God. The cosmos is the body and humankind is the spirit, and is thus immeasurably noble and beloved, not only in its potential but in the form which indicates that potentiality.[32]

Conventional sociological analysis can hardly entertain such an approach, since 'human sciences' must exclude so primal but unquantifiable a principle as love, that indispensable Ishmaelite gift which must be the foundation for an authentic and ego-free response to the *Ahl al-Kidhāb*. *Tanfīrīs*, sociologists and Strasbourg

---

30 Eric Ormsby, *Al-Ghazālī: Love, Longing, Intimacy and Contentment: Kitāb al-Maḥabba wa'l-shawq wa'l-uns wa'l-riḍā, Book XXXVI of the Revival of the Religious Sciences* (Cambridge, 2011).

31 Tirmidhī, Manāqib, 1.

32 William C. Chittick, *Imaginal Worlds: Ibn al-'Arabī and the problem of religious diversity* (Albany NY, 1994), 22, 35.

can simply not process the following advocacy of apparent madness from Bosnia's best-known theologian:

> There is no thought that does not tend toward the question of love. Although this is the case from the beginning to the end of existence, it is worth testifying that love remains indefinable by thought. The fullness of love is the same as emptiness of thought. To love is the same as to be mad. This is the case because comparison, measurement, and calculation—the essential attributes of reason—lose both their importance and their meaning in love.[33]

Ishmael, ecstatic even on public transport, is necessarily made a stranger by this madness; and his scriptures tell him that in the end-times he will be *gharīb*, exactly a stranger. Blessed, therefore, are the strangers, the hadith concludes.[34] He may seem to be banished from the secular desert, but he knows that at his journey's end lies the Sanctuary, the place of the embrace of diverse humanity in the Covenant. In a raging world of turbo-capitalism, face recognition software, biometric surveillance and runaway automation, the Ishmaelite, who 'hears God', is a hand-clapping gypsy, a Roma, a *Rind*, a Semitic nomad and wanderer; Ishmael, in the primal scriptural construction of the role, is precisely the one cast out by privilege, by elite races and lineages; for he is born of a Gentile mother, who is an African refugee and asylum seeker. He is the scriptural paradigm of worldly unchosenness, and sits in the rain at Calais waiting for the next truck; yet in the Great Sanctuary of Mecca, which holds the mortal remains of Abraham's first son, the world's poor and despised congregate in the love of God, recalling the universal love and beauty of the Primordial Assembly, the *bezm-i alast,* whose sign is the Stone. They congregate also in those ghetto mosques which are the most despised spaces in Europe's unreal cities: in Frankfurt basements they chant the divine name while skinheads hammer on

33 Rusmir Mahmutćehajić, *On Love in the Muslim Tradition* (New York, 2007), 7.
34 Muslim, Īmān, 333.

the windows. They are the sign and affirmation that God is, according to the well-known report, 'with the broken-hearted'.[35] Amid the Pharaonic world-arrogance of biocidal capitalism, the Ishmaelite underclass, despised by left and right alike, stigmatised as foreign, or phobic, or sexist, or terroristic, continues to love God, in other words, to be normally and traditionally human.

Here, then, is a hint, or perhaps a specifically Sufi sign, of the direction our theology of atheism should take. The atheist neighbour begins with the premise that there is nothing ultimately meaningful about human existence, and hence no real nobility; the Ishmaelite starts with the *imago dei* which is scripted as every man and woman, who are therefore to be loved. It is therefore for the believing minorities, energised by this privileged anthropology, to reach out, to reopen, as Rumi has it, God's hospital, to find accommodations and forms of living together, since the believer has objective reasons for doing these things, knowing that the Other's worth is intrinsic, not constructed. The citizen who sees humanity only as the blind watchmaker's latest production should be treated not with scorn but with compassion, as an exile from a world which since a time millennia before the Celtic stone circles has always been understood as sacred. Perhaps this re-enchantment which is the vocation of Europe's Ishmaelite underclass resembles that of the hero-saints of late antique Christianity, who lived under the triumphalist order of pagan Rome. Then, too, the civic religion of officialdom required forms of compliance troubling to the Abrahamic conscience. The parallel may be interesting, but *mutatis mutandis*. *Maḥabba* must be there, but hard monastic vows of asceticism and celibacy will not be part of the method; since Ishmael's is a way of celebrating God's gifts and of full sociality. He is suspect in the new Rome's eyes, but he will not respond by retreating into a hermitage. Instead, he will seek to heal and to build: as Gilis suggests, the demographic fe-

35 Al-Murtaḍā al-Zabīdī, *Itḥāf al-Sāda al-Muttaqīn sharḥ Iḥyā' ʿUlūm al-Dīn* (Cairo, 1311AH), VI, 290.

cundity of Ishmael in Europe, the land which defines him as its Other, is no ironic accident but is a divine initiative, for Ishmael comes with a 'collective mission to testify', carrying the 'decisive proof' (*ḥujja bāligha*) of the Qur'an, which restores the heart's ease (*sakīna*) to a continent where hearts are agitated and all are terrified of death.[36] It is precisely because of Europe's spiritual emergency that Ishmael has arrived.

This Sufi conception, directed towards rescue and healing, which makes life for minorities not only bearable but exquisite by teaching the glorious legibility of life and the intrinsic value of the Other, has nothing to do with Islamist ideological reshapings of Islam. These may impress anxious half-Westernised community leaders, bourgeois technocrats with shallow roots in our heritage; and because their Movement Islam originated among ideologues of the hurt anti-colonial generation it has an anti-Western instinct and a tendency to ideologise *dīn* which makes it assertively insistent on grievance issues and a parallel lives solution. These are the Islamisms which, as Wael Hallaq continues to remind us, are inauthentic Europeanised hybrids which, in the Muslim world, fail consistently, and must always fail, because they seek an impossible state.[37] The most apocalyptically failed of them all, Daesh Salafism, stands evidently at the opposite pole to the inclusive and authentically scriptural policy we have recalled, and represents Islamism in a state of enraged self-destruction, utterly unsuited to minority or any other form of existence. Such *tanfīr* is incapable of humility and of self-blame, and sees the unbeliever only as the reassuring object of scorn and the confirmation of pride; yet inwardly it is itself a form of unbelief.

> In former times the unbelievers worshipped idols and prostrated themselves to them. Today we do the same thing [...] we have many other idols within ourselves, such as greed, self-will, spite, and envy, and we obey them all.

36 Gilis, *Intégrité islamique*, 21-2.

37 Wael Hallaq, *The Impossible State: Islam, politics, and modernity's moral predicament* (New York, 2014).

> Therefore, outwardly and inwardly we act the same as the idol-worshippers, but we consider ourselves Moslems![38]

Humility and self-reckoning (*muḥāsaba*) must be core virtues when understanding and dealing with the problem of unbelief. Arrogance will never serve us; it 'defies the Truth'[39] and obstructs *tawḥīd* itself.

Unfortunately the voices of hyper-reified false scripturalism are growing louder. Western governments have maintained their *liaison dangereuse* with the Saudi fundamentalists for so long that the agenda of divisive *tanfīr* is gaining ground in our communities. An authentic and uncompromising Islamic response to the challenges of our situation must be rooted in a rejection of the fundamentalism which has been aided and abetted by government ministers hell-bent on the sale of weapons of mass destruction. *Daʿwa*, invitation, not *tanfīr*, repulsion, is the criterion of real Prophetic action; and to prevent the further importation of *tanfīrī* Islam we must tirelessly invite the European chancelleries to end their Faustian pact with the extremists.

But to sum up: the theology we need in order to make sense of our situation and to deal sensibly with the Islamophobia, the *niqāb* bans, the school indoctrination and the job discrimination which we face, needs to adopt as its watchword the Qur'anic verse, *East and West are God's, so wheresoever you turn, there is the face of God.* (2:115) The Ishmaelite living a minority life is not an epiphyte, a rootless plant growing on a larger organism which alone has roots. Ishmaelites are not in exile in a strange land, as believers they are never abroad, for the Man of Praise indicates that one of the *khaṣā'iṣ*, the unique traits, of his community is that 'the whole earth has been made a mosque for me.'[40] In this Prophetic optic the land of Europe, however secular, is already a *masjid*: it is the Ishmaelite's brow, not the atheist's, which touches the European earth.

So we are exiles from humanity's current inhumanity, and from the desolating winds of atheistic post-normativity; we are not exiles

38 Rūmī, in Chittick, *Love*, 152.

39 Abū Dāūd, Libās, 26; Tirmidhī, Birr, 60.

40 Bukhārī, Tayammum, 1.

from our good-hearted neighbours or their best traditions and motives; as the hadith says, 'Wisdom is the lost riding-beast of the believer; wherever he finds it, he has the most right to it.'[41] For al-Fuḍayl ibn ᶜIyāḍ, 'the company of an irreligious man of good character is preferable to me to that of an ill-natured man much given to worship.'[42] What is decently European and recognisably moral is also Islamically interesting. Even where the sun of faith has set, some light may linger in the sky, and secular neighbours may practice virtues inherited from monotheist ancestors whose true justification they have forgotten. And as al-Ghazālī says in one of the most challenging perorations which conclude his *Revival of the Religious Sciences*, we should not despise *any* descendent of Adam, since outward appearances may entirely veil the presence of a true saint.[43] According to a Naqshbandī counsel: 'Whomsoever you see, assume that he is Khiḍr!'[44] Even if we are mistaken, and our companion is no saint, the *fiṭra,* innate faithful goodness, is not completely lost in anyone; the spark of the spirit, *rūḥ*, cannot be extinguished.[45]

But to realise this we need to reduce the superficial outward signs that suggest to secular Lahabists that we *are* exiles. For faith to prevail over its alternative, it must not be veiled by strangeness.

41 Tirmidhī, ᶜIlm, 19; Ibn Māja, Zuhd, 15; for variants see Sakhāwī, 310-21.

42 Abū Ḥāmid al-Ghazālī, tr. T.J. Winter, *On Disciplining the Soul* (Cambridge, 1995), 14.

43 Abū Ḥāmid al-Ghazālī, tr. T.J. Winter, *The Remembrance of Death and the Afterlife* (Cambridge, 1989), 210.

44 ᶜAlī ibn Ḥusain Ṣāfī, tr. Muhtar Holland, *Rashaḥāt ᶜAyn al-Ḥayāt, Beads of Dew from the Source of Life* (Fort Lauderdale, 2001), 248.

45 For the great mufti of Damascus the believer's self-purification and goodness should benefit all humanity, since we are 'to maintain the breast's purity from all evil, for one must not sleep or wake while in one's heart there is harmfulness towards any of God's creatures at all, even if that creature is an unbeliever [*kāfir*] in God. For unbelief [*kufr*] is an attribute of the unbeliever, not his essence; and so is faith.' ᶜAbd al-Ghanī al-Nāblusī, in S. Akkach (ed.), *Letters of a Sufi Scholar: the correspondence of ᶜAbd al-Ghanī al-Nābulusī (1641-1731)* (Leiden, 2010), 115, 143.

Many British Muslims are torn not between two poles but between three: because to Islamic *dīn* and a fissile modern Britishness there is added the further complex of a specific Muslim culture. It is largely the older generation which suffers from this three-way stretch. The young increasingly abandon folkloric forms and values in favour of an Islam which is understood as *dīn* rather than just as a mimetic aspect of ethnic inheritance. This tendency, in its many affirmative modes, should be accelerated, since our cultured despisers, who understandably judge by appearances, frequently object to the spectacular outward tokens of foreignness and the ethnic exotica of the places where grandmothers were born. Put crudely, a sharia-compliant headscarf of British inspiration is less likely to invite attack than headgear which proclaims adherence to the culture of a fair but distant land. A man walking the cold and rainy streets of Frankfurt in desert clothes is inviting all who see him to the *tanfīrī* conclusion that the ways of Islam do not belong. The same applies to a Muḥarram procession in Stockholm whose forms belong in the Lucknow chouk. *Tajwīd* and *adhān* modes ought to be local and not imported.[46] There exists no Sharia requirement to make a public statement that Islam is an alien religion. In fact the Sharia usually mandates the opposite, epiphytic Islam being almost a contradiction in terms. Too many tropes beloved of mosque elders tend to convey to passers-by the defiant non-Europeanness of the community they represent, and the passers-by may even be entitled to their indignation.[47] If the idea of Ishmael as witness and healer of a Godless culture is accepted, then courtesy and good-neighbourliness must be the signs of his authenticity, not the triumphant vaunting of an ancestral homeland. If the need for courtesy and witness is not understood then the need for survival in times of increasing

46 It is easy to forget that *tajwīd* and *adhān* always followed local melodic traditions in the premodern Islamic world. See, for one example, Zilia Imamutdinova, 'The Qur'ānic recitation traditions of the Tatars and Bashkirs in Russia: evolution of style,' *Performing Islam* 6 (2017), 97-121.

47 Muslims should recognise that there can be such a thing as a 'decent populism'; see Goodhart, 6.

secularity and prejudice should be seriously considered instead. This is the agenda of a more interesting integration: while rejecting Blairite demands for conversion to extreme social beliefs we must revive the ancient Islamic practice of incorporating *ʿurf*, local customary norms, into our lived Muslim experience, wherever and whenever this does not challenge a revealed requirement. This is part of the vital but currently-ignored process of vertical integration, particularly germane since it does not assume the existence of religious belief in the environment which engenders it.

ʿUrf is an acknowledged source and factor of Islamic rulings in all four Sunni schools: one of the best-known *fiqh* maxims is 'what is known by custom is like what is legislated by revelation' (*al-maʿrūfu ʿurfan ka'l-mashrūʿi sharʿan*).[48] 'Specific custom' (*al-ʿurf al-khāṣṣ*) refers to generally-practiced customary norms which may fluctuate from country to country, generating one of the reasons for necessary variations in Sharia interpretation and practice, on the question of divorce, for instance.[49] Outside the race temples and some fundamentalist environments which reject classical jurisprudence, distinctive European Muslim customs, habits and expectations already exist as anthropological realities, as is appreciated by any second-generation Berlin Kurd who visits the land of his parents. This is not simply a matter of assimilation and weakening, but reflects the natural and time-honoured Islamic process of putting roots into new soil, of moving beyond the epiphytic culture of migrant mosques and into a habitat which is easier to occupy and which is also the necessary prelude to *daʿwa*. *ʿUrf* is an immensely important Sharia force; although it cannot overrule a regulation specified in a plain text of revelation, it can and must shape most other aspects of authentic Ishmaelite living.[50]

48 Mohammed Hashim Kamali, *Principles of Islamic Jurisprudence* (Cambridge, 1991), 284; for the authority of custom under the maxim *al-ʿāda muḥakkama*, 'custom is to be implemented', see Khadiga Musa, *A Critical Edition of ʿUmdat al-Nāẓir ʿalā al-Ashbāh wa'l-naẓā'ir* (Sheffield and Bristol, 2018), 408-36.

49 Amjad Mohammed, 107, 120.

50 If this Sharia principle is utilised, local idioms should profoundly inform

Here is a further good reason why Muslim insiders need to develop an active pastoral theology which can account for the new atheistic populism and respond with a fully Islamic moral compass, rather than either joining the ranks of the *enragés* or bowing the head and pusillanimously submitting to the Outsider's social gaze. That gaze feels increasingly chauvinistic, expecting a slavish self-dislike and abnegation that, if the assumptions of democratic Europe which prevailed before the rise of atheistic coercive liberalism are to be respected, should in fact be considered unnecessary as well as oppressive. A majority cannot realistically or sensibly demand a cringing self-flagellation and the endless whimpering of *mea culpas* from its most significant minority.

The final aspect of any confidently non-Fearful policy towards *Ahl al-Kidhāb* scrutiny and stigma must be to accept the liberal state's invitation to all citizens to join the national conversation about the public good. Availing themselves of this opportunity, believers of all religions need to be far more insistent than they have been in arguing against the alleged public benefit of atheism and secularity. It would be easy and entirely rational to deploy the insights of Durkheim's *Suicide* to call upon secular states to adopt a preferential attitude towards religion as opposed to materialistic worldviews, not on grounds of truth, but because of the positive physical and mental health outcomes associated with religion[51] and its signal benefits for social cohesion, whether within or outside the communal group. Secular individualism's negative entailments should be clearly understood by policymakers, particularly in the

Muslim styles in Europe. For former European colonies, however, Islam's concern for the oppressed will involve the revival of precolonial vernaculars, such as First Nation culture in North America and Aboriginal abstract art in Australia. In the United States, the realisation that Ishmael was half-African must always entitle African-Americans to a particularly honoured role in Muslim communities.

51 See for instance Lisa Miller *et al.* 'Neuroanatomical Correlates of Religiosity and Spirituality, A Study in Adults at High and Low Familial Risk for Depression', *JAMA Psychiatry* 71.2 (2014) 35-128.

context of a society whose systems are currently presiding over a steadily declining social infrastructure (across Europe communities are witnessing the closure of public libraries, post offices, banks, bookshops, bars, and local shops, while retail is being automated): exactly what Lévi-Strauss meant when he described anthropology as an 'entropology', mapping a 'process of disintegration.'[52] Paradoxically it is only in the context of a society still rich in social capital and larger structures of belonging that individualism can responsibly be advocated; this was one of the conclusions of Robert Putnam's *Bowling Alone:*

> Individualism need not lead to depression as long as we can fall back on large institutions—religion, country, faith. When you fail to reach some of your personal goals, as we all must, you can turn to these larger institutions for hope [...] but in a self standing alone without the buffer of larger beliefs, helplessness and failure can all too easily become hopelessness and despair.[53]

Other themes for the re-enchanters might include Ishmael's demonstrable historical capacity to protect a diversity of epistemes and forms of life, something which is of evident benefit to human flourishing. For Lévi-Strauss, globalisation and secularity cannot sponsor this and must spawn a monoculture, where 'the rainbow of human cultures will vanish into the void created by our own frenzy.'[54] Coercive liberal politicians determined to impose a single template of social beliefs should be invited to consider more pluralistic alternatives, of which Islamic history offers many suggestive, though never immaculate, examples.

Such Ishmaelite arguments in the public square are likely to be met with scepticism; however this is apt to be rooted in Eurocen-

52 Claude Lévi-Strauss, tr. John and Doreen Weightman, *Tristes Tropiques* (Harmondsworth, 1976 edition), 543.

53 Martin Seligman, quoted in Robert D. Putnam, *Bowling Alone: the collapse and revival of American community* (New York, 2000), 264-5.

54 Lévi-Strauss, *Tristes Tropiques*, 544.

tric pride rather than in Enlightenment reason or any serious reflection about the public benefit. As several recent studies have shown, Sharia discourse on ethics and law is well-equipped for inclusion in Rawls' 'overlapping consensus' in which our public conversations must be held, rooting itself in universally-accessible public benefit arguments.[55] Lahabist notions of the irrationality of 'law-bound' Semitism make no headway against Islam's historic insistence on ratiocination and the determining of public interest (*maṣlaḥa*) and the purposes of a morally-intelligible deity. By contrast, the atheist struggles to contrive an ethical basis for the overlapping consensus: Rorty insists that we have no good philosophical reasons to support humanistic ethics, but that we should do so nonetheless, since they are no more arbitrary than anything else.[56]

Although our ethico-legal heritage can and must be deployed in the secular public square to enrich national conversations, we have suggested that our theological answer, to be authentically rooted in Muslim experience, is ultimately grounded not just in belief but in the love of God and of His signs in a world where everything is a *shāhid*, and in the awareness that His decree prevails more reliably than 'social laws', and that thanks to this 'madness' there is always an abundance of hope. The presence of this hope is verified by an inner strength manifested as forgiveness, compassion and love, virtues difficult for hypocrites, timeservers and private cynics, and impossible for 'social scientists' to incorporate into their reductionist models and their notoriously unreliable predictions. The *fiqh* may struggle at first to create a complete system of engagement with an atheistic culture, but *maḥabba* is operative already. And *maḥabba*, together with a mature and sociologically-informed adaptation of

55 Anver M. Emon and Matthew Levering, *Natural Law: A Jewish, Christian and Islamic Trialogue* (Oxford, 2014); Andrew F. Marsh, *Islam and Liberal Citizenship: the search for an overlapping consensus* (Oxford, 2009); Mohammad Fadel, 'The True, the Good and the Reasonable: the Theological and Ethical Roots of Public Reason in Islamic Law,' *Canadian Journal of Law and Jurisprudence* 21 (2008), available at http://ssrn.com/abstract=1085347.

56 Richard Rorty, *Contingency, Irony and Solidarity* (Cambridge, 1989), 46-7.

local *ʿurf* and *ʿāda*, and an awareness of the Prophetic indispensability of a *daʿwa* orientation, must create a juridical culture which moves beyond the simple concession-based logic of 'minority *fiqh*', to generate a fully-authentic Islamic rule-making system which will allow us a style of life faithful to revelation and also viable as a mode of rich conviviality with a sad and stressed culture which enjoys an abundance of everything except the indispensable.

CHAPTER 9

Seeking Knowledge: the multiple horizons of British Islamic studentship

1. TURNING EAST

THE FIRST PART of this chapter adopts the form of a travelogue, a kind of Alan Whicker documentary in which the commentator picks his way through landscapes ravaged by neglect and conflict to point out the wonders of what used to be, and to report, perhaps, on rebuilding efforts here and there that presage recovery, or at least the appearance of a worthwhile surrogate. Our traveller through the ruined *Dār al-Islām* will not be a tourist, he is no Washington Irving dreaming of the Alhambra of Boabdil; for we mean to accompany a seeker who is on a quest for learning, a pilgrimage, even, he is a Majnūn seeking only his lost true Laylā; Ferhād crying out for Shīrīn. I propose to follow the steps of a twenty-first century British or European *ṭālib ʿilm*, a 'seeker of sacred knowledge', as she or he attempts to resume the iconic Muslim custom of *riḥla*, an epistemic quest for the Holy Grail of the true *isnād* and *ijāza*, and, therefore, for the authentic sage. As such students survey the sorry map of today's *umma* and contemplate the ruins of, as Montgomery Watt put it, 'the glory that was Islam', what roads can they travel, and what institutions of learning still survive which might allow a reliable comprehension of classical Muslim texts and habits of thought?

Such errants obey the Laylā and Majnūn script in indicative ways: in Niẓāmī's version of the perennial tale parents argue with him and counsel sanity, family honour and staid propriety, yet the youth insists on his wild and seemingly senseless odyssey. In the wasteland of today's unreal cities parental scolding is often shriller by far, as our culture has been monetised, instrumentalised and incentivised by anxiety-inducing performance indicators and career benchmarks. Among the young, mental plagues such as depression spread steadily; Britain, like America, has become a Prozac Nation; to some it seems that things fall apart, the centre cannot hold. Yet our mad rover still leaves his home in an unsatisfactory Ilford or Small Heath, following the rumoured fragrance of a Proserpine who is alive and still fair, but hidden underground during the present winter of the world. Hundreds of such young madmen now roam the earth, and budding British neophytes of this sort have become a familiarly exotic sight in Deoband, Cairo, Malaya, and the madrasas of Touba Darussalam. A seemingly inexorable demography may be relied upon even to increase their number in the coming years: a 2017 Pew Research report suggested that British Muslims, today 4.1 million, will number 13.4 million by the year 2050.[1] And they are diverse: the Office of National Statistics tells us that ten percent of British Muslims are black, and almost eight percent of them are white.[2] They are also young; and it is the young who catch Majnūn's disease, and defy tribe and logic to seek knowledge of a transcendent beauty.

Let us ignore the fundamentalists among them, and the traumatised identity-seekers, and the Fearful who thirst for simple answers to help them cope with an overcomplicated world. Those also-rans are like Salāmān in Mollā Jāmī's tale *Salāmān and Absāl*, who since his adolescence had been in love with his nursemaid Absāl, who

1 'Muslim population of the UK could triple,' *Daily Telegraph*, 29 November 2017.

2 Office of National Statistics, 2012.

symbolises the comforts of the ego and the world. The identity-seeking seeker on a quest for sacred truth is in fact pursuing his own infantile lower self, which he must immolate before he can begin his true journey.[3]

Instead let us see where the *real* errant, spurning the false temptress who has held back so many, might go if he seeks what may be seen as a faithful extension of premodern Muslim educational normativity, defined simply as what historians recognise as a very rough matrix of recurrent curricular and pedagogic patterns in our learned culture. He has heard of the abiding beauty of the scriptures, and the peacefully intoxicating *fiqh* to which they lead, and that a deep delight is available from the classical texts and a rich experience of joining a centuries-old mature tradition of commentary and gloss. Has this beloved been scarred, or slain by modernity; has it thrown acid in her face; or is she simply heavily veiled and secluded in some Eastern oasis or lost city of brass, a Samarkand imagined and awaiting its discoverer? Hamza Yusuf, we are told, found her in Mauretania, or at least a Mauretania of thirty years ago. But does she still live, though held captive by a foreign empire, and by the global reductionism of a totalising Mammon whose agency is everywhere?

Shahab Ahmed, for one, helps us to doubt this. For him the mental culture of modern Islam is no longer the true Laylā; she is wrinkled, demented, almost or actually dead. After noting furiously the recent demolition of the historic cities of Mecca and Madina which represents a wider symbolic erasure of centuries of cumulative culture and institutions, he writes this:

> The considerable loss of the multidimensional spatiality of Revelation is increasingly the *leitmotif* of modern Islam—and is precisely what makes it difficult for the practitioners of modern Islam to conceptualize pre-modern Islam in a

3 Abd al-Rahman Jami, tr. Edward Fitzgerald, *Salaman and Absal* (London, 1904), 41.

> manner that coheres with a human and historical phenomenon that they conceptualize as Islam.[4]

Even her outer fabric is gone; and mostly forgotten as well. Most thoroughly forgotten, in his eyes, and of vital importance to the definition of our quest, is the fact that a spirit of plurality and difference formed a determining facet of her subtle charm. She can be helpfully described in a thousand ways. Ahmed argues for something akin to Marshall Hodgson's famous although rather obvious idea of the 'Islamicate', which denotes every characteristic aspect of Muslim cultures, but collapses the Islamicate into Islam, which should be interpreted as being everything that Muslims have defined as their relationship to what they imagine Islam to be. Hence it includes the study of Persian kingly wisdom, the Arabic Plotinus, botany, and borrowed midrashic tales. To impose our own assumption that Islam is ultimately a regulated exercise in Qur'anic commentary is, he says, a characteristic elision of modern Muslim ideologies with an elderly Orientalism. It forms part of the invention of essentialised, dehistoricised religion decried by Cantwell Smith, and, more recently and thoroughly, by Tomoko Masuzawa.

Our British Majnūn, however, while hopefully respectful of the old culture of difference, is unlikely to be incentivised by such a fuzzy and all-inclusive definition of what he seeks, which reduces it to a field of signifiers which are determined only by each other and become fully explicable only in faculties of history and sociology. Ahmed's deconstruction evokes an elite discourse which feels so irked by Islam and its conventionally-associated duties that it has brilliantly devised a theory which proves that it does not in fact exist. Our Majnūn, by contrast, is seeking a narrative with claims to transcendent truth and soteriological promise. And here we need to propose an alternative to Ahmed's effective abolition of the religion. What if we were to imagine a vision of the *uṣūl*, and the deep human reasons of those *uṣūl*, which did in fact enable and even

4 Shahab Ahmed, *What is Islam? The importance of being Islamic* (Princeton, 2015), 537.

advocate a heterogeneity which might not embrace all the cultural features Ahmed is pleased to put in his grab-bag of Muslim things, but most of them, and particularly the most humanly important? Ahmed seems to assume an eternal tension between the nomocentric boundary-loving ulema and the hard facts of a heteronomic Muslim cultural history. He does show that *fuqahā'*, like Ebussuud, could cautiously acknowledge the 'paranomian', alternative and nonjuridically-detailed routes to accessing saintly charisma and Muslim kingship. But we will need a further analysis to help our Majnūn, who may not just tolerate but love the jurists as the indispensable custodians of the citadel of a religion of law; those same jurists whom Ahmed disdainfully describes as trapped in a 'confined undertaking'.

A first example. We have already cited Mollā Jāmī. Recent scholarship on the so-called Timurid Renaissance of which he formed a part has demonstrated his normativity in a hugely urbane and cosmopolitan Herat sociality which united the sultan Ḥusayn Bayqarā, Mollā Kāshifī (the belle-lettrist and eulogiser of the Ahl al-Bayt via an epic litany which ingathered Sunni and Shiʿi), and the elegant Chagatai poet ʿAlī Shīr Navāī.[5] Mollā Jāmī, correspondent of Muḥammad al-Fātiḥ and a hero for Ottoman grand muftis, was another Herat polymath, who wrote a manual of irrigation techniques, a major grammatical text, and the *Haft Awrang*, the versified 'Seven Thrones' of which the *Salāmān and Absāl* forms one part. He combines the systems of Bahā' al-Dīn Naqshband, Ibn ʿArabī, Ibn Sīnā, Taftāzānī and Plato; he knows the diversity of the *fiqh* and the four-part harmony of the *madhhabs*; he writes an epic poem on the death of Alexander the Great and praises the old Persian kings: he is a renaissance man of Islam; and yet he remains Mollā Jāmī, staple of the *madrasa* syllabus across the Islamicate republic of letters. Diversity, hybridity, polyphony and agglomeration were woven inseparably into the fabric of Timurid

5 Cf. Ilker Evrim Binbaş, *Intellectual Networks in Timurid Iran: Sharaf al-Dīn 'Alī Yazdī and the Islamicate republic of letters* (Cambridge, 2016).

learned culture, and this in no way challenges the existence or the coherence of the juridically-rooted Islamic.

Consider another case, this time taken from the Arab universe, investigated in a remarkable study by Konrad Hirschler, who by studying a medieval Damascene book catalogue has documented the cosmopolitanism of the scholars and patrons associated with Middle Eastern libraries. Noting the eirenic temper and intellectual curiosity of Syrian jurists in the thirteenth century he writes: 'This tolerance made it possible to accept opposing systems of values and norms without necessarily insisting on the exclusive truth of one's own system. Intellectual life in these societies was thus less characterised by the quest for the one and only truth than by searching for probable and likely answers.'[6] Hirschler's point is that the polyvalence of the culture was integral to the urbane jurists' understanding of what Islam was. Theirs was hardly a 'limited undertaking'. The narrative of *ijāza* Islam and the centuries-long conventions of commentary creation, which our seeker seeks, forms a stable component and underwriter of 'Islamic' diversity, not a restrictive aberration within it.

Another case is documented by Fozia Bora, a former research fellow at the Cambridge Muslim College. Her study of Mamluk historiography demonstrates the willingness of Muslim scholars to transcend sectarian polemic and to seek to offer an accurate and fair-minded account of the views of Muslim others, including the Ismaili Fatimid dynasty hitherto regnant in Egypt and Syria.[7]

Still more evidence is supplied in the 2011 monograph by Thomas Bauer entitled *The Culture of Ambiguity*, which is becoming something of a classic in the field.[8] Bauer documents the refined and intellectually-curious culture of the premodern *fuqahā'*, who

---

6 Konrad Hirschler, *Medieval Damascus: plurality and diversity in an Arabic library* (Edinburgh, 2016), 129.

7 Fozia Bora, *Writing History in the Medieval Islamic World* (London, 2018).

8 Thomas Bauer, *Die Kultur der Ambiguität: Eine andere Geschichte des Islams* (Berlin, 2011).

inhabited what he terms an 'ambiguity-tolerant' religious space in which legal and theological options were multiple and exegetes frowned upon zealotry and exclusivist closure. For instance, considering medieval Islam's acceptance of different vocalised readings of the Qur'anic text, Bauer shows how the leading Qur'anic expert of the medieval period, Ibn al-Jazarī (d.1429), understood the Qur'an's textual variations, the *qirā'āt*, as a divine gift. He then contrasts this with the modern Salafi jurist Ibn ʿUthaymīn (d.2001) who attempted to advocate for a single authorised version of the text.[9] Similarly he explores the Qur'anic commentary of al-Māwardī (d.1058), who accepted that the scripture's text could be interpreted in many diverse ways, and compares this eirenic approach with the same Ibn ʿUthaymīn's insistence that only one meaning can ever be correct. The shift from an 'ambiguity-tolerant' Islam to an 'ambiguity-intolerant' alternative synchronised with the advent of modernity, as defensive Muslims sought to combat *anomie* and scientific challenges with a simplified and unified truth. He dates the transformation to the last century and a half, although he acknowledges that classical Islamic understandings still prevail among the remaining traditional scholars; indeed, such an acknowledgement almost describes a tautology.

In this world of polysemy, enabled or even enforced by a God who had bestowed complex scriptures which often seemed difficult to interpret and which (particularly in the early period) were richly open to argument, Muslim intellectuals wondered whether most or even all possible interpretations, if reasonably and sincerely held, might be acceptable to Heaven. One tendency, which the jargon called the *mukhaṭṭi'a*, proposed that only one interpretation was in fact correct. *Al-ḥaqqu fi'l-wāḥid,* truth is in the one view, they held to be a self-evident truth. Yet for the majority this attitude came to be discarded in favour of the conclusion of another group, styled the *muṣawwiba*, who believed that every qualified jurist's conclusions were in some sense correct and approved by God. Sohaira

9 Bauer, 68-71.

Siddiqui, another associate of the Cambridge Muslim College, has written lucidly on this.[10] Perhaps this sometimes served to make a virtue out of necessity, but it deeply coloured premodern Islam's understanding of societal and legal norms and the divine purposes towards humanity, which was to flourish in diversity and ongoing debate. In many ways it sat well with other ubiquitous tendencies in the culture, such as the so-called command ethics of Ashᶜarism, which held that moral truths are not magically and discernably intrinsic in the material world but are determined by divine speech, which does, of course, manifest polysemy; speech permits ambiguity while matter cannot. It also cohabited with Sufi inwardness, which, in ways often convergent with Ashᶜarite apophaticism, frequently accepted the inevitability of diversity in strategies of describing the spiritual path and the design of liturgies. A typical Sufi poem ran: 'Our expressions are diverse, but Your beauty is One, and all these words point to that same beauty.'

> *ᶜIbārātunā shattā wa-ḥusnuka wāḥidun*
> *wa-kullun ilā dhāk al-jamāli yushīru.*[11]

So our Majnūn, if he is hoping to find normativity, must seek out as one of the signs of its true presence this learned culture which tolerates and even rejoices in multiple answers, so that when he comes to lead a community he will be equipped for versatility and tolerance. He will avoid at all costs the Fearful retreat into a comforting search for monochromy. For Traditional Islam, Truth is to be known, but its pathways and expressions are likely to be many, for God's path is *dīn*, not ideology. He or she (for women today increasingly attempt this errantry, adding to the consternation of parents) must seek the face of the thousand aspects. This will not require a collapse into Ahmed's definition of 'Islam', which is so inclusive as

---

10 Sohaira Siddiqui, 'Sunni Authority's Legitimate Plurality', https://www.oasiscenter.eu/en/sunni-islam-many-authorities

11 ᶜAlī al-Qārī, *Mirqāt al-mafātīḥ sharḥ Mishkāt al-Maṣābīḥ* (Beirut, 1422/2002), IV, 1715.

to constitute a kind of epistemicide, dealing with the annoyingly persistent challenge of Islam by abolishing it; but the 'limited' juridical understanding of it is not a monovocal alternative; on the contrary it should be seen as the civilisational metanarrative which was the prism for much of the more 'secular' and multilayered culture which he documents. With this 'post-Orientalist' but emphatically non-fundamentalist thought in mind we keep company with our traveller, to pick our way through the wrecked vistas of modern Islamic education.

If the search for a culture of ambiguity is to be determinative, we must evidently begin with the disturbing fact that the curricula of modern Third World nation-states know little of the old polyphony, and, more generally, bear scant resemblance to the general tendencies, pedagogic methods and societal concerns of pre-modern Islam. For example the modern Pakistan national system supplies an Islamic Studies module whose elements avoid *dīn* as traditionally understood, and instead bear the overwhelming impress of Islamist ideology. The Required and Recommended Reading lists offer texts by writers such as Sayyid Quṭb and Yūsuf al-Qarḍāwī; Mawdūdī's books are the most numerous.[12] At no point are Pakistani pupils given a sense of continuity with the majestic spiritual and theological depth and diversity of their heritage: the syllabus seems to insist on an impoverished and agitated orphanhood instead. Such a paradigm, dismissive of Hindustan's Muslim civilisation, might produce dichotomising and alienated ideologues insistent on a univocal Islam, but is bereft of the humane and subtle beauty of classical Muslim culture, and can hardly be expected to nurture thinkers, scholars and institutions which might hold the attention of a *ṭālib* ᶜ*ilm* intent on discovering authentic Islamic teaching. In his or her disillusionment the *ṭālib* might be tempted by the Subcontinent's independent madrasa sector, but this too has been reformed in complex ways, and often represents a fossilised memory of mid-19th century reactive

12 Federal Public Service Commission, *Revised Syllabi for CSS Competitive Examination CE-2016*, 18-19.

and polemical revisions to older and richer programmes.[13] Here, also, the Raj has cast a very long shadow.

Thus is the academic decline of key provinces of the *Dār al-Islām*, which are now increasingly unaware of the lost richness of their intellectual patrimony, thanks to a form of compound ignorance (*jahl murakkab*). However when we turn instead to some Levantine places favoured until the onset of the 'Arab Spring' by dozens of British students, we find that the madrasas themselves have been ruined in a more literal way. Many UK *ṭullāb* will fondly remember the Maʿhad al-Fatḥ college in Damascus. Now its major scholars form a diasporic community, and seem unlikely to see their city and their houses again. In Iraq, al-Imām al-Aʿẓam University once maintained five thousand students at its sub-campus in Mosul. In 2013 the *tanfīrīs* drove in, demanded the keys, and gave the scholars twenty-four hours to leave; they and their students tried to continue in makeshift accommodation in Erbil, over the front line in Iraqi Kurdistan. When they visited the trenches not far away, in scenes perhaps a little reminiscent of Europe's First World War, they could hear the Maghrib prayers being recited on both sides of Islam's new and great divide. The *mawlid*'s historically-evolved commemoration began centuries ago in Mosul; but more recently under *tanfīrī* influence those who celebrate it huddle secretly in private houses, for the zealot *mukhaṭṭi'a* armed with knives prowl the streets after dark, vigilantly watching for infractions. Attempting to revive classical learning under such conditions is only for the brave.

Most of Yemen, too, has imploded in *fitna,* civil strife and invasion. And following the Western 'takedown' of the Libyan dictator, a country where some Western Muslims once trained has been fought over by a remarkable ninety-three factions, surely one of the most complex and fissiparous civil wars in history.[14] In this way,

13 Yoginder Sikand, *Bastions of the Believers: madrasas and Islamic education in India* (New Delhi, 2005).

14 Frederic Wehrey, *The Burning Shores: Inside the Battle for the New Libya* (New York, 2018).

four major Arab countries are now academically as well as economically, politically and spiritually shattered.

But a further disincentive is hard to mistake, not only in the Arab world but across the *Dār al-Islām*, and this we might call curricular heteronomy. Wael Hallaq has reminded us of the structural gulf which must separate Sharia from traditional sultanic power.[15] The jurists are to be of communities, they are not agents of the ruler; there is no caesaropapism; this is the judge's law, *kadisgericht,* whose decentred informality so horrified Weber. With the madrasas it is likewise. In premodern times occasional sultanic *waqf*-founding might endow madrasas promoting a particular theology or law-school regarded as politically expedient. The Seljuk vizier Niẓām al-Mulk is the oft-cited example; the Ottoman sultan Or<u>h</u>ān Ghāzī with his first madrasa in Iznik might be another. The curriculum, however, was determined by the class of ulema and muftis. Hence the historic role of the madrasa as a bastion of the people's culture and values against the depredations of power; in the madrasa the moral Muslim self was cultivated, to speak freely from the judge's chair or the mosque pulpit. The scholars and their scholarship comprised society's voice, and the sultan could only listen, and perhaps tremble. In Muslim society the *vox dei* tended to be ventriloquised by the *vox populi*, while the sultan's voice remained just another Muslim voice.

Hallaq's work intends to show the absolute structural incompatibility of Sharia with the Westphalian order and the nation-state, and his argument is persuasive; but his logic may readily be extended to show that the centralising post-colonial polities of the Muslim world have also subverted the historic Sunni insistence on what we might call academic freedom. Faced with the colonial French manipulation of religious leaders, a policy akin to what the Pentagon nowadays calls 'religion-building', Ahmadou Bamba had cried: 'Do not kneel before the rulers',[16] and famously laid his pen

15 Hallaq, *Impossible State.*

16 Michelle R. Kimball, *Ahmadou Bamba, a peacemaker for our time* (Kuala

next to a French cannon in St Louis,[17] writing his great poem *Yā dha'l-bishārati* to indicate his confidence in God's support for independent and unbowed scholars who could speak truth to power, and who knew that God's religion ought to side with the helpless.[18] His terrible exile in Gabon which followed was a nineteenth-century *reprise* of a very long tradition of scholarly resistance, an epic which had seen Mālik ibn Anas flogged by one Abbasid 'Commander of the Faithful', who had unsuccessfully instructed him to change his fatwa on involuntary divorce.

State actors across the Muslim world now actively seek agency in *fatwa* production and madrasa curricula, often clutching the fig leaf of counter-radicalisation.[19] In Saudi Arabia in 2010 King Abdullah issued a decree giving the state-appointed Saudi Council of Senior Scholars a legal monopoly over fatwa-making in his realm. Independent scholarship there is all but impossible under the basilisk gaze of this compliant council. Salman al-Odah was arrested in September 2017 for upbraiding this seeming *trahison des clercs*. Others followed him into exile or the gulag. The sermons of a caesaropapist clerisy insisted that the state's boycott of Qatar, for instance, was Islamically-mandated. The rest is silence.

Mosque assembly and the freedom to preach are also increasingly circumscribed: the 2016 attempt by Egypt's military rulers to impose a single Friday sermon across the country's mosques had to be rowed back in the face of popular and Azharite resentment, but the effort may be repeated. In Morocco, state control of religious curricula is now ubiquitous, with 'imam training' increasingly centralised in locations such as the vast Muhammad VI Institute in Rabat whose curriculum is vetted by civil servants. This Moroccan spiritual *dirigisme* by the national elite, the *makhzen*, is of quite recent origin,

Lumpur, 2019), 85.

17 Kimball, 195.

18 Kimball, 193.

19 Cf. Alexandre Caeiro, 'Ordering Religion, Organizing Politics: the regulation of the fatwa in contemporary Islam,' in Zulfiqar Ali Shah (ed.), *Iftā' and Fatwā in the Muslim World and the West* (London and Washington, 2014), 73-88.

and has been, in the first instance, reparative in its purposes. Under Hassan II a notion arose that traditional religion would continue to decay and should be replaced by a kind of hygienic literalism strategically imported from the Gulf, which it was thought would be more 'modern' and less 'superstitious', as well as more politically pliant. However the literalism brought another set of problems in its train. In his article 'The (Re) Fashioning of Moroccan National Identity', Michael Bensadoun writes this:

> Hassan II [...] encouraged the penetration of Wahhabism in mosques and schools to strengthen the religious legitimacy of the monarchy. The sociologist Mohamed El Ayadi analysed the effects of this policy on Moroccan young men, blaming the education system for diffusing anti-Western and anti-Semitic feelings.[20]

Following the rise of fundamentalism in the Maghreb the *makhzen* is now anxiously backtracking, seeking to rebuild Ashᶜarī, Mālikī and Sufi tradition in a substantially ruined pedagogic landscape in which the old madrasas and *zāwiyas* have been closed for decades and their endowments taken by the state; the success of this project is still far from assured.

What if the thoughts of our lovelorn but by now discouraged wanderer should turn away from the troubled Maghreb to distant Pakistan, perhaps the land of his ancestors? The thin gruel offered by the Pakistan state syllabus has already been discussed. The Dār al-ᶜUlūm curriculum there has also been noted: it often bears the visible impress of a reactiveness both to British Victorian disdain and incursion, and to *soi-disant* Salafist pedagogies which typically prefer the mnemonic and reiterative aspects of brain function over those dedicated to analytic thought. The Dār al-ᶜUlūms, therefore, tend to focus heavily on the 'what' rather than the 'why': an evidently precarious strategy in a world bristling with direct concep-

20 Michael Bensadoun, 'The (Re) Fashioning of Moroccan National Identity,' pp.13-35 of Bruce Maddy-Weitzman and Daniel Zisenwine (eds.), *The Maghrib in the New Century: Identity, Religion and Politics* (Gainesville, 2007), 27.

tual challenges to religion. Here, too, the heavy hand of the state lies upon the wheel: in 2018 the Pakistan government, driven by security concerns, announced that it was taking control of thirty thousand independent madrasas and imposing a new curriculum determined by the Ministry of Education.[21]

Similarly, in Bangladesh there has existed since 1979 a Madrasa Education Board, a quango which has augmented the essentially Deobandi curriculum of the Alia madrasas with what it calls 'modern subjects', generating a two-track epistemology in which fossilised traditional topics are left largely undisturbed, and which attempts little conceptual interaction with new subject areas such as science and Bangladesh Studies. State surgery aims at excision and addition rather than at achieving the subtle metabolic adjustments which might allow the transplants to take and to engender an integrated and holistic syllabus. In 2017 the government appointed a committee to review their *fiqh* textbooks, and, in characteristically ham-fisted fashion, removed the chapter on *jihād*, despite the protests of Alia madrasa teachers that it was necessary for students to be able to differentiate classical normative teachings on *jihād* from modern militancy. In a further intervention the Awami League government moved to take independent, non-Alia madrasas, the so-called *qawmī* madrasas, under some form of centralised ideological oversight. A further government commission is offering to accredit madrasa degrees in exchange for the acceptance of a new state curriculum. The *qawmī* madrasas, which currently educate an estimated 1.4 million students, follow a Dars-i Niẓāmī syllabus which culminates, for a few, in the *dawra-yi ḥadīth*. This is now to be recognised as a master's degree. Since this is an entirely traditional, memorisation-based course (*naqlī* not *ʿaqlī* in the classical parlance), very considerable pedagogic and philosophical augmentation will be required. The aim, transparently, is to reduce and perhaps finally eliminate the fully-independent heritage of madrasa learning. If

21 https://www.reuters.com/article/us-pakistan-madrasas/pakistan-plans-to-bring-30000-madrasas-under-government-control-idUSKCN1S517Z

students wish to enter the job market they must study an approved curriculum; there is therefore a risk that the state will increasingly function as a *mujtahid,* picking the texts and determining right religion.[22] Little scope is likely to remain for the culture of ambiguity.

An analogous process is observable also in Singapore. In the same year of 2017 the Singaporean government formally established an Asatizah Recognition Board which issues permits to preachers and religious teachers, and disciplines or retires those whose messages are deemed unacceptable or who teach without authorisation. Such a permit is required for teaching even one other person, unless it be a family member. Overseas speakers, if their subject is religion, must apply for a separate permit, supplying the text or at least the substance of their lecture in advance.[23]

Through such processes the madrasa world stands in danger of being mis-oriented. It continues its historic function in mediating between power and parishes, but increasingly represents the former to the latter, not *vice versa*. Recurrent and thus normative historic structures are being steadily inverted, as religious authority is standardised and monopolised or at least made subaltern to the corporate modern state. If premodern Islam was never theocratic (insofar as the structures of state and religious authority were largely segregated) but was certainly not secular either, an ironic entailment of this Third World étatism is a type of elision of sacred and profane authority and knowledge production. The culture of ambiguity is abolished in favour of the model of an ideological religious or secular state recognising strictly homogenised sacred narratives deemed favourable to regime survival. Atatürk was the precursor, with his paradoxically simultaneous creation of a secular polity and

22 Masooda Bano, 'Madrasa Reforms and Islamic Modernism in Bangladesh,' *Modern Asian Studies* 48 (2014), 911-939; 'The Qawmi Conundrum', *Dhaka Tribune,* 8 January 2018.

23 Hisham Hellyer, 'What lessons can be learned from Singapore's religious regulatory framework?' *The National* (Abu Dhabi), 21 January 2018; cf. also muis.gov.sg

a nationalised religious hierarchy. In this way the governments have ironically adopted a model not so very different from that of the Islamists whom they are fighting. Once more, ideology has won a victory over *dīn*.

A clear-headed Western seeker may find it difficult to locate his beloved in such establishments. His own government may even tacitly approve the official regulation of colleges overseas and the censorship of the learned, imagining that this forms a useful part of the emerging global security architecture, rather than a deeply destabilising method of alienating the young from mainstream religion and reducing its diversity. If students happen to encounter fully traditional scholars, they may realise that the Islam which is officially taught may be seen as a composite, engineered product influenced by the often maladroit simplifications and reflexes of national elites acting in self-defence. Even if students are persuaded that such a product is usable, it is liable to incorporate inconsistent inputs and asymmetries which cannot settle comfortably as the grounds of a coherent and credible theology. If regime survival, rather than love of God and the believers, sways exegetic choices, and influences the operation of *qiyās, istiḥsān, maṣlaḥa*, and *ʿurf*, then *fiqh* as classically understood has come to an end, and countries with singular religious authorities directed by the ruler, which penalise independent shaykhs who teach in the traditional manner, have wounded their *sanad*, their chain of transmission, with all antecedent Muslim learning.

Some of our British Majnūns find their way to Saudi Arabia, where visas are straightforward thanks to Western governmental intimacy with the Wahhābī state. Michael Farquhar has given us a detailed picture of the government's closure of the traditional independent madrasas of Mecca during the early 20th century and their replacement with state fundamentalist institutions with centrally-managed curricula;[24] so seekers looking for a fully

24 Michael Farquhar, *Circuits of Faith: Migration, Education and the Wahhabi Mission* (Stanford, 2017).

traditional pedagogic context in the Holy City of Islam will have arrived several decades too late.

An average Laylā-seeker who visits Saudi state campuses and makes enquiries at the admissions office will already be aware of the so-called Madkhalī/Nawāqiḍī tension which energises much modern Salafism. The Saudi agencies and colleges tiptoe across a narrow bridge stretched over the current fundamentalist inferno. One sceptic calls them 'arsonists and firefighters',[25] and during the height of the Daesh crisis Saudi scholars such as al-Sharīf al-ᶜAwnī and ᶜĀdil Kalbānī pointed out the genetic links which linked the Saudi theology to that of Daesh. After all, did not Daesh use Saudi textbooks in their schools, rather than books from any other Muslim country? There is, moreover, the recurrent testimony of penitent *tanfīrī* extremists who blame Salafism itself for terrorism.[26] Uneasily aware of all this, the Saudi authorities have been revising their curricula in a generally Madkhalī direction.[27] While this remains, in the view of mainstream scholarship, a polemical and exclusionary reading of Islam, it is not an advocacy of terrorism, and Muslims and others should be clear about this. Nonetheless, a twofold problem for British seekers remains. Madkhalism is a hard version of *mukhaṭṭi'a* Islam, ambiguity-intolerant, and very disinclined to affirm diversity. And the *mukhaṭṭi'a*, we have suggested, tend to attract the suitors of Absāl, not of Laylā: they are typically looking for reassurance, not beauty. Secondly, there is the poorly-studied phenomenon of sudden conversions from Madkhalism to Surūrism or the Nawāqiḍiyya: the so-called 'Salafi Snap'.[28] Research has

---

25 Scott Shane, 'Saudis and Extremism: "Both the Arsonists and Firefighters"', *New York Times*, 25 August 2016.

26 E.g. the case of Manṣūr Nuqaydān, a former Saudi extremist who now campaigns against Wahhabism; see Commins, *Wahhabi Mission*, 198-9, 201.

27 For Madkhalism see Farquhar, *Circuits of Faith*, 106-7.

28 For a claim that the considerable traffic between 'quietist', 'political' and 'violent' Salafi movements results from an inherent closeness see Andrea Brigaglia, 'The Volatility of Salafi Political Theology, the War on Terror and the Genesis of Boko Haram,' *Diritto e questioni pubbliche* 15 (2015), 175-201.

shown how apolitical Saudi-backed schools in Somalia in the early 1990s, known as the Ittiḥād schools, mutated very suddenly into nurseries for the movement that became known as Shabāb.[29] Similarly, Boko Haram founder Muḥammad Yūsuf began his preaching at the Ibn Taymiyya mosque in Maiduguri having been instructed in Madkhalism by graduates of Madina University, but converted to a Nawāqiḍī interpretation.[30] ᶜAbd al-Raḥmān ᶜAbd al-Khāliq, one of the most newsworthy Egyptian radicals, also studied in Saudi universities; as did Turkī Binᶜalī, the 'senior scholar' of Daesh. Overall, since the Arab Spring observers have reported a slow but steady migration of Salafi discourse in an intransigent political direction.[31] Salafism, then, is seen by most ulema as one of Islam's less stable isotopes, hostile to the generous diversity and versatility of classical Sharia, and this will ensure that our seeker of classical Muslim authenticity and usefulness for European *daᶜwa*, after inspecting the Saudi campuses, is likely to frown, shake his head, and continue his quest elsewhere.

2. TURNING WEST

One evident elsewhere is of course the modern Western universities, some of which maintain, usually in rather small departments, programmes in what is called Islamic Studies. As instability mounts in the Middle East and as curricula are increasingly subject to regime encroachment, it seems evident that the Majnūns of Europe are considering this option more seriously than they might have done twenty years ago. This entails, for a Western Muslim, a kind of *hijra* within, not to faraway colleges in a ruined *Dār al-Islām* but

29 Michael Woldemariam, *Insurgent Fragmentation in the Horn of Africa: rebellion and its discontents* (Cambridge, 2018), 260.

30 Alex Thurston, 'Ahlussunnah: A preaching network from Kano to Medina and back,' in Masooda Bano and Keiko Sakurei (eds.), *Shaping Global Islamic Discourses: The Role of al-Azhar, Medina, and al-Mustafa* (Edinburgh, 2015).

31 Laurent Bonnefoy, 'Quietist Salafis, the Arab Spring and the politicisation process,' 205-218 of Francesco Cavatorta and Fabio Merone (eds.), *Salafism after the Arab awakening: contending with people's power* (London, 2016).

to a different habitat where freedoms are ironically more actual, and in fact claim to be zealously guarded. Remember the poem of ʿAbdullāh ibn al-Ḥārith, given refuge from Quraysh in Ethiopia:

Each of God's servants is today pressed hard,
in Mecca's vale, defeated and tempted.
We have found God's earth to be wide,
saving us from humiliation, shame and abasement.[32]

Could it be that under the painfully damaged conditions of the modern *umma* a paradoxical *hijra from* rather than *to* the *Dār al-Islām* and its ravaged institutions is now to be counselled? Morocco, Saudi Arabia, Bangladesh and elsewhere are, after all, locked into what Seamus Heaney, musing on Northern Irishness, called the 'tight gag of place'. Their particularities are oppressively parochial; controversial views are suffocated to death by local culture as well as by nervous authorities and factions; and in their classrooms an awareness of trends important to the European Muslim situation, or even the global reality, may be attenuated, distorted, or entirely absent.

What can we say about Islamic Studies in the Western academy? Here one uses the adjective 'Western' in the now familiar non-geographic sense, for one can now take many courses in Islam at, for instance, the Abu Dhabi campus of New York University, where every student has to take at least one Islamic Studies module. This is rather a distinguished programme, it seems, where the ambiguity-tolerance of premodern Islam is recognised; hence one can become acquainted with texts by Ibn ʿArabī, Rūmī, Bayḍāwī and Rāzī, and other medieval thinkers typically shut out by fundamentalists and the diversity-averse. Students can take modules in subjects usually ignored by madrasa curricula, such as Islam's understanding of disability, for instance, or Islamic art and architecture. The lecturers are mainly non-Muslim Americans, and the approach is rooted in Islamic Studies as presented in American area studies or religion departments, reflecting a policy which seems increasingly favoured in the Gulf region. Will this be perceived as a viable alternative?

32 ʿAbd al-Malik ibn Hishām, *al-Sīra al-Nabawiyya* (Cairo, 1428/2007), I, 202.

Considering the 'Orientalist' syllabus, in contrast to the syllabi of 'Islamic universities' which claim clarity about their object of study, one is forced to return again to the question of modern approaches to the great theodrama of Islamic civilisation, in its diachronic and synchronic heterogeneity, as these threaten the viability of the often carelessly-reifying adjectives 'Muslim' and 'Islamic'. The culture of ambiguity is a sign of authenticity, but cannot erase the religion's entire metanarrative. We have already noted how Shahab Ahmed delights in interrogating these markers as supposed relics of an older theological objectification, and proposes that Muslimness needs to be dissected into an indefinite field of drifting moods and cultural shapes. In the academy, while some Orientalist departments still seek to conserve the study of a medieval canon, traditionally Abbasid in its focus, as the most proper concern of Islamicists, we note the bewildering and growing proliferation of the study of aspects of the Islamicate not only in religion departments but in an increasingly broad range of arts faculties, including philosophy, theology, history of science, sociology, politics, and even European history. Moreover, 'Islamic Studies' now routinely recognises that societies as well as texts deserve to be studied.

Still, most Islamic Studies departments remain conservative in their instincts and tend to make claims for some form of coherence in their discipline, which still purports to research and teach 'Islam'. The absurdity of deconstructing Islam into nonexistence has not yet prevailed. Yet in these faculties a further inhibition appears for Muslim seekers. Orientalism, its roots lodged deep in philology (a Humboldtian calling *par excellence*), has often been intransigently insistent on its outsider status and a *de facto* objectification of Muslims and other 'Eastern' peoples. With the sky-hooks derided by Richard Rorty it tries to swing high above the personal commitments and experience of *engagé* insiders to survey historical Muslim acts and writings from the position of Olympian aloofness which is thought to prevail in the seminar room. Aaron Hughes still campaigns to maintain the totalising purity of this ideological view, which must exclude and stigmatise all insider perspectives.[33]

In contrast to this widespread Islamic Studies episteme, Jewish and Buddhist insiders tend to dominate their own respective departments, and often write explicitly as adherents, in faculties in which the idol of positivist fideism served by Hughes seems to have decisively fallen. Take, as an indicative example, a recent *festschrift* by Damien Keown, *Buddhist Studies from India to America: essays in honour of Charles S. Prebish*. A reviewer offers this observation, commonplace now in the field: 'It is interesting how many scholars within Buddhist Studies, including Charles Prebish himself, are also practitioners of Buddhist paths, which makes difficult any division into "academic" and "insider" perspectives'.[34] It is very instructive to compare an Islamic Studies journal with its Buddhist Studies equivalent, to observe the radical divergence in paradigms, with the former publication often self-consciously defending an old insider-outsider dichotomy which serious Buddhist studies seems to have left far behind.

To its great detriment, then, Islamic Studies is, with some exceptions, discordant with the more general practice in the study of 'Eastern' religions, often being governed by a nineteenth-century secular bias which claims that experience of a religion is likely to distort the understanding of it. It is as though a student of nautical engineering believed that those who actually board a ship or steer it must necessarily lose some objectivity, perhaps due to overexcitement, or some other inappropriately affective experience. Only the outsider's view is held to comprise the coveted non-'normative' view from nowhere; Ishmaelite insiders, like children, should be seen but not heard.

Humboldtian campuses, including the new American outstations in the Arab world, can thus appear to present an old-fashioned magisterial exegesis on behalf of an Enlightenment imperium of

33 Aaron Hughes, *Theorizing Islam: Disciplinary Deconstruction and Reconstruction* (London, 2012).

34 Denise Cush, book review in *Buddhist Studies Review* 27 (2010), 118-121.

letters. Much is lost when this becomes stiff and ideological. Apart from their unique empathy, many insiders enjoy practical advantages, including native linguistic fluency, a broad rather than hyper-specialised knowledge of the literatures, and an ability to recognise scriptural and canonical allusions in texts which secular Orientalists often miss; but in the eyes of traditional Orientalism this counts for nothing, or even, on occasion, serves to intensify the outsider's misgivings and, perhaps, sense of insecurity. In the Emirates, a land of insiders, outsider discourse is to monopolise pedagogy, at least in these gated communities of Occidental reason.

It is not only Muslim practitioners who are underwhelmed by this sort of positivist totalism, which in the name of Enlightenment paradoxically diminishes the right of scholars and students to speak with their own voices. Andrew Rippin, for one, sees the engagement of active Muslims in Western Islamic studies as a generally positive development, the alleged clash of paradigms and commitments having been overdramatised and exaggerated.[35] Consider, moreover, the more systematic critique deployed by Mike Higton's book *A Theology of Higher Education*. For Higton, who assails the discriminations of the secular positivistic academy: 'the university that they envisage does *not* actually allow each citizen to speak on his own behalf if he is not allowed to speak as the member of the particular, positive religious and secular traditions that have shaped him. The very stricture that the Romantic theorists erect in order to preserve free sociality is one that makes it impossible.'[36] It is not tolerable that only views from nowhere are tolerable.

Despite the continuing prosperity of the paradoxical and self-defeating 'insider/outsider' narrative, the Western academy has also and characteristically internalised a kind of Averroist double truth on the nature of religious claims; there *are* University spaces in which views from a monotheistic somewhere are entertained.

35 Andrew Rippin, 'The Reception of Euro-American Scholarship on the Qur'an and *tafsir*: an overview,' *Journal of Qur'anic Studies* XIV (2012), 1-8.
36 Mike Higton, *A Theology of Higher Education* (Oxford, 2013), 78.

Orientalism historically and persistently sticks with the Kantian and Berlin model; but in America and Europe, if not in the new outpost campuses in the Gulf, there are also Faculties of Theology, which in complex ways appreciate that scholarship is enriched when religious traditions deploy fully academic skills in order to explore their own paradigms and heritage. These faculties are for historical reasons dominated by Christian enterprises, and the advocacy or exploration of Muslim truth *as possible truth* is still seldom envisaged within their walls. Despite this, surely here we see a rich opportunity, which offers not a sally-port for an unscholarly fideism but an invigorating broadening of the episteme. This possibility, of a Muslim theology sited in modern universities and benefiting from a real culture of academic freedom and heuristic multiplicity, seems to be reinforced by the current decay of the elderly Humboldtian ideology.

To underline the obsolescent status of the older Orientalist discrimination we note that the dominant philosophical turn of recent years provides a strong accessory to the progressive interrogation or abolition of the discipline of Islamic Studies as an objective exercise in historiography by the detached Western self. Deleuzians and their allies influentially challenge the Enlightenment assurance about any truth as bearing fixity and a relationship to public reason, for this, Deleuze would have us think, is nothing but 'a region carved out of the irrational', for 'underneath all reason lies delusion and drift'.[37] Even in the natural sciences facts are thought to be significantly attributable to those who advocate them; the truths to which Islamic or any other Studies incline, however forensically supported by apparatus and annotation of the various kinds required in the guild, are only cultural facts, attributed always to their authors, and this perhaps accounts for the flux of thesis and antithesis in intellectual fashions and ideas, for instance, about the origins of Islam. Our findings inhabit a metaphysical bubble floating in the spume of principial chaos; where medieval and also Enlightenment

37 Gilles Deleuze, *Desert Islands and Other Texts 1953–1974* (Paris, 2003), 262.

universities of the Humboldtian type assumed an orderly physical creation which philosophy should mirror and match, the quantum revolution seems increasingly to be the ontological ground of the modern humanities, where movements are never decisive, and everything oscillates.

The wider Western culture which is the academy's life support system seems to cohere with this. Occidentals no longer look to humanities departments for guidance towards truth; they resemble ornaments which accompany what is *de facto* the real business of a research university, which is enhancing physical knowledge and wealth creation, with the Business School increasingly accorded special status and privileges. In this way any relic of a non-mercantile unifying principle has been lost.

> The very term 'university' means many-looking-towards-one, and is related to the term 'universe', the whole of reality. Thus the name no longer seems appropriate to such a fragmented modern institution whose unity is provided only by a financial administration and perhaps a sports team.[38]

Higton agrees: having discussed the internal contradictions of the Kantian model he documents what he sees as the virtual collapse of the Humboldtian vision of a university as a coherent community of seekers after public truth. The pursuit of truth now seems set at the margins, thanks to the monetizing of the academy, or because of hyperspecialisation and weak interdisciplinarity, or because of the ambient postmodernising culture in which the pursuit of truth is simply dismissed as a fool's errand. For Higton,

38 Benedict Ashley OP, *The Way Towards Wisdom: an interdisciplinary and intercultural introduction to metaphysics* (Notre Dame, 2009), 20. Cf. also Guénon, *Crisis*, 76: the Western academy recognises only rationalism and utility, and hence is individualistic; there is no principle of metaphysics which might unite us.

> fragmented expertise is the coin of such a university, not truth. Any strong version of a commitment to truth—strong enough, that is, to guide the university past the lure of problematic funding sources, to drive it beyond fragmentation, to offset the temptations of the purely pragmatic and utilitarian—turns out [...] to flounder when removed from the water of robust conceptions of the human good, and so to be among those things bound eventually to become extinct in the realm of attenuated public reason.[39]

Stanley Hauerwas has further pursued this discussion of the failure of the Humboldtian academy to secure the pursuit of public truths, on the basis of a thesis that universities require a symbiosis with what Alastair Macintyre calls a 'learned public.' Universities were once thought to pursue truth in order to train students in virtuous service to society. Kant's assumption was that this wider society would naturally exhibit a 'care for truth', a common coin in his world. In the twenty-first century, however, this common coin has been debased or abolished in favour of other forms of credit. Populist politicians trade on the emotions of electorates and ignore academic advice. Body beliefs have long shoved metaphysics aside (the Rortyan shift from epistemology to politics); the only truth is compliance with current doctrines about sexual identity, so we witness, as Peter Conrad has it,

> the so-called 'crisis in the humanities', which has dehumanised the study of literature by reducing authors to producers of texts and reducing those texts to position papers with agendas that interest us only if they contribute to contemporary debates about gender, sexuality and ethnic difference.[40]

Hence the spate of recent academic hoaxes, in which academics have successfully placed nonsensical articles in refereed journals, simply by recycling jargon and defending the most recently-articulated

39 Higton, 111.
40 Peter Conrad, *The Guardian,* 19 February 2012.

body beliefs.[41] Truth, in this world, is an obsolete category; compliance with consensual dogma has replaced it.

For Hauerwas, 'a university able to resist the mystifications legitimated by the abstractions of our social order will depend on a people shaped by fundamental practices necessary for truthful speech.'[42] For Hauerwas, and also Higton, the radical decay of a general public sense of what truth might be underlines the legitimacy and even the importance of a renewed *theological* project within the academy. Our culture of 'liquid modernity' cannot supply the external measures of the public good which the Enlightenment academic schema presumes. For Hauerwas, religion contributes 'by developing a people capable of bearing the burden of honor and truthfulness, a people without which the university, as I conceive its task, cannot exist.'[43] Higton further accepts that such a blood transfusion into a truth-starved, instrumentalised modern academy gripped by constructivist grievance cultures cannot be a purely Christian perquisite: thinkers of all traditions must offer their own capacities for the production of virtue and of the incentive to seek truth. And a university cannot be allergic to Muslim paradigms in a time when these are so demonstrably essential to the full discussion and determination of the public good.

The fact that we are startled or inclined to cynicism when told that the modern Western university began as a project for the location of public truth reminds us how far the Occident has

41 Following enthusiastic peer reviews, the feminist geography journal *Gender, Place and Culture* unwittingly published one of these hoax papers, entitled 'Human Reactions to Rape Culture and Queer Performativity in Urban Dog Parks in Portland, Oregon'. Another article accepted by the feminist journal *Affilia* reworked a chapter of *Mein Kampf* using feminist terms. See for these hoaxes and a discussion of the decadence of much body-belief culture, Helen Pluckrose *et al.*, 'Academic Grievance Studies and the corruption of scholarship,' in *Areo Magazine* (online), 2 October 2018.

42 In Higton, 126.

43 In Higton, 127.

travelled downhill from that ideal.[44] In the context of Islamic Studies, however, it should be evident that the remnants of the *wissenschaft* ideology which demands that I participate only as myself, and not as, for example, a Marxist, or a Christian, or an Ashʿarī, are no longer philosophically strong enough to suppress the plurality of a modern Islamic Studies programme or to limit its horizons. Orientalists uncomfortable with this need not surrender to an abject constructivism, but should at least pick up a primer on modern philosophy.

We should look, then, to the growth of Islamic Studies within theology schools, not as a replacement or rival to the older and more limited Oriental Studies project, but as a necessary and very contemporary opening up of the epistemic horizon.[45] In various complex ways this is already in progress: the significance of the work of Yahya Michot, for instance, at Hartford Seminary, who successfully combines an unmistakeable voice from somewhere with trenchant academic rigour, is one case in point. Sherman Jackson at the University of Southern California has been another. Universities such as Edinburgh, Brandeis and Yale have also provided space for Muslim theologians; and the German government has funded five new departments of Islamic theology to parallel the historic Protestant and Catholic faculties, where Islamic ideas are allowed to participate in the shaping of the students' intellectual life and to contribute to the quest for public truth in a way inconceivable in the more cloistered Oriental Studies enclaves.[46] In these institutions work is underway which seems set fair to challenge the

44 In 2009, British universities were placed not under a Ministry of Education, but under the new Department of Business, Innovation and Skills.

45 Y. Ellethy, 'Enseigner la théologie islamique: l'exemple néerlandais,' 177-99 of Francis Messner and Moussa Abou Ramadan (eds), *L'enseignement universitaire de la Théologie musulmane. Perspectives comparatives* (Paris, 2018).

46 Bekim Agai and Armina Omerika, 'Islamic Theological Studies in Germany: A Discipline in the Making', in Michael Kemper and Ralf Elger (eds.), *The Piety of Learning: Studies in Honor of Stefan Reichmuth* (Leiden, 2017), 330-54.

corrosive post-truth episteme which is becoming the *leitmotif* of the contemporary humanities.

A specifically Muslim style of intellectuality in the Western academy is starting to grow into a salient and influential fact which is exercising a reach in the less free 'Islamic world' as well, and its access to contemporary examinations of Muslim texts and proof-claims and an awareness of the 'culture of ambiguity' equips it to offer an alternative to local homogenised, nationalised or fundamentalist Islamic interpretations. Our world is so replete with tragic ironies that we scarcely wince when told that Western universities often seem to be better and safer habitats for Muslim research and creative thinking than their equivalents in the East. Here, too, we find a strong argument to support Muslim theology in Western academies.

However universities are not all about research; and our *ṭālib ᶜilm* will still hanker after an undergraduate theological and juridical training of reasonable comprehensiveness and relevance; and few if any Western universities can yet accommodate that. Hence the urgent need for carefully hybridised spaces which can fully benefit from academic freedom and contemporary research methods while still offering an education which recognises the curricular and vocational interests of insider students. One of these, it seems, might be the College of Islamic Studies on the Education City campus in Qatar. Another candidate is the Ibn Haldun University in Istanbul. Neither seeks to replicate either a siloed madrasa thoughtworld or a Faculty of Oriental Studies. The Cambridge Muslim College and Zaytuna College in California also attempt to invigorate Muslim pedagogy by standing at the *majmaᶜ al-baḥrayn*, the isthmus, between the two oceans of discourse, insisting not simply on a toleration of proximity but on a creative and mutually-helpful dialogue.[47] One result is, crucially, the return of a culture of diversity as intrinsic to the authentic and uncompromising Muslim pursuit of truth,

47 Alison Scott-Baumann and Sariya Cheruvallil-Contractor, *Islamic Education in Britain: new pluralist paradigms* (London, 2015), 24, 46, 145, 148.

and the rejection of the new totalitarian narratives of a singular Islam, whether or not this is curated by a state.

Assuming that we need not entirely abandon the Kantian hope that humanities graduates might be useful, to what extent might such alumni aspire to join the public conversation? Although truth-seeking seems increasingly to be supplanted by materialist instrumentality and paradigms shaped by body beliefs, university training does not automatically lead to civic positions in which the academically-enlightened dispense influential public policies. Muslim alumni who suppose that graduating with an Islamic Studies degree will ease access to a mandarinate which offers counsel to state and society report that they are quickly disabused. Academic area studies expertise was largely overruled or ignored during the run-up to the 2003 invasion of Iraq. In 2017 Arabs and Muslims confronted another sobering fact when the American government's Middle East portfolio was handed to Jared Kushner, a thirty-seven year old estate agent who had never been a civil servant, still less a scholar. Twenty-first century Western policy formation has probably been shaped more by Cambridge Analytica than by the University of Cambridge; there is much on this phenomenon, and more, in Zeynep Tüfekci's excellent study *Twitter and Tear Gas*;[48] Tom Nichols' book *The Death of Expertise* is also sobering and very timely.[49] Despite Rorty's turn from epistemology to the political, academic Islam experts, like other professionals, are increasingly ignored by public decision-makers.

Not only fundamentalists but just about every citizen now lives in a knowledge silo vulnerable to online manipulation,[50] and this shapes the social context for the postmodern crumbling of the brave Kantian assurances about universal autonomous reason and the pos-

48 Zeynep Tüfekci, *Twitter and Tear Gas: The Power and Fragility of Networked Protest* (New Haven, 2017).

49 Tom Nichols, *The Death of Expertise: The Campaign against Established Knowledge and Why it Matters* (New York, 2017).

50 Recall Steve Bannon's comment that President Trump 'reads to reinforce'; see Michiko Kakutani, *The Death of Truth* (London, 2018), 28.

sibility that truth might be discerned through the weaving together of the discoveries of a community of free minds, following which enlightened social and political directions will naturally arise. Western universities, in the eyes of many writers, are ruined, cast down into the individualistic abyss of postmodern irony and self-exculpating isolation. But there is a silver lining here comprising useful energies generated by the force of the implosion: we have found that theology, with increasing confidence, is taking a second wind.

So is this, finally, journey's end? Is our dismal tour of ruins East and West to have a happy terminus? Will our British seeker, like the Sīmurgh of ʿAṭṭār's *Conference of the Birds*, find the lost beloved in himself and at home? That remains only in prospect, not in fact; for these tender new shoots visibly rising from the ashes left by fundamentalist or modernist forest fires need careful nurturing. The rising zeitgeist, lost in polarised absolutes, is increasingly populist and hence impatient with pluralities, ensuring that a diversity-averse Islam and a Humboldtian exclusivism about paradigms will continue to prosper and to impede creativity. Institutions must, moreover, fight to remain free from political and commercial intervention. But however tentative may be their efforts, a few colleges stand on the horizon; not cities of brass, certainly, but refuges for a few, and indicants of something demonstrably achievable for European Islam. Whether their students have found their beloved as they imagined her to be is for posterity to judge—but even then, all discourses of authenticity must remember that tradition without change is not tradition at all.

CHAPTER 10

Creation Spirituality

for Matthew Fox

ONE OF THE TENSIONS favoured by the religious iconography of traditional Europe is the representation of the nature/grace dichotomy by the figure of the Green Man. This recurrent image, most often taking the form of a hieratic face sprouting acanthus or oak leaves from mouth and cheeks, appears in a startling number of our historic churches. In Britain, well-known examples may be observed at Rochester Cathedral, Bolton Abbey, and St Magnus' Cathedral on Orkney; but thousands upon thousands of others show their faces across Western Europe, lurking in the capitals of columns, ogee arches, and even beneath misericords.

Folklorists often identify this half-hidden, often satirical, yet often severe and staring visage as a pagan survival, a fertility symbol of the spring, a Jack-in-the-Green, a Robin Hood;[1] and some of the iconography certainly recalls themes associated with Nordic deities such as Odin. Modern neo-Paganism, as it calls itself, in its curious belief that primordial initiatic traditions can be resurrected for use by hipsters and millenials, has often conscripted the Green Man in this sense. As Europe casts off its Christian inheritance, these half-banished sprites seem to have climbed down from the

1 Carolyne Larrington, *The Land of the Green Man: a journey through the supernatural landscapes of the British Isles* (London, 2017), 226; William Anderson, *Green Man: the archetype of our oneness with the earth* (London and San Francisco, 1990), 28-9.

cobwebbed vaults of parish churches to find an honoured place in our secular dystopia, where a frequent hope is that through a highly-selective reversion to pagan and shamanistic ideas we can heal the alienation from ourselves and from nature which technology has imposed upon us.

The more scholarly literature, however, tells a more interesting tale. Although there exist late Roman equivalents to the Green Man, for instance at Nero's palace in Rome, these are quite different from those which appear from the twelfth century onwards in Christian churches. Evidently they represent specific deities, usually Sylvanus, Bacchus, or Dionysus, bearing an ecstatic and intoxicated aspect. Art historians point to a significant transformation which seems to have synchronised with the rather sudden intrusion of the Man into ecclesial architecture in the twelfth century after he had almost disappeared during the so-called Dark Ages. The physiognomy of the Roman deities, who in any case had not survived the collapse of the empire, is now replaced with something less occult and wild, and more unsettlingly esoteric. Beyond this, however, the foliate head remains an enigma. Why, amid the triumph of Christianity, should this eminently un-Biblical figure have invaded the churches in the first place? The Green Man is there in medieval folklore: in the English legend of Sir Gawain and the Green Knight, for instance, and in the names of countless pubs. But why is he in church?

One answer connects to the emergence of the Gothic style itself. In much of its form and, partly, in its sacral logic, this new idiom, ironically perhaps the only fully Christian style of building in the West, was enabled by the Crusades, during which era Muslim and Levantine Christian masons and master-craftsmen were brought to the Latin lands to catalyse the sudden aesthetic and engineering breakthrough which we identify with the Gothic genius. The Ishmaelite DNA of this style was necessarily disavowed by the prelates, who sought other tributaries, such as the Platonising cosmology of Denys the pseudo-Areopagite. However in spite of this disavowal the beginning of the High Middle Ages was unmistakeably characterised by an Islamic fecundation.[2] In this context of cultural borrowing and syncretism, which also gave England its morris (Moorish) dances, we can perhaps begin to see tokens of the conflation which existed in monastic minds between images of the pagan and the Saracenic; indeed, for medieval Christians Islam was simply another manifestation of the pagan principle: it was of the flesh, of nature, while Christianity was of the spirit: the great crusading war-cry since the time of the *Chanson de Roland* had been *Chrétiens ont droit et païens ont tort*. So we can perhaps understand this presence, amidst the gargoyles and the startlingly licentious and carnal figures which grimace and frolic in the ecclesial shadows, as the icon of an Augustinian polemic against nature, represented unconsciously by the Saracenic enemy: Islam is of the body, the Church is of grace; they are perfect antinomies; the stare of the Green Man and his inextricability from vegetation are there to show the triumph of the altar: through the miracle of the sacrament the shadows have been chased away, as the flesh is defeated by the sinless New Adam in whose immunity to concupiscence we are all invited to share.

The Gothic style, in which Latin Christendom finally found its soul, which had never been purely expressed by the essentially pagan, civic and static language of the Romanesque,[3] is a gift from the Muslim East, bestowing the wonder of fan vaults, novel geometries, ogival arches culminating in a sign to heaven, and stained glass windows with their evident and effective symbolic indicativity. Even the practice of double genuflection seems to be a Crusader

2 Anderson, 76.

3 The basilica (a form which early Levantine Islam also adapted to its ends) originates in Roman royal and civic building, not the sacred architecture of ancient Rome. The replacement of horizontal archivolts by cross-vaulting and barrel vaulting did not fully veil this secular origin. The appearance of the Gothic remedied the crisis: 'the Romanesque church building is earth in its lower reaches, Heaven in its height. Around the space in a Gothic church, Heaven itself descends like a mantle of crystalline light.' Titus Burckhardt, tr. Keith Critchlow, *Chartres and the Birth of the Cathedral* (Ipswich, 1995), 35.

importation. But in this Islamic upliftment of the European soul, which gifted to Western Christendom what is perhaps its most celebrated aesthetic expression,[4] we find also the intrusion of the Green Man, this peeping staring visage, bespeaking, according to our speculation, the Christian mason's insistence that unregenerate nature stands in opposition to Eucharistic grace.

So here, on this view, the Gothic church, an open book in which the unlettered peasant reads the story of salvation, reminds worshippers of the crusade of Grace against Nature (we might say, of St Denys against Dionysus) and ultimately of Christ's sacrifice, which for the Latin mind was perfectly represented by the tormenting of a body and the liberation of spirit. Through mortification we may repent and escape the gravitational forces of *eros*, fecundation and of death, whose symbols are banished to squeak and gibber in the shadows. In heaven 'there is no marriage' (Matthew 22:30) and the body is to be made unlike itself; and the lives and even the bodies of the righteous in this world below are to be proleptic signs of that paradisal state. Thus the celibacy of the clergy and of all the saints. The Green Man, implicitly Ishmaelite, opposes all of this, and tries to stare it down with his Medusa grimace; but his power has been overthrown.[5]

But for us there is more still going on here, and to grasp it we need to shift our optic to consider a more modern diagnostic of the human situation. In his remarkable book *Green Man, Earth Angel,* Tom Cheetham presents a contemporary analysis of the Man's

---

4 In the Slavic East, the high point of ethereal spiritual architecture also was reached following the fecundating touch of Muslim design: the density of the early Byzantine was made luminous once the Central Asian and Tatar influence touched the art of Kiev and Moscow. St Basil's is said to take its inspiration from the Mosque of Kul Sharif in Kazan, which Ivan the Terrible had destroyed. One could make a comparable point, without risk of subjectivism, about the illuminating touch of Islam on the architecture of Hindu temples.

5 As demonstrated explicitly in Exeter Cathedral, where the Virgin is shown trampling the head of the Green Man; see Kathleen Batsford, *The Green Man* (Cambridge, 1978), 20.

significance.[6] He focuses on Henry Corbin (d. 1978), Sufi interpreter to the Eranos fellowship and probably the most philosophically-minded of Orientalists, who was famously entranced by Ibn ᶜArabī and by the ways in which the Andalusian master's characteristic doctrine of the creative imagination might offer one route to the resuscitation of European soul-thought, which was reeling from the impact of the Enlightenment and from the consequent and catastrophic Darwinian political ideologies of the mid-twentieth century. The translator of Heidegger, Corbin recognised in the German philosopher's account of being and alienation a critical lack: the principle that Ibn ᶜArabī calls the Breath of the Compassionate, *nafas al-Raḥmān*. This is the primordial but eternal divine exhalation which brings being out of not-being, and which is concurrently, when rightly understood, Being itself.[7]

For Ibn ᶜArabī this Breath forms an isthmus between the human order and the realm of divine fullness. Like verdure it exists between earth and sky, and partakes of both. It manifests most characteristically as the Muhammadan, life-affirming and thus 'green' presence which allows access to the inner meaning of the world's 'signs' and forbids us to stop only at their outward surface. It performs the same hermeneutic function with the Qur'an, transforming and transcending the reductionist philological and historicising techniques that dissect the organism of the word as though it were a dead thing. Its symbol is the eight-pointed star, which denotes the intersection and mutual definition of the fourfold heavenly and earthly planes; and as such it becomes fundamental to Muslim sacred geometry. The loss of this principle, Corbin suggests, has comprised the great defining drama of the West in its downward journey from the symbolic to the conceptual, and from Christianity to profane externalism.[8] Fundamentalism

6 Tom Cheetham, *Green Man, earth angel* (Albany NY, 2005).

7 William C. Chittick, *The Sufi Path of Knowledge: Ibn al-'Arabi's metaphysics of imagination* (Albany NY, 1989), 127-30; Cheetham, *Green Man*, 121.

8 Cheetham, *Green Man,* 121.

(which is approximately the Reformation principle) turns out to be a synchronous and closely-related phenomenon.

Corbin again offers us a critical message. For him, as for Louis Massignon, the inner sanctum of the Qur'anic text is the 'apocalypse' of Sūrat al-Kahf, the Chapter of the Cave. Here a sequence of three sapiential and initiatic tales is recited, each reminding us of the inadequacy of a purely exoteric reading of phenomena existing in time and space: that which is from eternity must have depth as well as breadth. In the heart of this Qur'anic sacratum we find the enigmatic tale of the pilgrimage of Moses to the 'meeting-point of the two seas' (*majma*ᶜ *al-baḥrayn*). In the Qur'an's telling Moses does not travel alone; instead, this paradigm of halakhic probity and moral and physical strength begins his journey when he encounters and asks to accompany a guide, who shows him, through a series of three baffling and apparently unethical acts, the limitations of the external Law. Scripture is not here invalidating the legislation which Moses is apparently being asked to challenge, but is reminding us that exterior rulings and readings are at best a needed point of view; even to smash a poor fisherman's boat can be revealed as a moral and wise action once the full context is disclosed.[9]

This condensed and dream-like narrative requires, to borrow Corbin's language, a retrieval of the symbolic over the conceptual manner of discourse; it recalls, in Lévi-Strauss's discrepant vision, the *pensée sauvage,* the 'untamed thinking' that cannot be excluded without self-alienation and that seems somehow to be integral to our healthy selves. Linearity and a mechanistic view of causation do not give humanity a suitable approach to the experienced deepness of being and morality. Sūrat al-Kahf enables an Islamic thinking which is both a sign of aboriginal and pre-axial holism and an indispensable reminder that formal religion is not all that religion must be. Moses' companion allows the commentator, the jurist, and the ethical philosopher to ground their interpretations

9 Sūra 18:60-82; Cheetham, *Green Man,* 122; Norman O. Brown, *Apocalypse and/or Metamorphosis* (Berkeley CA, 1991), 69-94.

in the 'uncreated' ontology of the text and not only its *ẓāhir*, its plain sense. He is therefore a Mullah Nasrudin, or a *rind*, a pride-puncturing dervish whose unfamiliar way of experiencing the divine compels us to think afresh about God, thereby casting a protective shield against sclerotic habituation or the reduction of religion to fundamentalism.

Mosaic externalism thus seems implicitly out-narrated by this *ʿilm ladunnī* (18:66), this esoteric wisdom, or, to be truer to the unusual Qur'anic phrasing, the knowledge that is from and of the Divine closeness. Moses is enabled to bear the shock of the disclosure of legal approximativity by his longstanding prophetic awareness of the limitations of purely horizontal perception. The revelation's doughty emblem of legal probity and defiance of state tyranny, he had defeated Pharaoh's magicians by showing them a supernatural act of a higher order than theirs: his staff, which, in the Qur'an's discourse, became a snake by God's leave (20:69-70). Thus does the prophetic soul see that cause and effect, and the whole gigantic web of causation which we take to be a first-order truth and the basis for our every action in this world, are merely convention, *ʿāda*, not a full and sufficient account: Moses is granted an intuition of quantum indeterminacy, as one might say in today's language. Causation, the *sabab* of which the Sūra speaks, is probabilistic at best, a very convenient rule of thumb.

The insight that the physical as well as the socio-legal cannot evade the judgement of a higher perspective is confirmed to Moses by his mysterious travelling-companion and mentor, and the commentary tradition names this personage 'al-Khiḍr', the Green One. Our Western Muslim theological tradition has much to say about this clearly essential figure, who alone, of all the entities under God, can be the guide of a prophet and can rightly correct his understanding and apparently out-narrate his Torah.[10] Here revelation explicitly indicates that mystical unveiling (*kashf*) is an essential

10 Tom Cheetham, *The World Turned Inside Out: Henry Corbin and Islamic mysticism* (New Orleans, 2015), 85-111.

deepening of our understanding of the surface of the physical and the scriptural worlds, thanks to the *ʿilm ladunnī* and the mercy (*raḥma*) which al-Khiḍr is given (18:66). We remain, however, bound by the Law: for his discourse of gnosis and compassion is not simply subversive of the linear and the ethical.

Henry Bayman, in his book *The Secret of Islam*, is inviting us to an inward perspective which can recognise the necessity of this Qur'anic surprise. He implicitly presents this esoteric guide to scriptural, cosmological and legal interpretation as an affective principle: the principle of love, *maḥabba*, which is an aspect of *raḥma*. This is what Bayman writes:

> Because Law is based on conscience and ultimately upon love, what is lawful in Islam is that which is informed by love. [...] the only action which is free of blame is that which is based on love, and the Divine Law is a compendium of such action or non-action. [...] Thus Islam answers the critical question: 'How should I behave towards beings?' in the following concise way: treat them as if you loved them [...] And for our convenience, Islam outlines in its prescriptions of Holy Law what such action is.[11]

This is Bayman's way of fully embracing Sharia while avoiding the trap of horizontality: God's law is not random but is always the articulation of philanthropy in its full and original sense of *raḥma*. This is the meaning of *futuwwa*, spiritual chivalry. And beyond this, when we need to ask the question of *how* to love, and *how* to know that our acts are loving, there is the Breath of the Compassionate, without whose touch ethics becomes just a point of view we feel comfortable with (modern relativism), or a matter of arbitrary divine command (monochrome, greenless piety). The interpretations of *qāḍī* and *muftī*, and tools such as *istiḥsān* ('juristic preference for equity'), rely on the application of external ethical

11 Bayman, *Secret*, 82-3. Bayman's own journey was shaped by Gustav Meyrink's Green Face image; see Henry Bayman, *The Station of No Station* (Berkeley, 2001), 2-3.

and compassionate criteria to ensure that any harsh outcomes of literalistic juridical method are removed. Hence spiritual discipline and the 'way of love' are indispensable preparations for a Muslim legal career: without the vertical, the horizontal path cannot be reliably straight.

Love, in this deeply sacramental sense of *raḥma*, is a disposition of being, more of an essence than an accident; the eight-pointed star is unshakeably integrated. Our lower world is also a scripture written by God, composed of signs, *āyāt*, in a *Qur'ān Takwīnī*, a Creation Qur'an, as Ibn ʿArabī says, distinct from but intertextual with the *Qur'ān Tadwīnī*, the Inscription Qur'an which the believer holds in his or her hands. The *Qur'ān Takwīnī* is always the manifestation of the Breath of the Compassionate, for nothing can exist without that Breath, which is Being itself. However human readings of the world may be perverted by the ego, until we only see dead matter and oppressive causal chains from which we could never escape; in this sense natural science dismays us with *jabr*, compulsion, without even the illusion of free will. Likewise, in the absence of the human sense of the Breath of the Compassionate we cannot read scripture; instead, we find only 'consonants without vowels', and thus we misread. Fundamentalism and all other deviant impositions on God's book flow from this contamination of the reader by ego and its psychic residues. Only the Green Hermeneut who counselled Moses can bestow the gift of presence, and hence of interpreting at sufficient depth.

Norman Brown, in his essay 'The Apocalypse of Islam', writes about al-Khiḍr as a transprophetic figure urgently required in today's linear, flat and literalising world.[12] And he notes that this mysterious personage, while recalling immortal esoteric guides in other traditions, such as Elijah, is, in an Islamic matrix, paradigmatically green. This is Islam's colour, indicated by the Prophetic oasis city of Madina and the green dome which rises over the enigma of the ongoing Prophetic presence. It is also the colour of the Nahdlatul

12 Brown, *Apocalypse*, 69-94.

Ulama, the world's largest Islamic organisation, which is committed to a traditional Islam of mercy, local wisdom and the holiness of nature.

We have connected this ontology to the riddle of Europe's Green Man. Historians sometimes suggest that the transmission was assisted through Ismaili influence, and that of esoteric Christian fraternities. Almost certainly the channels whereby such a tradition reached us will never be clearly discernable; yet what is important is that it took place.[13] The Green Man becomes a sign of nature, and hence, for the initiated, of the Breath of the Compassionate, until, with the Renaissance, he declines into a very different symbol of man's dominion over the natural order. More recently still, with contemporary neo-pagan appropriations he has reverted effectively to the role of circus-master or cabaret star for neo-Roman saturnalia.

In the Green Man mystery we might seem to be confronting an elision between a pagan and a Qur'anic motif, an association which for the Latins seemed self-evident but which to us appears impossible. Although the commentary literature may sometimes draw parallels with the figure of Hermes Trismegistus, the mysterious guide of the Qur'anic commentaries is certainly not understood as a pagan magus; in the context of the scripture's titanic struggle against Arab heathenry that would have entailed a wholly uncharacteristic relapse. An initiatic paganism is nowhere on the Qur'an's palette. Instead we find that the initiator, troublingly capable of 'correcting' the patriarch, is a purely monotheistic figure who seeks to purify and rightly interpret the law, rather than overturning it in the antinomian Dionysian manner, or finding a gnostic or magical 'true sense' of scripture which would subvert its plain sense.

At this point let us recall the very noticeable archaism of the Ishmaelite style of monotheism. Islam is very evidently not a paganism; but the site of its emergence is neither Jewish Palestine nor a Christian Levantine city partaking in the full sophistication of the ancient ecumenical culture, but is the Mother of Cities, seen as

13 Anderson, 75.

somewhat detached from the late antique world and very ancient in its religious style.[14] Unquestionably the Qur'anic text, while refuting Arab paganism and polytheism, recalls primordial and natural themes far more than, say, the Bible does. The early Meccan passages ceaselessly invoke the sun and the moon, the fertilising rain, the fecundating winds, the dyad of gender, the embryo, tree, mountain, ocean and plain. In part, of course, this conjuring with the natural world forms part of a rhetoric intended to undermine pagan Arab religion by attributing natural phenomena to the true transcendent deity rather than to individual and competing spirits. But it does this not by desacralising those phenomena but by intensifying their holiness and their theophanic indicativity, by insisting that they are signifiers of a God who is called *al-Qarīb*, the Near (2:186), and who declares that 'wheresoever you turn, there is God's Face.' (2:115)

Jaroslav Stetkevich, in *Muhammad and the Golden Bough*, notes the strikingly primordial quality of the Qur'an's litanies of nature, with God even swearing oaths by its phenomena. *Wa'sh-shamsi wa-ḍuḥāhā, wa'l-qamari idhā talāhā, wa'n-nahāri idhā jallāhā, wa'l-layli idhā yaghshāhā:* by the sun and its shining, by the moon when it follows it; by the night when it covers it; by the day when it makes it plain. These sequences, syncopated and incantatory in a way reminiscent of truly ancient deliverances by seers and entranced mediators, are very frequent. Again they can be seen as part of a strategy of firmly reattributing natural signs to the Semitic godhead, and hence of ascribing their luminosity to God alone. They are anti-pagan, but their form discloses the gigantic power of a new monotheistic deployment of so ancient and manifestly oral a literary form. The orality, recalling an unlettered age when speech, as Plato understood, was enchanted and therefore natural, underlines

14 Glen Bowersock, Garth Fowden and others have rightly challenged older ideas of Arabian isolation from the Hellenistic *oikomene*, but nonetheless, tribal Western Arabia formed a backwater with some very distinctive cultural forms.

the preternatural sense of place and of moment, of presence. Oral voicings are closer to the human lifeworld, being situational rather than abstract; they bring us closer to nature, which 'speaks' but cannot write; they are uniting, since they are heard in company, while writing can be considered privately and alone. Ashley Montagu observed that 'the more "literate" people become, the more they tend to become detached from the world in which they live.'[15] As Walter Ong surmised, this is, perhaps, the best meaning of 'the letter killeth': orality is the more natural, normative and sacral form of language.[16]

Stetkevych writes this of the Qur'an's Chapter of Joseph: 'Unlike the latter [Genesis account of Joseph] the Quranic rendition is not an ideology-saturated pretense of tribal history, and, for that reason, it is more detached and more archetypal—and thus closer to myth.'[17]

Detached and archetypal: this seems exactly right, and is surely a sufficient argument against those wayward speculators such as John Wansbrough who strain to place the genesis of the Qur'anic text in an eastern Mediterranean or Mesopotamian sectarian milieu. This is ruled out absolutely by a range of facts, including the complex internal symmetries of the text which negate any theory of a disorderly cumulation of pericopes,[18] the non-referentiality of the scripture's discourse (particularly the absence of any reference to the Arab conquests), and the striking archaism of its themes and voice.

Not only does the *Qur'ān Tadwīnī* reference the *Qur'ān Takwīnī* with frequently and hypnotically-chanted adversions to the great signs of virgin nature, but it takes a quite remarkable view of the

15 Cited in William A. Graham, *Beyond the Written Word: oral aspects of scripture in the history of religion* (Cambridge, 1987), 22. For the Qur'an's remarkable scriptural orality see Graham, 79-116.

16 Walter J. Ong, *Orality and Literacy* (2nd edition Abingdon, 2012), 74.

17 Jaroslav Stetkevych, *Muhammad and the Golden Bough: reconstructing Arabian myth* (Bloomington, 2000), 11.

18 Raymond Farrin, *Structure and Qur'ānic Interpretation: a study of symmetry and coherence in Islam's holy text* (Ashland OR, 2014).

sacral performativity of the created order. Here, particularly, it distinguishes itself from most ancient Hebrew narrative, in which life and fecundity tend to be celebrated in connection only with Palestine. It differs, also, from the dualisms of late Hellenistic religious culture, which typically relegate nature and its processes to the status of opponents of the divine light. With the Qur'an's insistence on the animated quality of nature we again seem to hear a strikingly primordial register of discourse.

For the Qur'an the cosmos is not inert and insensate matter but appears to be alive; not just some dimensions of it which are of an animal or vegetal nature, but the entire physical order of creation.

> *There is no thing which does not glorify Him with praise.* (17:44)
>
> *Do you not see that everything that is in the heavens and the earth glorifies God?* (24:41)

In several well-known and well-attested hadiths the Man of Praise takes pebbles in his hand, and his Companions are miraculously enabled to hear them eulogising God.[19] When walking on Mount Thabīr near Mecca the hill begins to tremble because of the spiritual presence of the one walking upon it; he scuffs it with his foot and says, *Askin Thabīr*; 'be still, Thabīr'.[20] In Madina he says: 'Uḥud is a mountain which loves us and which we love',[21] and the jurist Nawawī affirms that a metaphorical neutralisation of this startling claim is impossible to support from the Arabic words.[22] We inhabit a mysteriously animate world, and human language is not just a medium of informatic exchange but a means of affirming reciprocity with nature.

Regarding the animal kingdom we encounter a very distinctive

---

19 Abū Dāūd, Witr, 34.

20 Nasā'ī, Ihbās, 4.

21 Bukhārī, Iᶜtiṣām, 15.

22 Yaḥyā al-Nawawī, *Tahdhīb al-asmā' wa'l-lughāt* (Cairo, n.d.), I, 17: *wa-hādha'l-ḥadīthu ᶜalā ẓāhirihi idh lā istiḥālata fīhi wa-lā yultafatu ilā ta'wīli man awwalahu.*

Prophetic virtue ethic of compassion and respect. Here are some representative and very familiar hadiths:

> A dog was once panting by a well, almost dead with thirst. On seeing it, a harlot of the ancient Israelites removed her shoe, dipped it in the water, and gave it to drink. For this, God remitted her sins.[23]
>
> It is a great sin for a man to imprison the animals which are in his power.[24]
>
> Once when we were travelling with God's Messenger, may God bless him and grant him peace, he left us for a short while. We beheld a *ḥummāra* bird with two chicks, and we took the young fledglings. The *ḥummāra* hovered with fluttering wings, and the Prophet returned, saying: 'Who has injured this bird by taking its young? Return them to her'.[25]
>
> There is no-one who without reason slays a sparrow or anything higher, but that God shall ask him about it.[26]
>
> The Prophet, may God bless him and grant him peace, forbade that animals should be set to fight each other.[27]

In some other hadiths we find the Founder apparently communicating with animals, as in the story, narrated by Abū Dāūd, in which the Man of Praise enters an enclosure where a camel is experiencing a fit of groaning, with its 'eyes streaming'. Unafraid, he walks over to it and rubs its ears, and it calms down. He asks whom the camel belongs to, and a man identifies himself as its owner. The Prophet says: 'Do you not fear God concerning this beast which He has let you own? It complained to me that you starve it and tire it by overworking it and using it beyond its capacity.'[28]

Scripture also presents the natural world, and its animals, as

23 Bukhārī, Anbiyā', 54.

24 Muslim, Zakāt, 48.

25 Ibn Ḥanbal, I, 404; Abū Dāūd, Jihād, 112.

26 Nasā'ī, Ḍaḥāyā, 42; Ibn Ḥanbal, II, 166.

27 Abū Dāūd, Jihād, 51; Tirmidhī, Jihād, 30.

28 Abū Dāūd, Jihād, 44.

instinctively concerned to protect the Prophet and the Ishmaelite sanctuary: the Sūra of the Elephant seems to document this, where the elephant of the invading king Abraha refuses to march against the City, while Abraha's armies are shattered by stones dropped by a flock of birds. In Madina, likewise, the site for the Prophetic mosque is chosen not by human agency but by the Prophet's white camel, al-Qaṣwā.[29] The texts seem to imply that the animal communities were signalling their awareness that the Prophet would protect and recognise them and their place in the order of creation.

Again there is something primordial in the Qur'anic assertion that other species are communities which in some authentic way are like us.[30]

> *There is not an animal in the earth, nor a bird flying on two wings, but that they are nations like yourselves. We have neglected nothing in the Book. Then unto their Lord they will be gathered.* (6:38)

Each species is an *umma*, a nation or community, and, even more remarkably, it is in some authentic way like us. Commentators argue over this radical and unsettling text: Qurṭubī, for instance, states that it means that animals are like us in that they have rights. Rāzī holds that they resemble us in having certain physical capacities and behavioural traits; while Shāh Walī Allāh of Delhi holds that each species has a divinely-ordained *sharīʿa* which naturally corresponds to its form.[31] In all cases the exegetes accept that life on earth comprises what Aldo Leopold calls a 'biotic community', whose member peoples are interdependent and intersubjective.[32]

In the Sufi commentaries, informed, as it were, by the Khiḍr

29 Lings, *Muhammad*, 21, 123.

30 Cf. Tim Winter, '"Nations like yourselves": some Muslim debates over Koran 6:38,' in Andrew Linzey and Claire Linzey (eds.), *The Routledge Handbook of Religion and Animal Protection* (London, 2019), 163-172.

31 Dahlawi, *Conclusive Argument*, 115.

32 For this concept, remarkably resonant with Islamic definitions, see Aldo Leopold, *A Sand County Almanac and Sketches Here and There* (Oxford, 1949), 204.

principle, we find a more dramatic account of this. Here is Rūzbehān Baqlī (d.1209) in his commentary entitled *ʿArā'is al-Bayān*:

> God created the animals, birds, predators and insects with the primordial nature [*fiṭra*] of monotheism and instinctual knowledge of Him, which is why He speaks to them and has [...] created for their minds pathways to His eternal presence and secrets. It is by that Presence that they live. Their whistling, lowing, singing, and roaring are from the sweetness of the spiritual world which is reaching them, and the manifest lights of His glory. They long lovingly for God and to taste the oceans of His mercy.[33]

So animals possess a spiritual awareness, and the sounds they make are their attestation to God's beauty and unity. He continues with these words:

> All the nations share a basic created nature in being composed of the four elements, and are made with animal and spiritual natures, and are equal in eating and drinking, motion and congregation, the qualities of the self and properties of identity, such as desire, anger, passion, and pride; this equality [*tasāwī*] is based in the stuff of the primordial nature [*fiṭra*], according to which God made them, as He has said: *From it did We create you, to it do We return you, and from it We shall bring you forth one more time* (20:55). [...] They all have their drinking-places in the ocean of God's speech and His eternal words which indicate the paths of His unity: the nature of animals, birds and insects and predators is mingled with knowledge of their Maker and Creator, whose qualities and essence they know; this discourse is not difficult or insufficient for them to understand.[34]

The Muslim internal library is well-stocked with this biophiliac and

---

33 Rūzbehān al-Baqlī al-Shīrāzī, *ʿArā'is al-bayān fī ḥaqā'iq al-Qur'ān* (Cawnpore, 1300AH), 205.

34 Rūzbehān, 205.

lyrical vision of a cosmos ontologically engaged in a joyful act of praise. With no Augustinian doctrine of original sin and no pathologising of *eros*, Islam has always been insistent in its regard for the inviolability of the order of nature. This may be what Herder had in mind when he described Islam as shamanistic:[35] it attributes to the material world a real presence, not only of a single vibration of the sacred, but of ubiquitous and beautifully-variegated local instantiations of holiness, sometimes explicitly animated, and always implicitly existing in a state of praise. However the fearful and occult aspects of shamanism are notably absent: historians note the pessimism of the *jāhilī* Arabs;[36] whereas Islam, 'saturated with sexual vivacity,'[37] and with 'a remarkably easygoing attitude to the body and its urges'[38] was notably life-embracing and upbeat; the Man of Praise 'loved optimism.'[39] The prevalence of the symbol of the crescent moon in later Islamic history, replete with its evident feminine and fecund resonances, appears like a confirmation of Islam's appropriation and retrieval of very ancient, pre-axial ideas of the sanctity of sublunary nature and the epiphanic value of periodicity.

Islamic art diverges in its modes of celebrating this principle, yet certain constants are remarkably evident. Far from Mecca, in Java, say at the shrine-mosques of Sunan Kudus or Gunung Jati, one savours the genius and ubiquitous applicability of the Qur'an's retrieval of the primordial. In these places there is nothing of the Arabian, and yet the scriptural vision is radiantly upheld. They appear as ancient sanctuaries, sites of a timeless wisdom and initiatic stillness harmoniously integrated into the tropical ecosystem which surrounds them; and this makes them perfect matrices for the *ṣalāt*, which, as Rod Blackhirst has noted, is designed as a universal

35 Einboden, 27.

36 Izutsu, *Ethico-Religious Concepts*, 45-54.

37 Ze'ev Maghen, *Virtues of the Flesh: Passion and Purity in Early Islamic Jurisprudence* (Leiden, 2004), x.

38 Maghen, ix.

39 Muslim, Salām, 113.

geometric and cosmic ritual.[40] In Islam the sacral act is guided by the cosmos, by the motions of sun and moon; and the cyclicity of the prayer, by which man begins upright in heaven, 'falls' to earth, and then ends in the balanced position of *jalsa* between the two, which is the caliphal posture, is fully integrated into the motions of the solar system. Muslim worship is cosmological, affirming our reciprocity with the universe, the holiness of nature and the enchantment of the cantillated narrative; in its cyclical movements we move from air to the clay from which we are made, and to which the symbolically defiant forelock is necessarily pressed, after which, thanks to the act of prayer itself and the peaceable surrender which it enacts, we find that balance is restored. The prayer's orality, ensured by the strict prohibition on reading, calls to mind the free and unlettered purity of the Prophetic soul, and hence the 'time before time' before the cognitive disjuncture which so alarmed Plato, when writing began and the ancient, more normative spiritual objectivity and perspicuity began to be veiled. The *ṣalāt*, then, the 'reminder' (20:14) which, inaugurated by the chant 'God is Greater', takes us back to the cyclical and the numinous, is the ideal liturgical enactment of *fiṭra* and hence of humanity's habitation of the middle world which unites the transcendent and the immanent.

Hence as well as the strict and crystalline geometries which adorn mosques and shrines, we encounter the swirling subtleties of the vegetal motifs which likewise call *al-Qarīb* to mind. In synergy with an art of cool and algebraic transcendence Islam hosts a luxuriant culture of immanence, of al-Khiḍr; Islam's prophetic recovery of sacred time, in which sun and moon determine the life of sacred spaces, has constantly and in a spiritually satisfying way inspired architects and craftsmen to use formal geometry side by side with stylized biomorphic spirals. Representing Islam's simultaneous affirmation of transcendence (*tanzīh*) and immanence (*tashbīh*), this

40 Rodney Blackhirst, 'Symbolism of Islamic Prayer', at http://themathesontrust.org. See also William Chittick, *In Search of the Lost Heart: explorations in Islamic thought* (Albany NY, 2012), 23-6.

combination is, possibly, the most recurrent and also theologically Islamic feature of the multiple idioms of Islamic art.

This applies in the public square as well. In premodern sultanic cultures we find a hospitality to Qur'anic principles of ancient kingly wisdom; the supreme ruler for scripture is Solomon, who also builds the *masjid*; the drastic misunderstanding which separates holy and profane realms is impossible in such a world. Huston Smith has put this very clearly in the introduction to Nasr's book *Ideals and Realities of Islam*:

> We have seen that the Qur'an incorporates the social order into the religious. This is, on the one hand, a recovery, it having been so included in all early—'whole'; tribal and ethnic—cultures. The inclusion is likewise logically indicated; the sacred/profane dichotomy may be required as an expedient in times and places, but it can never from the religious point of view be considered normative. Buddhism and Christianity, the other universal and missionary religions, do not embrace society. The ethnic religions—Hinduism, Judaism and, in a different way, Confucianism and Shintoism—do, but with a specificity which makes them unexportable.[41]

So Islam is tradition-mindedness incarnate; its life-affirming forms of worship, notably, which shape the faithful life, are astoundingly stable, having changed not at all since the religion's earliest times, and recall still older principles. And this stability, and the reassurance and protection which stability brings in times of liquid modernity, doubtless offer a further explanation of the popularity of Islam, evident despite rising levels of hostility from its cultured despisers around the world. This is part of the charism of Ishmael: powerful elites demand conformity and compliance in the hope of banishing Ishmael's annoying and retrograde conspicuousness from sight; but those demands seem only to strengthen the believer and to vindicate his sense that his life for God and for justice is more meaningful than any subaltern compliance with a fleeting modernity could ever be. A

41 Seyyed Hossein Nasr, *Ideals and Realities of Islam* (London, 1966), vii.

religion which affirms *tanzīh* and *tashbīh* preserves both the uniquely compelling idea of monotheism, and the no less compelling human need for reintegration within the natural matrix.

The Green Man, in Europe, does not look down with disapproval upon the Muslim prayer; he is there, as we have suggested, as one who participates in that prayer, upbraiding the grim theologies which see nature as 'fallen' and in enmity towards grace. In our own time he deplores a widening ignorance of sacred things and a fanatic passion for consumption. His expression laments the monoculture's chronic 'deficit of signifieds.' Grimacing or laughing from the despised margins, he is still present in our postmodern Europe. He is, from one perspective, Ishmael himself, the 'heir according to the flesh'. He lives in social housing, sweeps the trains and builds Mercedes and Renault cars to return value to shareholders whom he will never meet. As Ishmael he is the type of the outcast and disdained; and he is summoned to reconnect with the most authentic and florescent dimensions of his sacred heritage, if he is to be true to himself, and thus to discharge his vocation in Europe, which must be to point to the sanctity of the world, to heal, and to unite.

Ishmaelites in our spiritually-devastated continent are called to be this organic fecundating principle, a rain, a leaven in the dough. Like the Green Man and his folkloric epigones who in medieval times were, in a sense, the first wave of Muslim immigrants to the West, they are holy dissidents, possessed of a wisdom which is not merely linear; in Europe they are here to dispute what Charles Taylor calls the felt flatness of secularity and to bear witness to a world of contours. Europe's green men and women are prophetic reminders and witnesses to humanity's natural abode in heaven, in the source of all life; in the homeland of all biology which is paradisal; their symbol is the crescent moon, which calls forth the dew. In this way they belong more truly than people exiled from faith in Abraham's God could ever belong: a European Muslim of Moroccan, Turkish or Indonesian parentage, by accepting the reality of God, is more a part of Europe's deepest and most irreplaceable heritage than any secular populist could ever claim to be. This is what we have called 'vertical integration': belongingness is most surely defined by a positive continuation with the deep strata of local identity, not by compliance with current secular and individualistic fashions: *nolite conformari huic seculo:* 'be not conformed unto this world.' Europe, in its recurrent and most profound identity, is Christian in many different ways; and Jewish, also in different ways; the idea of Abraham's God and the assurance of heaven have formed the essence and heart of European life. With this we cohere; but the primordiality of Muslim forms roots Ishmael still more surely in Europe's still deeper life, connecting very visibly with some pre-Biblical and pre-axial concepts of natural sacrality. Yew trees should soon be planted around every English mosque, where the sun slanting through windows joins worshippers to the harmonious armillary of heaven and illuminates a cosmic worship which has eluded the New Age pilgrims at Stonehenge.

Thus the Man helps us to make the claim that Muslims belong here, to the real, deep Europe. Secular politicians, whatever their opportunistic and desperate claims, have no more than shallow roots; despite their noisily-vaunted 'horizontal integration' they are, in very many cases, aliens, foreigners, recent immigrants from Planet Atheism. Contrast them and the hateful columnists with the green men and women who have a family life which recalls how Europe used to be. Figures now show that more than half of British people see family and friends less than once a month;[42] while only twenty percent eat a meal at the family dining table at least once a week.[43] This is certainly not the Ishmaelite and Hagarene

42 'Half of Britons socialise with family and friends at most once a month', *The Guardian*, 17 June 2019. Perhaps reminding us that this developing asociality seems particularly acute among secular liberals, Germaine Greer comments: 'I don't have any enduring relationships of any sort except with animals and plants' (*Times Literary Supplement,* 4 January 2019); cf. also Kate Millett's autobiographical remarks in *The Loony Bin Trip* (London, 1991).

43 'Is eating at the traditional dining table becoming obsolete?', *Daily Telegraph*, 29 April 2014.

way, which assumes that three generations will live together in every house, and that everyone keeps up with relatives. Muslims are socially conservative in many ways that real Europeans of a more European age would have recognized and honoured. Thus we find the Prophetic 'green saying' that 'the whole earth is made a mosque for me'[44] to be true: we experience a real belongingness here, for we profess so much of what always constituted the deepest truth of European culture. All humans, irrespective of religious appurtenance, have a capacity to recognize and yearn for the *fiṭra*, and they should be able to see it in us.

> *The original pattern* [fiṭra] *of God, in accordance with which He originated man; there is no changing the creation of God.* (30:30)

We should be confident that a real, uncompromising, *fiṭrī* Islam will always gather an audience of respect, for like a majestic tree it puts down deep roots, which reach beyond even the Christian and Jewish to the religion of Abraham as *ḥanīf*.[45] Conversions, which are ongoing, are one sign of this. Nature shines, even as it cringes from modern man; and Islam tells our impoverished Europe why, and offers a ritual manner of response and participation.

But our green men and women, our *khulafā'*, offer more; and here we find scope for immediate political action. The Qur'anic celebration of the sacrality of nature and the rights of other species which are *umamun amthālukum*, 'nations like yourselves' united in a single biotic community, is precisely the vision which the Green Parties and the ecowarriors need: nature is not merely useful, and hence worth saving, it is sacred, a concert of God's signs, inviolable and glorious. In a famous hadith we are instructed: 'If the Hour comes while you are planting a tree, finish planting it',[46] implying that environmental repair is to be a characteristic aspect of faithful action during turbulent and ominous times. The epistemicide which is environmental destruction is resisted by the Man's

44 Bukhārī, Tayammum, 1.

45 'The believer is like an evergreen tree' (Bukhārī, Adab, 79).

46 Ibn Ḥanbal, III, 191.

adherents. Here, precisely, the Islamic caliphal vision shows Islam as the 'green deen' par excellence. We save the signs to save humanity from the spiritual as well as the physical emergency which is threatening us, and this is part of what God has determined to be Ishmael's saving and preserving role in Europe.[47]

With climate change corrupting the theophanic earth and stubborn epidemics emerging which are very likely the consequence of man's persecution of nature,[48] Muslims, with their strikingly biophiliac narrative of nature's *baraka*, should present themselves as therapists. Climate change activism has been secular, pragmatic or pseudo-pagan for too long, and has lacked a true spiritual heart. It has been dominated by the so-called 'flat whites'; and it is time for those with access to the vertical dimension, and of the whole range of ethnicities represented by Ishmael, to exercise a catalytic function. For Ishmael in modern Europe increasingly appears as the last vibrant refuge of the indispensable dictum that materialism killeth, while the spirit giveth life, a rule which is now disastrously impacting the biosphere. *Dīn* offers an alternative to the two Faustian *shahādas* of materialism, which comprise the moderns' claim that they are only part of nature, after which they proceed to destroy it.

Of course this may not be what our neighbours think we are. Mostly they are ignorant of our theology, our ethics and our spirituality. The race temples, the Fearful and the *tanfīrīs* have failed to convey any of these things. Often, too, neighbours do not choose to befriend us, although this is beginning to change. Ishmael is misunderstood, to everyone's detriment. For 'man is the enemy of what he does not understand'.[49]

To overcome this, then, forms part of the charism of Ishmael and an entailment of the *fiṭra*, for we are animals whose nature it is to communicate. There is much work to do. Firstly, we need to state,

47 Gilis, *Intégrité islamique*, 25.

48 'Coronavirus: "Nature is sending us a message," says UN environment chief.' *The Guardian*, 25 March 2020.

49 Abu'l-Ḥasan al-Māwardī, *Adab al-Dunyā wa'l-Dīn* (Cairo, 1975), 104.

more clearly than we have been able to do, that there is a normative and holy Islam, which is indeed the beautiful *dīn al-fiṭra*, exemplified, for instance, by the heritage of the Nahdlatul Ulama, and the mainstream library-rooted, mysticism-friendly, nature-loving heritage of our civilization. By contrast there are fundamentalisms, radical Islamisms, and lethal dreams of Islam not as *dīn* but as ideology. None of those modern surrogates has shown any interest in nature, still less in the Khiḍr principle which allows a deeper and initiatic knowing. The catastrophes of modern Islamist dysfunction, on the basis of which our neighbours rush to judge us, are the consequence of the bastardising of our discourse by narratives of postcolonial grievance and by illicit and unstable intrusions of formalist interpretation far from the Breath of the Compassionate. So our green men must grimace not only at the secular moderns, but at the grey men of *tanfīr*.

To lead this charge for all the *ummas*, including the sad remnants of the animal nations, let us remember the saints of our heritage, who were not 'moderates' in some insipid modern way, but were passionate and uncompromising champions of truth. Their interpretation of Qur'an and our holy tradition was shaped not by ego but by spirit, not by *nafs* but by *rūḥ*. Thus did Islam enter the hearts of so many great peoples in history. This miracle can happen again; for al-Khiḍr is immortal. But for that sun to rise in the West, we must turn again to the spirit and restore the *aḥsani taqwīm*, the best of forms, we must green ourselves by bathing in the light of nature, we must explain the beauty and cosmic harmony of our worship and our beliefs, we must be the cupbearers who carry the Zamzam water of Hagar to the thirsty throats of a Europe which has been materialistic for too long and is parched from heat and drought. In our greening of Europe is hope for reconciliation, blessing, and the repair of the most indispensable human capacity.

CHAPTER II

Zakat in the postmodern economy

WE CLOSE WITH a few reflections on the way the Zakat might function creatively and therapeutically in the rather outlandish context of the twenty-first century financial system. The question is, like most current Islamic questions, about the viability of continuity. One of the most evident features of Muslim religion is its resolute constancy, at times even immobility: which other world religion has maintained not just essential doctrines, but the details of its practice, intact from the time of its foundation? Like the prayer, Ramadan and Hajj, the pillar of Zakat seems strongly to partake of the Sharia's timelessness. In a world of accelerating and runaway change, Islam is a rock of ages; these are rules which are not made to be broken, ever.

Yet the Zakat, while required to remain faithful to the Founder's inaugural vision, seems distinct from the other Pillars. If the prayer is about worshipping God, the fast about self-mastery, and the Hajj about our reconnection with our sacred past and our sacred centre, the pillar of Zakat concerns our connection to society, in its apparently profane but indispensable economic dimension. Religion, a term said to spring from the Latin word *ligare,* meaning 'to bind', does not only bind us to heaven, but to our fellow-men: religion is an eminently social thing. Moreover, because the globalised world which we inhabit has changed in such extreme and disorienting ways, not least in the way it gives and takes our wealth, this Pillar of Islam finds itself confronted by greater challenges than those which currently stretch our other fundamental obligations.

Some of the Zakat principles seem entirely unthreatened by modernity, notably those which relate immediately to its purpose. Zakat has an inwardly and also an outwardly-oriented dimension. Within the soul it has the evident virtue of purifying us of accumulated residues of greed, avarice, and indifference to others. It is cathartic, a palpable tithe which renders the remainder of our worldly goods spiritually and morally available to us. It is a healing of our personal economies, a kind of fiscal *ḥijāma*. But as well as conferring this blessing, the Zakat connects us to all other human beings, with whom we are networked through our financial and legal dealings. The Sharia regulates and purifies those connections in a myriad other ways, but the foundation of our monetary social interactivity is to be this toll on our wealth. So important is economic justice to the Qur'an's vision of society that this *social* pillar of the religion is not about family, or neighbour, or Jihad; but relates to how *money* is stored, taxed, and exchanged.

It is in no sense a substitute for other forms of social action. The rules of Zakat distribution incorporate virtues of preferring family, neighbour, and those who risk their lives in the defence of the community. Still, the principle remains: Zakat is our third pillar, rather than, for instance, *ṣilat al-raḥim*, the bond of kindred. The entire social vision of a believing and just Muslim society reveals a characteristic emphasis on *economic* justice. 'I seek God's protection from a poverty that makes one forget, and a wealth that makes one harsh,' as the Holy Prophet remarked.[1] Some of the very first sūras to be revealed comprised severe warnings against avarice and the neglect of the financial wellbeing of the disadvantaged sections of Meccan society (sūras 83, 102, 107, for example).

'Your Lord enjoins justice', says the Book (7:29), and without economic justice there can be little justice of any kind. Hence, one may surmise, the titanic importance of this cardinal duty of our religion. The Muslims are, very characteristically, a people who are to value equity in the matter of wealth distribution, but who, as

1 Tirmidhī, Zuhd, 3.

metacitizens, take matters further: we go beyond the dry economic analysis of the Marxists to realise that we are not only to sympathise with the poor, but actually to *love* them. Such was the Man of Praise, who 'loved the poor and sat with them,'[2] and asked us to pray: 'Lord God, grant us love for the poor [*ḥubb al-masākīn*].'[3] Remember the lines of Aḥmad Shawqī:

> *al-ishtirākiyyūna anta imāmuhum*
> *law-lā daᶜāwī al-qawmi wa'l-ghalwā'u*
>
> You are the imam of the socialists;
> but for their excesses and their claims …
>
> *Fa law anna insānan takhayyara millatan*
> *ma'khtāra illā dīnaka al-fuqarā'u.*[4]
>
> Were a man to select a religion for himself,
> the poor would only choose your religion.

In medieval times the Zakat institution, which was often complemented by a vast infrastructure of *waqf* endowments distributed across the far-flung Islamic world, contributed very significantly to the alleviation of poverty and other kinds of want. From today's perspective those societies, like the community of the Man of Praise, were nevertheless characterised by limited levels of intricacy. Although medieval Islam invented some complex financial systems (words like 'cheque' and 'tariff' are of Arabic origin), the classical theory of Zakat assumed a society infinitely less convoluted and centrally-managed than our own globalised world of runaway turbocapitalism. Muslim jurists today furrow their brows at the proliferation of complex and often entirely parasitic financial instruments: long-short funds, macros, futures, derivatives, cryptocurrencies and credit default swaps. Vast corporations are dedicated exclusively to trading financial products which bet on currency or commodity movements at various points in the

2 Tirmidhī, Manāqib, 29; Ibn Mājah, Zuhd, 7.

3 Tirmidhī, Tafsīr Sūrat Ṣād, 2; Ibn Ḥanbal, IV, 66.

4 Shawqī, 26.

unstable future. Computers trade on market vacillations occurring at intervals of a thousandth of a second. Most fundamentally of all, money itself has become a commodity whose value and availability are shaped by the fiat of central banks.

Which of the myriad new forms of wealth are liable to which forms of Zakat is a question for the scholars. But the *fiqh* of Sharia-compliant operation in today's smoke-and-mirrors financial world is not our concern here. During their reactive search for 'Islamic' equivalents to the financial products of the modern market economy, Muslim thinkers must not neglect ways in which the principle of Zakat, in its broad and—God willing—timeless architecture, might bring a new moral force to bear in the freakish and unstable environment of modern casino capitalism.

Let us reflect for a few minutes on the oddness of today's global economy. In its volatility and sheer newness it seems to mirror so many other late-modern sources of stress and uncertainty, such as climate change, terrorism, the flux in social structures, gender identities and relationships, religious confusion, troll farms, novel viruses and the domination of world culture by politically-networked media corporations. Although in some ways it is connected to all of these other sorrows, in its inherent bizarreness it seems to stand in a class of its own; or, perhaps, it is simply ahead of the downward curve.

This oddity, and the precarity which it veils, are not sufficiently known to the general public. In little more than a generation, financial laws and processes which underpinned the world economy for at least two centuries have been abolished or allowed to mutate strangely. Vast bubbles grow thanks to a thousand new forms of credit and of credit upon credit. In the intoxicated years before the 2008 crash, traders had piled into securitised high-risk mortgages, easily deceiving themselves and the rating agencies about the evident risks. Today as then the British reader works through the financial columns and assumes that despite all the hyperactive commotion, business is proceeding as usual and that no systemic collapse is possible. Market leaders cannot imagine how they could profit from challenging this complacency.

Why are we so ignorant, in an age of mass communication when with a few effortless clicks we can access the deregulated stock market, check the metrics, and even trade shares for ourselves? When the traditional branch bank manager of the Captain Mainwaring type seems unnecessary because we can manage our accounts online, and create and structure our own assets and borrowing? Thanks to the online revolution we can step right inside the great financial institutions; the system's chronic leakiness even allows us to read the most furtive emails of the creative tax consultants at Mossack Fonseca. The infrastructure seems reassuringly, though by no means deliberately, transparent; and yet it is extremely murky as well; it is not only all the young trees competing for the light that prevent us seeing the fire in the forest: the forest floor is only very dimly lit.

One reason is that the political direction of the whole apparatus seems to partake in the same quantum indeterminacy, as the information revolution has coincided with the success of what Benjamin DeMott calls 'junk politics'.[5] This is the politics of the upbeat mood-music soundbite, which delivers an endorphin hit to voters disoriented and jaded by a world of infotainment, Instagram and tweets. With our attention spans shrivelling we need ever quicker and quirkier thoughts from the politicians. A considered parliamentary speech on justice is nobody's news, but clumsiness is telegenically charming. So too are the indecorous secrets of a politician's private life. The increasingly HD quality of visual media and the hard-fought competition with sophisticated entertainment direct our senses to the captivatingly two-dimensional: when he ran in the 2019 European elections, did people think of Silvio Berlusconi's strategy for reducing Italy's sovereign debt, or the lurid Rubygate scandal which showed him as a 'relatable' Italian man?

5 Benjamin DeMott, *Junk Politics: the trashing of the American mind* (New York, 2003).

Like the arts and much else in our late modernity, politics increasingly finds itself more accessible when able to replace truth and value with celebrity style. What is cool is what is modish, new and interesting. Junk politics cannot easily direct us to reflect in a measured way on social inequities, or the real reasons for Palestinian anger or for climate change; and hence these serious affairs are shelved or dealt with only tokenistically. Like us the politicians do not want to look long into the eyes of such deep and difficult issues; like their voters they are quietly fearful of a universe in which Providence is thought to be no longer active. Instead they exploit the indulgent, distracted habits of a generation disquieted by the deep meaninglessness of things, and who crave regular gulps of laughing gas. This is why the most successful junk politicians make everything personal. Even acute scandal no longer shocks if it has been amusingly spun: a Prime Minister can install his girlfriend in Downing Street and smirk, as long as we are sufficiently entertained by his frolics.

The Obama presidency was also a case in point. What was really new about his policies? Did he in fact close Guantánamo, promote Middle Eastern democracy, or tackle income disparity or unemployment, as he had foretold? We no longer remember, but we enjoyed his 'audacity of hope'; the actual past has receded quickly into unreality; in a troubling and disappointing world we did not really hope for audaciousness, but only for some new caressing of our dopamine receptors. For Britain, Tony Blair inaugurated the UK version of the same feelgood 'truthiness'. As this Labour politician armwrestled the economy in a neoliberal direction, what he stood for was veiled behind a susurration of newly-spun emotive and faux-sincere soundbites calibrated to catch the current atmospherics. His successors, despite an ongoing British distrust of charismatic politicians, have not been able to ignore his example. They know that most of us glance only at headlines and images, and crave emotional reassurance, and fear analysis. The main argument against prospective London mayor Sadiq Khan was not policy-related at all, but comprised vague but attention-grabbing insinuations about alleged Islamist connections. This is the new normal in British politics.

DeMott writes that in this novel world of junk politics there is 'zero interruption in the processes and practices that strengthen existing, interlocking systems of socioeconomic advantage.' It 'maximizes threats from abroad while miniaturizing large, complex problems at home [...] It's a politics that, guided by guesses about its own profits and losses, abruptly reverses public stances without explanation.'[6]

While the media and the politicians distract us, the income disparities continue to widen. Now that there is no socialism, and no real conservatives (for what they used to conserve is now 'politically incorrect'), everyone who wishes to use her or his vote must choose parties which trade on our panic about the moment, rather than those with a long-term vision of equitable human flourishing or a sense of national identity and history. We switch parties, then, frequently and with hardly a qualm. This lack of ultimate vision obstructs the creation of a real public discourse about our shared future, including questions of wealth distribution, climate change, housing prices, job security, and the decline of family and neighbourhood. A still deeper question, which is how the corporate capitalist doctrine of perpetual growth might cohere with the scientific fact of finite natural resources, is too alarming to dwell upon. The deeper dysfunctions are simply too hard for the politicians, requiring as they do policies which reach beyond the electoral cycle, and a serious and potentially unpopular public conversation about the origin and content of values in an increasingly desacralised society.

The global financial system, grounded in the illusion that it is trading with measures of real intrinsic value, is veiled from us by the mirage machines of the media networks, spin-doctor chancellors, and the willingness of CEOs to ignore the real state of the markets in favour of the indices important to big shareholders

6 DeMott, x, ix.

and the media. CEOs, like ministers, come and go with increasing rapidity, and hence find it easy or even essential to resist the temptation to take a long view, and so they raise share prices for the current year by cutting R&D. This is certainly one key contributor to the volatility of the markets: most equity and commodity fluctuations are caused by irrational or very short-term herd impulses, or what is euphemistically called 'market sentiment', rather than by anything real, among fund managers concerned only to beat this year's index. This is further magnified by the reflexes of automated share-trading algorithms. Moreover, the FTSE is highly vulnerable to junk politicians who abbreviate and abbreviate their feelings about complex issues such as Brexit. But nobody actually *knows* anything at all. What will really happen to markets next year? Nobody knows: predictions by economists come true less frequently than those of astrologers. Every future seems both likely and unlikely. The mood, not even the medium, is the message in a liquid modern civilisation that adores Mammon but has no real idea how to control it.

In 2012 Slavoj Žižek gave a lecture in London under the title 'The Buddhist Ethic and the Spirit of Global Capitalism'.[7] He reflected on the fact that the most common form of religious practice in the City of London is now Buddhism, often in quite radical forms. The young bond traders on sixteen-hour shifts need to wind down and decompress, and hence 'mindfulness', Zen, or various incense-burning meditative therapies, have become their spirituality of choice. The Wren churches bustle with lunchtime clarinet recitals and parties of Chinese tourists, but Evensong among the teeming glass spires is thinly attended. The reason? The traders' cognitive frame is not monotheism-friendly. Theravada Buddhism holds that all is a void, nothing is intrinsic; values, life, soul, self, the body, money, bonds, the Nasdaq: all are unreal, humming in a state of endless playful flux like green figures dancing forever across a void. *Sunyata!* What more perfect model could there be for the modern numbers game?

7 https://Zizek.uk/the-buddhist-ethic-and-the-spirit-of-global-capitalism/

We borrow Euros that don't yet exist, and then trade on their future movements; with the profits, we trade again. Money bursts from this cornucopia of consensual illusion, this 'saving falsehood' (*upaya*): everyone seems to gain, and there is plenty more paper, and many more bond issues, so who will speak out? Why upset the market with predictions of a recession?

When sober, Washington and London elites are hardly oblivious to the dizzy precariousness of this arrangement. However any last-minute escape from the jaws of a new credit crunch that would make 2008 look like a picnic of *peris* would demand decisions that elected politicians, addicted as usual to the short-termism endemic in the election cycle, could not take without courting annihilation at the polls.

Yet the cash may not ferment and bloat forever. In a 2016 interview with CNBC the then Republican front-runner staggered viewers by letting something slip. He speculated about a possible need to force holders of US treasury bonds to (as the jargon goes) take a haircut, rather as savings account holders have done in the *ribā*-ruined Greek economy. They might lose ten or fifteen percent of their bond balances in a sudden and irreversible raid by the Fed.

This remarkable warning of state default is not the kind of thing politicians usually utter or threaten. The reaction of the establishment media, institutionally committed to the delusory print-money-forever usury boom, was to hit the panic button. The *Washington Post* condemned the speech as 'reckless'. In effect, it continued, the US government would be in a state of default. The collapse of confidence in the world's banker of last resort, the Federal Reserve, and in the worth of Treasury bonds, would trigger a global economic meltdown and a massive shift away from bonds into equities, hedge funds, property and precious metals. The dollar would weaken as a global reserve currency, perhaps to be replaced by the euro or even the renminbi. Even a ten percent haircut would, it seems, precipitate this *yawm al-ḥisāb* in the financial markets. 2008 and the 2000 dot-com bubble would dim into comparative insignificance.

The trouble is that everyone, even The Hillary, knows that the alternative is likely to be more apocalyptic still. Here is what Trump actually said:

> We're paying very low interest rates. What happens if that interest rate goes two, three, four points up? We don't have a country. If you look at the numbers, they're staggering.[8]

Trump, coming from left field, not a Beltway insider, had mentioned the unmentionable truth about the harlot called *Ribā*.

Servicing the US national debt is projected to exceed 280 billion dollars annually, even on the historically bizarre nil or near-nil interest rates decreed by the Federal Reserve. What if rates moved up to their historic post-war average of 4.6%? Any resumption of those traditionally normal levels would result in a jump in the interest repayments to over one trillion dollars, devouring a quarter of the federal budget.

What would happen, if that happened? The White House would be forced to borrow more money to cope with this increase in debt servicing, and a vicious circle would ensue, capsizing the entire American economy and, therefore, government, within five years. Military spending, currently $649 billion annually, would need to be slashed, slashing the American empire. All this, we recall, is the prophecy if rates only go up to their historical average. A return to the double-digit rates of the 1980s would pull the Armageddon lever far more rapidly.

Here in the UK we are no less exposed. On 12 May 2016 the Bank of England directors voted unanimously to maintain the base rate at half a percent, the lowest for three centuries, a level which had been held for an astonishing seven years. At such levels our £1.78 trillion national debt is just manageable. But even Mark Carney warned of an uptick in rates following any post-Brexit chaos. That, or any entirely unforeseen 'black swan' event, could push rates back towards their historical norms, and the aftermath of the 'corona crash' proved

---

8 http://www.thefiscaltimes.com/2016/05/06/Trump-Would-Risk-Full-Faith-and-Credit-US

depressingly accessible to such predictions. The national budget, already reduced by agonisingly deep austerity cuts, would have to take a further swingeing hit. The NHS, state pensions, and many social services, already struggling, certainly could not survive in their present form.

That is the scenario for the national debt. The implications of massive mortgage default among homeowners and buy-to-let landlords would be even more calamitous. In September 2019 the average UK household owed £2,603 in credit card debt, at an average interest rate of 20.1%.[9] A significant interest rate rise would unleash an unprecedented political and social emergency.

It is almost universally agreed that, like a corpse, the economy has been blowing bubbles. Cheap money for banks, quantitative easing, and a regulatory environment that despite the 2008 debacle remains historically permissive, have allowed debt to swell and metastasize. All this during a period of so-called European recovery which by most traditional indices has not been much of a recovery at all. The so-called 'equilibrium rate of interest', in which investment and savings correspond with full employment in a moderately inflationary environment is now extremely low, partly thanks to historically very depressed rates of inflation. The equilibrium rate is looking unprecedentedly faint and flat; neo-Keynesians are talking of a radical and stubbornly persistent form of 'secular stagnation.'

Everyone is in debt: students, homeowners, car-owners, cardholders: indebtedness, once a stigma, is the new normal; yet these same neo-Keynesians argue that the economy needs more stimulus in the traditional form of yet more credit injections. But again, the religion of economics is a broad church. Others have published a number of papers to defend the somewhat self-evident point that a surge in cheap money can *cause*, rather than resolve, a financial crisis.

These dissident economists have only one solution: raise the value of *ribā*. They are convinced that the world has been experiencing

---

9 themoneycharity.org.uk/money-statistics

real interest rates below zero, despite low levels of inflation. Lending money helps to store it and push it around, but makes a loss, not a profit. Already some European central banks have offered bonds with a negative interest rate, even before inflation is taken into consideration. So on this view, higher rates are called for to re-establish the equilibrium rate, so that investment and savings once more exist in a coherent and balanced relationship.

The ongoing boom-and-bust fairground ride of the new disaster capitalism is rushing us to an unguessable destination. Investors cannot tell at what point to get off. Are we looking at cycles, or at a structural depression? Nobody can tell us: the theorists can't agree; the situation is without precedent. But the harlot has more suitors than ever.

Whereas in premodern states, and certainly in Islamic political structures, central government's economic functions were limited essentially to matters of security and the regulation of the mint, the modern state has become a monster whose tentacles envelop every contour of the citizen's life. For all the proud rhetoric of freedom and rights, our education, justice systems, health, and other key dimensions of our existence are subject to meticulous state regulation and control. Money itself, the key indicant of value, is valued and created by the state's central bank. It is not hewn from mines in God's solid earth, but comprises scraps of paper whose fiduciary value is determined by government policy, which in turn is rooted in economic theories on which there is no consensus at all.

Here again Sharia systems insist on a real rather than an illusory freedom. A private currency whose worth lies largely outside the power of state banks to determine is to be the essential measure of exchange. In a manner superior to cryptocurrencies (whose claimed libertarian advantages have not convincingly outweighed the dire drawbacks of their volatility and their environmental impact), gold and silver, the *naqdayn*, allow private individuals considerable freedom from manipulation by states and corporate interests. The *naqdayn* also provide an insurance against unexpected haircuts, levies, and other state-imposed interferences with personal wealth. Finally, when the ATMs at last stop doling out cash, the *naqdayn* will come into their own: no politician or central bank can cancel their value and negotiability.

All this certainly seems to be of more relevance to Islamic banking than to Islamic charity and to Zakat. But perhaps we can begin to make the point that although we are conscientious and believing human beings who abhor the relativism of modern 'values' and the human suffering which spreads amid our contemporary Potemkin palaces, not least the misery already caused by environmental decay resulting from capitalism's addictions, we will find it challenging to create a fully Sharia-compliant banking system. It is true that the Islamic banks represent a vastly preferable alternative to conventional usury finance. This is not only because they try to invest ethically, avoiding investment in alcohol and other narcotics, for instance, but also because they tend to be comparatively well-capitalised and to avoid some of the more esoteric and parasitic financial instruments which make banks vulnerable in times of sudden recession. During the 2008 crisis the Islamic banks generally fared fairly well, although there were some embarrassing and revealing exceptions.

Unfortunately the money in which they hold their deposits is not the *naqdayn*, but euros and greenbacks. Hence they inextricably form part of the global net of fiduciary money, and as such they cannot really escape its volatility. Or, if the system goes down, its total collapse.

This is not to say that the experiment has been simply bogus, as claimed by some purists, a mere replacement of Western financial products with Arabic-sounding facsimiles. In our stressed global environment one is always looking for the least bad option. Sharia compliance is a matter of degree these days, and it behoves us to remember the religion's traditional realism, and the forgiving mercy of God. Utopians can be sure of nothing except disappointment.

Still, let us also consider that whatever the current scene might suggest, the Islamic economic vision is not limited to the provision of banking services. As we mentioned at the beginning of this chapter, the Third Pillar, which relates to justice, is not about banking at all, but about Zakat, a statutory purgation of our fiscal bloodstream. So perhaps the creation of institutions such as the National Zakat Foundation, benefiting from London's stringent charitable and financial regulatory environment, represents a more interesting area in which to develop our campaign to offer an ethical and also realistic alternative to the current unstable and injurious economic paradigm.

Islamic banks often, unfortunately, recycle assets among wealthy investors. Much of London's jagged new skyline is the outcome of Middle Eastern and Malaysian speculation. The Olympic Village was one example; the makeover of Battersea Power Station is another. There is One Hyde Park, Harrods, and Chelsea Barracks. The Shard was partly financed by Sharia-compliant instruments, and yet if one walks through the adjacent dismal and depressed streets it is by no means clear that the ethical gifts of Islamic banking have trickled down to the Southwark precariat, which relies not on Islamic banks, but on food banks. It is also likely to be the case that the influx of Gulf money into the safe haven of the London property market has contributed to the rise in house prices in the capital, with grave consequences for the young and the poor. The Islamic banks prefer to invest in Mayfair property portfolios rather than in the construction of affordable housing. None of this sounds particularly compliant with the vision of the Ishmaelite prophet, who longed to be resurrected among the *masākīn*, the poorest of the poor. A Zakat initiative, by contrast, would by definition make a difference to their neighbourhoods.

It is interesting to speculate about the amount of tithe-able money which is floating around London. Some is indeterminate in its status and actual location, thanks to the shell-within-a-shell tax avoidance stunts unveiled by the Panama Papers revelations. But even the visible wealth is startling. London is home to more ultra-high-net-worth individuals than any other city in the world.

This is the category of people with at least twenty million pounds at their disposal over and above the value of their main residences. There may be five thousand of them in London, and quite a few of them are Muslims, including some storied Russian oligarchs, friends or foes of Putin and his sprawling global estate. The *Sunday Times* Rich List names over fifteen Muslims. The chattels of their gilded lives are everywhere to be seen. A glitzy penthouse at One Hyde Park is home to a Ukrainian Muslim. *Haute couture* icons schedule culturally-specific appointments for Gulf ladies. The most spiffy hotels, such as the Dorchester and the Savoy, provide female butlers, prayer rooms, and halal chefs. London is a Muslim playground.

The super-rich individuals of this class account for an ever-growing share of global wealth. A recurrent feature of our age has been the progressive concentration of capital in few hands. According to *Forbes* magazine the world's sixty-two richest people own more than the poorest half of the earth's population; while between 2010 and 2016 the net wealth of that poorest half declined by over a trillion dollars.[10] In Europe, at the desperate end of the spectrum an increasing number of people are obliged to subsist on the minimum wage, or to work on zero-hours contracts or as long-term unpaid interns. The middle classes, too, find themselves squeezed, as less healthcare is available for free, and as they are obliged to support their children well into their twenties and even beyond. As Danny Dorling puts it in his book *Inequality and the 1%*, we are all being turned into service workers in a world that seems to exist for only a few individuals.[11]

London's ultra-high-net-worth scene is largely populated by foreign expatriates. Of these it is not clear how many are being approached to discharge their Zakat obligations, although some are visibly generous to secular charities, while some Muslim donors support the Royal Opera House or the Conservative party. There

10 'The sixty-two people who are as wealthy as the poorest half of humanity combined', *The Independent*, 18 January 2016.

11 Danny Dorling, *Inequality and the 1%* (London, 2015).

is surely mileage in the idea that they should be called upon to support, say, anti-extremism initiatives in the Muslim community, far from the dire bungling of Whitehall or what Stephen Toope calls the 'fundamental threat' of the Prevent agenda.[12] After all, several Gulf states historically carry the main responsibility for the funding of global fundamentalism, the potash which has fertilised the soil from which al-Qaida, ISIS and Boko Haram have grown. Why should they not also fund charities and mosques which try to challenge the extremists? As yet they have not begun to do this, preferring to pay PR companies to devise exculpations. They recall the public image of Exxon executives as they try as hard as they can to avoid paying for their own oil spillage. Their petrodollars have supported global fundamentalism, considerably destabilising Western Muslim communities in the process; it is not unreasonable to ask them and their citizens now to spend some money on the mainstream Islamic alternative which is the only demonstrably efficient inoculation against the pandemic of *tanfīr*.

Unfortunately, many Muslim expatriates in London appear allergic to the idea that if they fast in Ramadan and pray punctually in the Dorchester mosque, they are also equally liable for Zakat. Ṣalāt is euphonic with Zakāt; they are twin sisters, and those verses fail to work musically when missing one voice in the duet. The Islam of these 'Herods in Harrods' is unbalanced; it is an Islam which fails to rhyme or charm, and the impact on their sleek yet withered selves is often very evident in their faces.

Wealth normally hardens the heart. Research into student responses to poverty and suffering shows that the brains of individuals from wealthy backgrounds, who did not need to work or take student loans, tend to respond very distinctively, often showing activity in areas of the brain associated with disgust. Their reaction to seeing images of the poor is often indistinguishable from their reaction to photographs of piles of uncollected garbage. It seems

12 'The reality of Prevent,' *Varsity*, 27 April 2018.

that wealth and privilege tend not only to harden the heart, but to rewire the brain, and thus to de-Ishmaelize the soul.[13]

Zakat, therefore, presents itself as a moral and economic therapy of a radical kind, pushing Muslims back into the orbit of their spiritual forebear. Progressive income taxes have failed to limit the widening gulf which, to the detriment of both, separates rich from poor; social services and health care continue to be cut. Here revelation has proposed a different type of solution, which links the spiritual to the socially just.

Zakat is effectively a net wealth tax. It is true that there are exemptions: one's own private home, for instance. But the one-pound-in-every-forty annual tithe remains immensely promising. Consider the amount which could be raised from Britain's Muslim millionaires. According to the Muslim Council of Britain there are more than ten thousand of them. This would represent two hundred and fifty million pounds a year for charity purely in Zakat terms. One should, moreover, not neglect the fourteen thousand Muslim-owned businesses in London. Over a third of small to medium enterprises in London are said to be owned by Muslim entrepreneurs.[14] What is the Zakat liability there?

Already, according to the Charity Commissioners, Muslims are *per capita* the most generous charitable givers in the UK.[15] A full operationalising of a national Zakat system could build this Muslim pre-eminence substantially and even spectacularly higher. Moreover, Zakat and *ṣadaqa* are not simply about charity. These religious statutes have not only a charitable object but a larger redistributive function, justified not only morally but psychologically, since it is evident that real wealth is what the Man of Praise called 'soul-

13 Cf. Lasana T. Harris and Susan T. Fiske, 'Dehumanizing the Lowest of the Low: neuro-imaging responses to extreme out-groups', *Psychological Science* 17 (2006), 847-853.

14 'London's Mecca rich,' *Evening Standard*, 30 October 2013.

15 'Muslims "are Britain's top charity givers"', *The Times*, 20 July 2013.

wealth' (*ghinā al-nafs*), and that monetary riches do not usually correlate with happiness.[16]

This forms part of the wider philosophy intrinsic to Islam's social vision. While mercantile activity is encouraged, the long-term accumulation of capital is obstructed by several Sharia mechanisms. One of them is our system of inheritance tax. Marx's analysis of the emergence of capital in Europe should make little headway in observant Muslim societies, since there is no principle of primogeniture. An English duke's estate is inherited by the eldest son; the others make their way in the world as best they can. By contrast the Qur'anic inheritance rules divide an estate multiply: all children inherit, and often further relations as well. Moreover a third has to go to others outside this family circle, and often this will be willed to *awqāf* of various types. So in premodern Istanbul, for instance, where a Western European city's land would be largely divided among aristocratic and mercantile families, a high proportion of the city was owned by *awqāf*, whose revenues could only be used for charitable ends.[17] This established a public commons system of accessible assets such as mosques, hospitals and soup kitchens, which were controlled neither by the state nor by the market.

Speaking of one type of charity, the Qur'an determines that recipients will be 'relations, orphans, paupers and wayfarers', adding 'so that this wealth should not be circulated between the wealthy among you.' (59:7) Wealth must be ploughed back, into lower and disadvantaged segments of society: the homeless, the familyless, the refugee, the asylum seeker. These are all perennial categories of human need, and those in each category have a right, *ḥaqq*, over the assets of the fortunate.

The advantages of a tax on wealth, rather than simply on income, are not a uniquely Qur'anic teaching. In 2014 a literary sensation erupted when French economist Thomas Piketty published

---

16 https://www.princeton.edu/news/2006/06/29/link-between-income-and-happiness-mainly-illusion

17 Barnes, *Introduction to Religious Foundations*.

his *Capital in the Twenty-First Century*.[18] Piketty's concern is with income disparity. He points out that when dividends on capital exceed the economic growth rate, the rich will grow richer. This will, ultimately, threaten the entire global system. The solution is not an income or sales tax, but must take the form of a tax on wealth.

Piketty almost seems to be echoing classical Islamic thinking when he goes on to suggest that a shift away from income taxes to a wealth tax would not only reduce wealth differentials but would energise the economy. Money left idle would be subject to an annual haircut, forcing assetholders to invest in profitable enterprises. These would in turn generate a higher revenue, since income taxes would be proportionately lower. Parasitical investment would be replaced by a more active investment strategy that focussed on real asset growth rather than the circulation of funds among passive investment vehicles. The result, Piketty believes, would be an end to our era of secular stagnation and the return of a more healthy economic model based on tax as a negative reinforcer. Passive assets would suffer, while economic activity would be rewarded, with positive consequences for employment, investment, company dividends, and global trade.

Piketty's thesis is not likely to be actioned. Even in the world's largest economy, the United States, Donald Trump's suggested national haircut which would pay off the national debt in a single year, would, as the terrified critics noted, galvanise massive capital flight into other asset classes and overseas markets, even though this would be mitigated by the fact that America sensibly operates a global tax regime, taxing citizens wherever they and their assets are domiciled. Piketty's context is France, which actually applies a wealth tax: any French citizen with total assets above 1.3 million euros is subject to an annual levy of up to 1.5%. Unfortunately the net outcome has been capital flight, particularly to London, now home to over a hundred thousand French tax exiles.

This is the usual argument used against the idea of a wealth tax.

---

18 Thomas Piketty, *Capital in the Twenty-First Century* (Cambridge MA, 2014).

But it does not apply to Zakat, which is global and universal. A Muslim believer is obligated whether his money is sitting in his kitchen jar or in a shell company in the Cayman Islands. The Sharia thinks in global terms.

Let us remember a further interesting and sadly-neglected fact. We tend to think of the Zakat level as fixed at a flat rate of 2.5%. However the Sharia raises this on certain asset classes, notably the category known as *rikāz*, which essentially denotes wealth with no previous owner which exists underground. Here, although the *madhhabs* diverge somewhat, we find generally that mineral wealth, on extraction, attracts a zakat charge of up to 20%, the *zakāt al-rikāz,* or *zakāt al-maᶜdin.*[19]

In 2008, al-Azhar's Institute of Islamic Research issued a fatwa about this. Oil wealth, like other mined mineral wealth, is to be considered *rikāz*, and hence the mufti called on oil-rich Gulf states to pay a flat rate of 20% on all oil assets once these are removed from the ground. The revenues would be used to uplift the economies of poorer Muslim countries, and to relieve the suffering of the poor and refugees.[20]

It would not be right to say that this proposal met with an ecstatic reception in the Gulf region. Nonetheless, the higher-rate Zakat asset classes are specified by the classical Sharia manuals. The timeless relevance of these texts is very conspicuously shown when we consider how seismic would be the impact of such an annual levy, if applied virtuously and efficiently to relieve countries like Bangladesh and Mali, where a single dirham goes a long way. The hoarding of assets in London property portfolios, and the speculative purchase of Damien Hirst artworks, football clubs, and shares in Apple and Fox News, would be dented, returning asset prices to

19 The rulings vary between schools, but see ᶜAbd al-Raḥmān al-Jazīrī, tr. Nancy Roberts, *Islamic Jurisprudence according to the Four Sunni Schools* (Louisville KY, 2009), 824; Yūsuf al-Qarḍāwī, tr. Monzer Kahf, *Fiqh al-Zakat: A Comparative Study* (London, 1999), 278-86.

20 *Rūz al-Yūsuf*, 4 June 2008.

something more recognisably normal. The global economy would benefit, as the new import demand in the countries being developed by *rikāz* financing would support base industries and stimulate trade, particularly within the OIC countries.

Note another neglected consequence of this type of Zakat. It specifically taxes mineral wealth, including fossil fuels. An effective hike of 20% in oil, coal and gas extraction costs would represent an effective subsidy in the same value to sustainable alternatives. There is no *zakāt al-rikāz* or *zakāt al-maᶜdin* on hydroelectric dams, wind farms, and photovoltaic arrays. Where these are private investments they will at most be liable to the ordinary 2.5% Zakat rate.

More, much more, could be said. We live in times as interesting as they are precarious. Our postviral and postmodern future is unprecedentedly hard to guess, and sensible experts seem in most cases to have stopped trying. But it is reasonable to anticipate the ongoing significance of London as a centre for global and Muslim wealth. As the nations of the Middle East implode, whether due to political turmoil or climate change, their elites are increasingly likely to move to our shores. This is an opportunity which British Muslims should recognise. London is set to be the world capital of Muslim wealth, and quite possibly of Islamic banking as well. With institutions such as the National Zakat Foundation also located here, it is set fair to be a hub of authentic and transformative Islamic benevolence and wealth-sharing. We must hope and pray for its continued thriving, wisdom, and compliance with heaven's law.

BIBLIOGRAPHY

Abd-Allah, Umar. 'Islam and the Cultural Imperative', at http://www.artsrn.ualberta.ca

Abisaab, Rula Jurdi. *Converting Persia: religion and power in the Safavid empire* (London: I.B. Tauris, 2004).

Adraoui, Mohamed-Ali. 'Salafism in France: ideology, practices and contradictions', in Roel Meijer (ed.), *Global Salafism: Islam's new religious movement* (London: C. Hurst and Co., 2009), 364-83.

Agai, Bekim and Omerika, Armina. 'Islamic Theological Studies in Germany: A Discipline in the Making', in Michael Kemper and Ralf Elger (eds.), *The Piety of Learning: Studies in Honor of Stefan Reichmuth* (Leiden: Brill, 2017), 330-354.

Ahmed, Shahab. *What is Islam? The importance of being Islamic* (Princeton: Princeton University Press, 2015).

Amerio, Romano. *Iota Unum: a study of changes in the Catholic Church in the XXth century* (Kansas City: Sarto House, 1998).

Almond, Ian. *The New Orientalists: postmodern representations of Islam from Foucault to Baudrillard* (London: I.B. Tauris, 2007).

Alshech, E. 'The Doctrinal Crisis within the Salafi-Jihadi Ranks and the Emergence of Neo-Takfīrism,' *Islamic Law and Society* 21 (2014), 419–52.

Alvi, Hayat. 'Diffusion of Intra-Islamic Violence: the impact of Salafi-Wahhabi ideologies', *Middle East Review of International Affairs* 18 (2014), 38-50.

Anderson, William. *Green Man: the archetype of our oneness with the earth* (London and San Francisco: HarperCollins, 1990).

Anidjar, Gil. *Acts of Religion* (London: Routledge, 2002).

Anṣārī, Khwāja ʿAbdullāh, *Munājāt*, in *Ibn Ata'Illah, The Book of Wisdom, Khwaja Abdullah Ansari, Intimate Conversations*, introduction, translation and notes of the *Book of Wisdom* by Victor Danner, and of *Intimate Conversations* by Wheeler M. Thackston (Mahweh: Paulist Press, 1979).

Anzulović, Branimir. *Heavenly Serbia: from myth to genocide* (London: Hurst, 1999).

Arnold, T.W. *The Preaching of Islam: a history of the propagation of the Muslim faith* (Westminster: Constable, 1896).

Ashley, Benedict, OP, *The Way Towards Wisdom: an interdisciplinary and intercultural introduction to metaphysics* (Notre Dame: Notre Dame University Press, 2009).

Ashworth, Jacinta, and Farthing, Ian. *Churchgoing in the UK* (Teddington: Tearfund, 2007).

ʿAsqalānī, Ibn Ḥajar al-. *Fatḥ al-Bārī sharḥ Ṣaḥīḥ al-Bukhārī* (Riyadh: Dār al-Salām and Damascus: Dār al-Fayḥā, 3rd ed. 1421/2000).

Audi, Robert (ed.), *Cambridge Dictionary of Philosophy* (Cambridge: Cambridge University Press, 1995).

Awliya, Nizam Ad-Din, tr Bruce B. Lawrence, *Morals for the Heart* (New York and Mahweh: Paulist Press, 1992).

Azraqī, Muḥammad ibn ʿAbdallāh al-, ed. Rushdī al-Ṣāliḥ Malḥas. *Akhbār Makka wa-ma jā'a fīhā min al-āthār* (Madrid: Dār al-Andalus, 197?).

Baldwin, Tom. *Ctrl Alt Delete: how politics and the media crashed our democracy* (London: Hurst, 2018).

Bangstad, Sindre. *Anders Breivik and the rise of Islamophobia* (London: Zed, 2014).

Bano, Masooda. 'Madrasa Reforms and Islamic Modernism in Bangladesh,' *Modern Asian Studies* 48 (2014), 911-939.

Barnes, Robert. *An Introduction to Religious Foundations in the Ottoman Empire* (Leiden: Brill, 1987).

Batsford, Kathleen. *The Green Man* (Cambridge: D.S. Brewer, 1978).

Baubérot, Jean. *La laïcité falsifiée* (Paris: La Découverte, 2012).

Baudrillard, Jean. 'No Pity for Sarajevo', in Thomas Cushman and Stjepan G. Meštrović (eds.), *This Time We Knew: Western responses to genocide in Bosnia* (New York and London: New York University Press, 1996), 79-89.

Bauer, Thomas. *Die Kultur der Ambiguität: Eine andere Geschichte des Islams* (Berlin: Verlag der Weltreligionen, 2011).

Bausani, A. 'Religion under the Mongols,' pp.538-549 of the *Cambridge History of Iran,* V (Cambridge: Cambridge University Press, 1968).

Bayḍāwī, ʿAbd Allāh al-. *Anwār al-tanzīl wa-asrār al-ta'wīl* (Istanbul: al-Maṭbaʿa al-ʿUthmāniyya, 1329AH).

Bayman, Henry. *The Secret of Islam: revealing the compassionate Koran* (Berkeley CA: North Atlantic Books, 2004).

—— *The Station of No Station* (Berkeley: North Atlantic Books, 2001).

Bayramoğlu, Fuat. *Hacı Bayram-ı Veli: Yaşamı, Soyu, Vakfı. Cilt II: Belgeler* (Ankara: Türk Tarih Kurumu, 1983).

Binbaş, Ilker Evrim. *Intellectual Networks in Timurid Iran: Sharaf al-Dīn Alī Yazdī and the Islamicate republic of letters* (Cambridge: Cambridge University Press, 2016).

Binns, John. *An Introduction to the Christian Orthodox Churches* (Cambridge: Cambridge University Press, 2002).

Birgivī, Muḥammad ibn Pīr ʿAlī (ed. Muḥammad Ḥusnī Muṣṭafā), *al-Ṭarīqa al-Muḥammadiyya wa's-sīra al-Aḥmadiya* (Aleppo: Dār al-Qalam al-ʿArabī, 1423/2002).

Beier, Mattias. *A Violent God-Image* (London: Continuum, 2003).

Belloc, Hilaire. *The Great Heresies* (London: Sheed and Ward, 1938).

Bennett, Alan. 'The Laying On of Hands', in *Four Stories* (London: Profile, 2014), 1-78.

Bensadoun, Michael. 'The (Re) Fashioning of Moroccan National Identity,' pp.13-35 of Bruce Maddy-Weitzman and Daniel Zisenwine (eds.), *The Maghrib in the New Century: Identity, Religion and Politics* (Gainesville: University Press of Florida, 2007).

Blackhirst, Rodney. 'Symbolism of Islamic Prayer', at http://themathesontrust.org

Blankinship, Khalid. 'The early creed', in Tim Winter (ed.), *The Cambridge Companion to Classical Islamic Theology* (Cambridge: Cambridge University Press, 2008).

Blumenthal, Max. *The Management of Savagery: How America's national security state fuelled the rise of Al Qaeda, ISIS, and Donald Trump* (London: Verso, 2019).

Bonnefoy, Laurent. 'Quietist Salafis, the Arab Spring and the politicisation process,' 205-218 of Francesco Cavatorta and Fabio Merone (eds.), *Salafism after the Arab awakening: contending with people's power* (London: Hurst, 2016).

Bora, Fozia. *Writing History in the Medieval Islamic World* (London: I.B. Tauris, 2018).

Bradbury, Malcolm. *Mensonge: My Strange Quest for Henri Mensonge, Structuralism's Hidden Hero* (Harmondsworth: Penguin, 1998).

Brigaglia, Andrea. 'The Volatility of Salafi Political Theology, the War on Terror and the Genesis of Boko Haram,' *Diritto e questioni pubbliche* 15 (2015), 175-201.

Brown, Callum. *The Death of Christian Britain: Understanding Secularisation 1800-2000* (London: Routledge, 2000).

Brown, Norman O. *Apocalypse and/or Metamorphosis* (Berkeley CA: University of California Press, 1991).

Bruce, Steve. *God is Dead: Secularization in the West* (New York: Wiley-Blackwell, 2002).

Bunt, Leslie. *Music therapy: an art beyond words* (London and New York: Routledge, 1994).

Bulliet, Richard. *Islam: the view from the edge* (New York: Columbia University Press, 1995).

Burckhart, Titus, (tr. Keith Critchlow), *Chartres and the birth of the cathedral* (Ipswich: Golgonooza Press, 1995).

Butler, Hubert. *In the Land of Nod* (Dublin: Lilliput, 1996).

Butler-Sloss, Elizabeth (chair). *Living with Difference: community, diversity and the common good* (Cambridge: Woolf Institute, 2015).

Byford, Jovan. 'Bishop Nikolaj Velimirović: "Lackey of the Germans" or a "Victim of Fascism"?', in Sabrina P. Ramet and Ola Listhaug (eds.), *Serbia and the Serbs in WW2* (Basingstoke: Palgrave Macmillan, 2011), 128-54.

Caeiro, A. 'Theorizing Islam without the State: minority *fiqh* in the West', in M. Diamantides and A. Gearey, *Islam, Law and Identity* (London: Routledge, 2011).

——'Ordering Religion, Organizing Politics: the regulation of the fatwa in contemporary Islam,' in Zulfiqar Ali Shah (ed.), *Iftā' and Fatwā in the Muslim World and the West* (London and Washington: The International Institute of Islamic Thought, 2014), 73-88.

Carr, Raymond. *The Spanish Tragedy: the civil war in perspective* (London: Weidenfeld, 1977).

Champion, Justin. *The Pillars of Priestcraft Shaken: The Church of England and its Enemies, 1660–1730* (Cambridge: Cambridge University Press, 1992).

Cheetham, Tom. *Green Man, earth angel* (Albany: State University of New York Press, 2005).

—— *The World Turned Inside Out: Henry Corbin and Islamic mysticism* (New Orleans: Spring Journal, 2015).

Chesterton, G.K. *The Flying Inn* (London: Methuen, 1914).

Chittick, William. *The Sufi Path of Love: the spiritual teachings of Rumi* (Albany NY: State University of New York Press, 1983).

—— *The Sufi Path of Knowledge: Ibn al-'Arabi's metaphysics of imagination* (Albany NY: State University of New York Press, 1989).

——*Imaginal Worlds: Ibn al-'Arabi and the problem of religious diversity* (Albany NY: State University of New York Press, 1994).

——*In Search of the Lost Heart: explorations in Islamic thought* (Albany NY: State University of New York Press, 2012).

Choudhury, Tufyal. 'British by Dissent: alternatives to jihadi narratives of identity, belonging and violence among Muslims in Britain', 191-215 of Jeevan Deol and Zaheer Kazmi (eds.), *Contextualising Jihadi Thought* (London: Hurst, 2011).

Cigar, Norman. *Genocide in Bosnia: the policy of 'ethnic cleansing'* (College Station: Texas A&M University Press, 1995).

Coates, John. 'Symbol and Structure in *The Flying Inn*', *Chesterton Review* 4 (1978), 246-59.

Commins, David. *The Wahhabi Mission and Saudi Arabia* (London: I.B. Tauris, 2006).

Contreras, Francisco J. 'Hostilidad anticristiana en España', 91-107 of Jaime Mayor Oreja et al., *¿Democracia sin religión? El derecho de los cristianos a influir en la sociedad* (Barcelona: Stella Maris, 2014).

Cook, Michael. *Commanding Right and Forbidding Wrong in Islamic Thought* (Cambridge: Cambridge University Press, 2010).

Copsey, Nigel. *Contemporary British Fascism: the British National Party and the quest for legitimacy* (London: Palgrave, 2008).

Çoruh, Hakan. 'Friendship between Muslims and the People of the Book in the Qur'ān with Special Reference to 5:51', *Islam and Christian-Muslim Relations* 23 (2012), 505–13.

Cragg, Kenneth. *Semitism: the whence and the whither, 'How dear are your counsels'* (Brighton: Sussex Academic Press, 2005).

Dahlawī, Shāh Walī Allāh al-, tr. Marcia K. Hermansen, *The Conclusive Argument from God* (Islamabad: Islamic Research Institute, 2003).

Dajani, Samer. 'Ibn 'Arabī and the Theory of a Flexible Sharia', *Journal of the Muhyiddin Ibn Arabi Society* 64 (2018), 78-81.

Daniel, Norman. *Islam and the West: the making of an image* (Revised edition Oxford: Oneworld, 1993).

Daniels, Roger. *Prisoners without Trial: Japanese Americans in World War II* (Revised edition New York: Hill and Wang, 2004).

Dawson, Christopher. *Enquiries into Religion and Culture* (New edition Washington DC: Catholic University of America, 2009).

De Botton, Alain. *Religion for Atheists: a non-believer's guide to the uses of religion* (London: Penguin, 2013).

De Jaeghere, Michel. *Enquête sur la Christianophobie* (Issy-les-Moulineux: Renaissance Catholique, 2006).

Deleuze, Gilles. *Desert Islands and Other Texts 1953-1974* (Paris: Semiotexte, 2003).

DeMott, Benjamin. *Junk Politics: the trashing of the American mind* (New York: Avalon, 2003).

Demiri (ed.), Lejla. *A Common Word: a resource for parishes and mosques* (Cambridge: Muslim Academic Trust, 2011).

DeWeese, Devin. *Islamization and Native Religion in the Golden Horde: Baba Tükles and Conversion to Islam in Historical and Epic Tradition* (Philadelphia:

Pennsylvania State University Press, 1994).
Divjak, Jovan. *Sarajevo, mon amour: entretiens avec Florence La Bruyère* (Paris: Buchet Chastel, 2004).
Dorling, Danny. *Inequality and the 1%* (London: Verso, 2015).
Eatwell, Roger, and Goodwin, Matthew. *National Populism: The revolt against liberal democracy* (London: Pelican, 2018).
Einboden, Jeffrey. *Islam and Romanticism: Muslim currents from Goethe to Emerson* (Oxford: Oneworld, 2014).
El-Yousfi, Amine. 'Conflicting paradigms of religious and bureaucratic authority in a British mosque', *Religions* 10 (2019).
Ellethy, Y. 'Enseigner la théologie islamique: l'exemple néerlandais,' Francis Messner and Moussa Abou Ramadan (eds), *L'enseignement universitaire de la Théologie musulmane. Perspectives comparatives* (Paris: Cerf, 2018), 177-99.
Emon, Anver M. and Levering, Matthew. *Natural Law: A Jewish, Christian and Islamic Trialogue* (Oxford: Oxford University Press, 2014).
Etzioni, Amitai. 'Flirting and Flag-Waving: The Revealing Study of Holidays and Rituals', *Chronicle of Higher Education* 49/16 (December 13, 2002), 16.
Fadel, Mohammad. 'The True, the Good and the Reasonable: the Theological and Ethical Roots of Public Reason in Islamic Law,' *Canadian Journal of Law and Jurisprudence* 21 (2008), available at http://ssrn.com/abstract=1085347.
Farīdī, Abū Fayḍān (Muhammad Riedinger), *The Broken Kashkul of Sufidom* (Karachi: Na'layn Publications, 2015).
Farquhar, Michael. *Circuits of Faith: Migration, Education and the Wahhabi Mission* (Stanford: Stanford University Press, 2017).
Farrin, Raymond. *Structure and Qur'ānic Interpretation: a study of symmetry and coherence in Islam's holy text* (Ashland OR: White Cloud Press, 2014).
Farris, Sara R. *In the name of women's rights: the rise of femonationalism* (Durham NC: Duke University Press, 2017).
Frazee, Charles A. *The Orthodox Church and Independent Greece 1821-1852* (Cambridge: Cambridge University Press, 1969).
Fromm, Erich. *The Anatomy of Human Destructiveness* (Harmondsworth: Penguin, 1977).
Gauthier, Léon. *Introduction à l'étude de la philosophie musulmane. L'esprit sémitique et l'esprit aryen: la philosophie grecque et la religion de l'Islâm* (Paris: E. Leroux, 1923).
Geaves, Ron. *Islam in Victorian Britain: the life and times of Abdullah Quilliam* (Markfield: Kube, 2010).
Ghazālī, Abū Ḥāmid al-. *Iḥyā' ʿulūm al-dīn* (Riyāḍ: Dār al-Minhāj, 1434/

2013 edition).
——*al-Mustaṣfā min ʿilm al-uṣūl* (Cairo, 1353/1937).
——(tr. Eric Ormsby), *Al-Ghazālī: Love, Longing, Intimacy and Contentment* (Cambridge: Islamic Texts Society, 2011).
——(tr. T.J. Winter), *Al-Ghazālī: The Remembrance of Death and the Afterlife* (Cambridge: Islamic Texts Society, 1989).
——(tr. T.J. Winter), *Al-Ghazālī: On Disciplining the Soul* (Cambridge: Islamic Texts Society, 1995).
Gilis, Charles-André. *L'Intégrité islamique, ni intégrisme, ni intégration* (Paris: Albouraq, 2004).
Gilroy, Andrea, and Lee, Colin (eds.). *Art and Music: therapy and research* (London and New York: Routledge, 1995).
Goodhart, David. *The Road to Somewhere: the new tribes shaping British politics* (London: Penguin, 2017).
Graf, Tobias P. *The Sultan's Renegades: Christian-European Converts to Islam and the Making of the Ottoman Elite 1575-1610* (Oxford: Oxford University Press, 2017).
Graham, William A. *Beyond the Written Word: oral aspects of scripture in the history of religion* (Cambridge: University of Cambridge Press, 1987).
Gray, John. *Al-Qaeda and What it means to be Modern* (London: Faber and Faber, 2003).
——*Straw Dogs: thoughts on humans and other animals* (London: Granta, 2002).
Grumezescu, Alexandru Mihai (ed.). *Therapeutic Foods: Volume 8* (Cambridge MA: Academic Press, 2017).
Goethe, Johann Von, tr. Eric Ormsby. *West-Eastern Divan, complete, annotated new translation, including Goethe's 'Notes and Essays' and the unpublished poems* (London: Gingko Library, 2019).
Gow, James. *Triumph of the Lack of Will: International Diplomacy and the Yugoslav War* (London: Hurst, 1997).
Guénon, René (tr. Marco Pallis and Richard Nicholson). *Crisis of the Modern World* (London: Luzac, 1975).
Gutman, Roy. *A Witness to Genocide: the first inside account of the horrors of 'ethnic cleansing' in Bosnia* (Shaftesbury: Element, 1993).
Hafez, Mohammed M. *Why Muslims Rebel: repression and resistance in the Islamic world* (New York: Lynne Riener, 2004).
Hakkı, Erzurumlu İbrahim (ed. Numan Külekçi). *Dîvân* (Erzurum: Harf, 1997).
Halkin, A.S. 'The Ḥashwiyya', *Journal of the American Oriental Society* 54 (1934), 1-28.

Hallaq, Wael. *Sharīʿa: theory, practice, transformations* (Cambridge: Cambridge University Press, 2009).

—— *The Impossible State: Islam, politics, and modernity's moral predicament* (New York: Columbia University Press, 2014).

Hamilton, Alastair. 'After Marracci: The Reception of Ludovico Marracci's Edition of the Qur'an in Northern Europe from the Late Seventeenth to the Early Nineteenth Centuries,' *Journal of Qur'anic Studies* 20 (2018), 175-92.

Hamming, Tore Refslund. *Fratricidal Jihadists: A Historical Examination of Debates, Contestation and Infighting within the Sunni Jihadi Movement* (London: ICSR, 2019).

Hampson, Michael. *Last Rites: the End of the Church of England* (Cambridge: Granta Books, 2006).

Harris, Lasana T. and Fiske, Susan T. 'Dehumanizing the Lowest of the Low: neuro-imaging responses to extreme out-groups', *Psychological Science* 17 (2006), 847-853.

Hartung, Jan-Peter. *A System of Life: Mawdudi and the Ideologisation of Islam* (New York: Oxford University Press, 2014).

Harvey, Ramon. *The Qur'an and the Just Society* (Edinburgh: Edinburgh University Press, 2018).

Hastings, Adrian. *The Shaping of Prophecy: Passion, Perception and Practicality* (London: Geoffrey Chapman, 1995).

Hawley, John. 'Naming Hinduism,' *Wilson Quarterly* 15 (1991), 20–34.

Haythamī, ʿAlī ibn Abī Bakr al-. *Majmaʿ al-zawā'id wa-manbaʿ al-fawā'id* (Cairo: al-Khānjī, 1352).

Heinisch, Reinhard, and Mazzoleni, Oscar. *Understanding Populist Party Organisation: the radical right in Western Europe* (London: Palgrave, 2016).

Hellyer, H.A. *Muslims of Europe: the 'other' Europeans* (Edinburgh: Edinburgh University Press, 2009).

—— 'What lessons can be learned from Singapore's religious regulatory framework?' *The National* (Abu Dhabi), 21 January 2018.

Higton, Mike. *A Theology of Higher Education* (Oxford: OUP, 2013).

Hirschler, Konrad. *Medieval Damascus: plurality and diversity in an Arabic library* (Edinburgh: Edinburgh University Press, 2016).

Hix, Simon. *What's Wrong with the European Union and How to Fix It* (Cambridge: Polity Press, 2008).

Holdbrooks Jr, Terry C. *Traitor?* (Lexington KY: Createspace, 2013).

Holmes-Katz, Marion. *Women in the Mosque: a history of legal thought and practice* (New York: Columbia University Press, 2014).

Houellebecq, Michel. *Platform* (London: Vintage, 2002).

——tr. Lorin Stein. *Submission* (London: Vintage, 2015).

Hughes, Aaron. *Theorizing Islam: Disciplinary Deconstruction and Reconstruction* (London: Routledge, 2012).

Ibn ʿĀbidīn, Muḥammad Amīn. *Radd al-muḥtār ʿalā al-Durr al-Mukhtār* (Beirut: Dār al-Fikr, 1405/1985).

Ibn al-Dabbāgh, ʿAbd al-Raḥmān (ed. Helmuth Ritter). *Mashāriq anwār al-qulūb wa-mafātīḥ asrār al-ghuyūb* (Beirut: Dār Ṣādir, 1379/1959).

Ibn Ḥanbal, Aḥmad. *al-Musnad* (Cairo: al-Maymaniyya, 1313).

Ibn Hishām, ʿAbd al-Malik. *al-Sīra al-Nabawiyya* (Cairo: Maktabat al-Riḥāb, 1428/2007).

Ibn Rajab, ʿAbd al-Raḥmān. *Jāmiʿ al-ʿulūm wa'l-ḥikam fī sharḥ khamsīn ḥadīthan min jawāmiʿ al-kalim* (Beirut: Dār al-Khayr, 1417/1996).

Imamutdinova, Zilia. 'The Qur'ānic recitation traditions of the Tatars and Bashkirs in Russia: evolution of style.' *Performing Islam* 6 (2017), 97-121.

Imber, Colin. *The Ottoman Empire 1300-1481* (Istanbul: Isis, 1990).

——*Ebu's-su'ud: the Islamic legal tradition* (Edinburgh: Edinburgh University Press, *ca* 1997).

Irwin, Robert. *For Lust of Knowing: the Orientalists and their enemies* (London: Penguin, 2007).

Iṣfahānī, Abū Nuʿaym al-. *Ḥilyat al-awliyā' wa-ṭabaqāt al-aṣfiyā'* (Cairo: al-Khānjī, 1932-8).

Izetbegović, Alija. *Islam between East and West* (3rd edition, Indianopolis: American Trust Publications, 1993).

Izutsu, Toshihiko. *God and Man in the Qur'an: semantics of the Qur'anic weltanschauung* (Tokyo: Keio Institute of Cultural and Linguistic Studies, 1964).

——*Ethico-Religious Concepts in the Qur'ān* (Montreal: McGill University Press, 2002)

Jāmī, ʿAbd al-Raḥmān (tr. Edward Fitzgerald). *Salaman and Absal* (London: De La More Press, 1904).

Jazīrī, ʿAbd al-Raḥmān al-, tr. Nancy Roberts, *Islamic Jurisprudence according to the Four Sunni Schools* (Louisville KY: Fons Vitae, 2009).

Jīlānī, ʿAbd al-Qādir al-. *Futūḥ al-Ghayb* (Cairo: Maktabat al-Azhar, 1330).

Jelavić, Barbara. *History of the Balkans: Eighteenth and Nineteenth Centuries* (Cambridge: Cambridge University Press, 1983).

Johnson, Luke T. 'The New Testament's Anti-Jewish Slander and the Conventions of Ancient Polemic', *Journal of Biblical Literature*, 108/3 (1989), 419-41.

Kakutai, Michiku. *The Death of Truth* (London: William Collins, 2018).

Kertzer, David I. *The Pope Who Would be King: the Exile of Pius IX and the Emergence of Modern Europe* (New York: Random House, 2018).

Keown, D. *The Nature of Buddhist Ethics* (London: Macmillan, 1992).

Khādimī, Muḥammad ibn Muṣṭafā al-. *al-Burayqa al-Maḥmūdiyya sharḥ al-Ṭarīqa al-Muḥammadiyya wa'l-sharīʿa al-nabawiyya fi'l-sīrat al-Aḥmadiyya* (Istanbul: Maktabat al-Busnawī, 1287AH).

Khair, Muhammed. 'Hegel and Islam', *The Philosopher,* Volume LXXXX No. 2 (Autumn 2002) at www.the-philosopher.co.uk.

Kimball, Michelle R. *Ahmadou Bamba, a peacemaker for our time* (Kuala Lumpur: The Other Press, 2019).

Kirmānī, Shams al-Dīn Muḥammad al-. *al-Kawākib al-Darārī fī sharḥ Ṣaḥīḥ al-Bukhārī* (Beirut: Dār Iḥyā' al-Turāth al-ʿArabī, 1401/1981).

Klein, Charlotte, tr. Edward Quinn. *Anti-Judaism in Christian Theology* (London: SPCK, 1978).

Lahham, Kerim. *The Roman Catholic Church's position on Islam after Vatican II* (Abu Dhabi: Tabah Foundation, 2008).

La Rochefoucauld, François de, tr. Norman Scarfe. *A Frenchman's Year in Suffolk: French impressions of Suffolk life in 1784* (Woodbridge: The Boydell Press, 1988).

Larrington, Carolyne. *The Land of the Green Man: a journey through the supernatural landscapes of the British Isles* (London: I.B. Tauris, 2017).

Lee, Umar. *The Rise and Fall of the Salafi Da'wa in America: a memoir* (St Louis: St Louis Stranger, 2014).

Leopold, Aldo. *A Sand County Almanac and Sketches Here and There* (Oxford: Oxford University Press, 1949).

Lewis, David Levering. *God's Crucible: Islam and the making of Europe* (New York: W.W. Norton, 2008).

Lewis, Franklin D. *Rumi Past and Present, East and West* (Oxford: Oneworld, 2000).

Levinas, Emmanuel, tr. Seán Hand. *Difficult Freedom: Essays on Judaism* (Baltimore: Johns Hopkins University Press, 1990).

Lévi-Strauss, Claude. *Race and History* (Paris: UNESCO, 1952).

——(tr. John and Doreen Weightman). *Tristes Tropiques* (Harmondsworth: Penguin, 1976).

Lindsey, B. and Hooper, J. 'Music and the Mentally Handicapped: The Effect of Music on Anxiety,' *Journal of British Music Therapy* 4 (1990), 19-26.

Lings, Martin. *Muhammad: his life based on the earliest sources* (Cambridge: Islamic Texts Society, 1991).

Lüdemann, Gerd. *The Unholy in Holy Scripture: the dark side of the Bible* (London: SCM, 1998).

Lunt, Theodore R.W. *The Story of Islam* (London: Church Missionary Society, 1909).

Lyons, Jonathan. *Islam through Western Eyes: from the Crusades to the War on Terrorism* (New York: Columbia University Press, 2012).

Madelung, Wilferd. 'The Spread of Māturīdism and the Turks,' *Actas do IV Congresso des Estudos Árabes et Islâmicos, Coimbra – Lisboa 1968* (Leiden: Brill, 1971), 109-68.

Maghen, Ze'ev. *Virtues of the Flesh: Passion and Purity in Early Islamic Jurisprudence* (Leiden: Brill, 2004).

Mahmutćehajić, Rusmir. *Bosnia the Good: tolerance and tradition* (Budapest: Central European University Press, 2000).

——*On Love in the Muslim Tradition* (New York: Fordham University Press, 2007).

Malik, Maleiha. 'Religion and sexual orientation: conflict or cohesion?' 67-92 of Gavin D'Costa, Malcolm Evans, Tariq Modood and Julian Rivers (eds.), *Religion in a Liberal State* (Cambridge: Cambridge University Press, 2013).

Manne, Robert. *The Mind of the Islamic State: ISIS and the ideology of the caliphate* (Amherst NY: Prometheus Books, 2017).

Marsh, Andrew F. *Islam and Liberal Citizenship: the search for an overlapping consensus* (Oxford: Oxford University Press, 2009).

Marshall, John. *John Locke, Toleration and Early Enlightenment Culture* (Cambridge: Cambridge University Press, 2010).

Matar, Nabil. 'John Locke and the Turbanned Nations', *Journal of Islamic Studies* 2 (1991), 67-77.

Matton, Sylvie. *Srebrenica: un genocide annoncé* (Paris: Flammarion, 2005).

Māwardī, Abu'l-Ḥasan al-. *Adab al-Dunyā wa'l-Dīn* (Cairo: al-Shaᶜb, 1975).

Mazower, Mark. *Dark Continent: Europe's Twentieth Century* (London: Penguin, 1998).

McCann, Craig J.J. *The Prevent Strategy and Right-Wing Extremism: a case study of the English Defence League* (London: Routledge, 2019).

Miles, Joanna, Mody, Parveez, and Probert, Rebecca (eds.). *Marriage Rites and Rights* (London: Hart Publishing, 2015).

Miller, Lisa *et al.* 'Neuroanatomical Correlates of Religiosity and Spirituality, A Study in Adults at High and Low Familial Risk for Depression', *JAMA Psychiatry* 35-128 (2014) 71.2.

Millett, Kate. *The Loony Bin Trip* (London: Virago, 1991).

Moaveni, Azadeh. *Guest House for Young Widows among the women of ISIS* (Mel-

bourne and London: SCRIBE, 2019).
Modood, Tariq. *Essays on Secularism and Multiculturalism* (London: Rowman and Littefield, 2019).
Mohammed, Amjad M. *Muslims in Non-Muslim Lands: a legal study with applications* (Cambridge: Islamic Texts Society, 2013).
Monteil, Vincent-Mansour. *Aux cinq couleurs de l'Islam* (Paris: Maisonneuve et Larose, 1989).
Mortimer, Sarah. *Reason and Religion in the English Revolution* (Cambridge: Cambridge University Press, 2010).
Mulalić, Nermin, and Risaluddin, Saba. *From Daytonland to Bosnia Rediviva* (London: Bosnian Institute, 2000).
Murad, Abdal Hakim (tr.). *Selections from the Fatḥ al-Bārī* (Bartlow: Muslim Academic Trust, 1421/2000).
——*Muslim Songs of the British Isles* (London: Quilliam Press, 2005).
——*Commentary on the Eleventh Contentions* (Cambridge: Quilliam Press, 2012).
Murata, Sachiko, Chittick, William C. and Weiming, Tu. *The Sage Learning of Liu Zhi: Islamic Thought in Confucian Terms* (Cambridge MA and London: Harvard University Press, 2009).
Musa, Khadiga. *A Critical Edition of ᶜUmdat al-Nāẓir ᶜalā al-Ashbāh wa'l-naẓā'ir* (Sheffield and Bristol: Equinox, 2018).
Nāblusī, ᶜAbd al-Ghanī al-. *al-Ḥadīqat al-Nadiyya sharḥ al-Ṭarīqa al-Muḥammadiyya* (Lahore: al-Maktaba al-Nūriyya, n.d.).
Nagle, Angela. *Kill All Normies: online culture wars from 4chan and Tumblr to Trump and the Alt-Right* (Alresford: Zero Books, 2017).
Nahouza, Namira. *Wahhabism and the Rise of the New Salafists: Theology, Power and Sunni Islam* (London: I.B. Tauris, 2018).
Nasr, Seyyed Hossein. *Ideals and Realities of Islam* (London: George Allen and Unwin, 1966).
Nawawī, Muḥyī al-Dīn al-. *al-Minhāj fī sharḥ Ṣaḥīḥ Muslim ibn al-Ḥajjāj* (Cairo: al-Maṭbaᶜa al-Miṣriyya bi'l-Azhar, 1347AH).
——*Tahdhīb al-asmā' wa'l-lughāt* (Cairo: al-Munīriyya, n.d.).
——*Sharḥ al-Arbaᶜīn*, presented by Louis Pouzet as *Une Herméneutique de la tradition islamique: Le Commentaire des Arbaʿūn al-Nawawiya de Muḥyī al-Dīn Yaḥyā al-Nawawī (m. 676/1277)* (Beirut: Dar El-Machreq, 1982).
Negarestani, Reza. *Intelligence and Spirit* (New York: Sequence, 2018).
Neirynck, Jacques. *Le siège de Bruxelles* (Paris: Desclée de Brouwer, 1996).
Nettelfield, Lara, and Wagner, Sarah E. *Srebrenica in the Aftermath of Genocide* (Cambridge: Cambridge University Press, 2014).
Nichols, Tom. *The Death of Expertise: The Campaign against Established Knowl-*

edge and Why it Matters (New York: OUP, 2017).
Nicholson, Reynold A. *Selected Poems from the Divani Shamsi Tabriz* (Cambridge: Cambridge University Press, 1898).
Niffarī, Muḥammad al-. *al-Mawāqif*, ed. A.J. Arberry (London and Cairo: Luzac, 1934/5).
Nussbaum, Martha C. *The New Religious Intolerance: overcoming the politics of fear in an anxious age* (Cambridge MA: Belknap, 2012).
Ong, Walter J. *Orality and Literacy* (2nd edition Abingdon: Routledge, 2012).
Ormsby, Eric. *Theodicy in Islamic Thought: the dispute over al-Ghazālī's Best of All Possible Worlds* (Princeton: Princeton University Press, 1984).
Pačariz, Sabina. 'Montenegro', in Oliver Scharbrodt et al., *Yearbook of Muslims in Europe*, 7 (2015), 409.
Pauwels, Teun. *Populism in Western Europe: comparing Belgium, Germany and the Netherlands* (London: Routledge, 2014).
Paxman, Jeremy. *The English: a portrait of a people* (London: Penguin, 1998).
Pérez, Joseph. *The Spanish Inquisition: a history* (London: Profile Books, 2004).
Perica, Vjekoslav. 'The Most Catholic Country in Europe? Church, State and Society in Contemporary Croatia', *Religion, State and Society* 3 (2006), 311-46.
Perlovsky, Leonid. 'Cognitive function, origin, and evolution of musical emotions,' *Musicae Scientiae* 16 (2012), 185-99.
Perry, Mary Elizabeth. *The Handless Maiden: Moriscos and the Politics of Religion in Early Modern Spain* (Princeton: Princeton University Press, 2005).
Perry, Whitall N. *A Treasury of Traditional Wisdom* (Cambridge: Quinta Essentia, 1991).
Peterson, Jordan B. *12 Rules for Life: an antidote to chaos* (London: Allen Lane, 2018).
Piketty, Thomas. *Capital in the Twenty-first Century* (Cambridge MA: Harvard University Press, 2014).
Pirenne, Henri. *Mohammed and Charlemagne* (New York: Norton and Co., 1939).
Pluckrose, Helen, *et al.* 'Academic Grievance Studies and the corruption of scholarship,' in *Areo Magazine* (online), 2 October 2018.
Pollis, Adamantia. 'Eastern Orthodoxy and Human Rights,' *Human Rights Quarterly* 15 (1993), 339-56.
Postman, Neil. *Technopoly: the surrender of culture to technology* (New York: Vintage, 1993).
Puar, Jasbir K. *Terrorist Assemblages: homonationalism in queer times* (Durham NC: Duke University Press, 2007).

Putnam, Robert D. *Bowling Alone: the collapse and revival of American community* (New York: Simon and Schuster, 2000).

Qarḍāwī, Yūsuf al- (tr. Monzer Kahf). *Fiqh al-Zakat: A Comparative Study* (London: Dar al-Taqwa, 1999).

Qārī, ʿAlī al-. *Mirqāt al-mafātīḥ sharḥ Mishkāt al-Maṣābīḥ* (Beirut: Dār al-Fikr, 1422/2002).

Quḍāʿī, Muḥammad ibn Salāma al-. *Musnad al-Shihāb* (Beirut: Mu'assasat al-Risāla, 1985).

Ramet, Sabrina P. *Balkan Babel: The Disintegration of Yugoslavia from the death of Tito to the War for Kosovo* (Boulder: Westview Press, 1999).

Rāzī, Fakhr al-Dīn al-. *Mafātīḥ al-ghayb* (Beirut: Dār al-Fikr, 1985).

Rees, Martin. *Our Final Century: a scientist's warning* (London: Arrow, 2004).

Reeves, Minou. *Muhammad in Europe* (Reading: Garnet, 2000).

Richardson, John E. *(Mis)Representing Islam: the racism and rhetoric of British broadsheet newspapers* (Amsterdam: John Benjamins, 2004).

Rippin, Andrew. 'The Reception of Euro-American Scholarship on the Qur'ān and *tafsīr*: an overview,' *Journal of Qur'anic Studies* XIV (2012), 1-8.

Risaluddin, Saba. *Case of the Zvornik Seven: ethnic cleansing of the legal system in Bosnia-Herzegovina* (London: Bosnian Institute, *ca.* 1998).

Rohde, Achim. 'Der Innere Orient. Orientalismus, Antisemitismus und Geschlecht im Deutschland des 18. bis 20. Jahrhunderts,' *Die Welt des Islams* 45 (2005), 370-411.

Rorty, Richard. *Contingency, Irony and Solidarity* (Cambridge: Cambridge University Press, 1989).

Rubin, Dominic. *Russia's Muslim Heartlands: Islam in the Putin Era* (London: Hurst, 2018).

Rūzbehān al-Baqlī al-Shīrāzī. *ʿArā'is al-bayān fī ḥaqā'iq al-Qur'ān* (Cawnpor: Navāl Kishwar, 1300AH).

Ryan, Nick. *Homeland: Into a World of Hate* (Edinburgh: Mainstream, 2003).

Saʿdī. *Kulleyyāt,* ed. Muḥammad ʿAlī Furūghī (Tehran: Enteshārāt-e Qafnūs, 1374 solar).

Ṣāfī, ʿAlī ibn Ḥusain (tr. Muhtar Holland). *Rashaḥāt ʿAyn al-Ḥayāt, Beads of Dew from the Source of Life* (Fort Lauderdale: Al Baz, 2001).

Sakhāwī, Muḥammad al-. *al-Maqāṣid al-Ḥasana fī bayān kathīrin min al-aḥādīth al-mushtahira ʿala'l-alsina* (Beirut: Dār al-Kitāb al-ʿArabī, 1405/1985).

Sanders, E.P. *Paul* (Oxford: Oxford University Press, 1991).

Schimmel, Annemarie. *Mystical Dimensions of Islam* (Chapel Hill NC: University of North Carolina Press, 1975).

Schuitema, Etsko. *The Millennium Discourses* (Johannesburg: Intent Publishing, 2011).

Scourfield, J., Taylor, C., Moore, G., and Gilliat-Ray, S. 'The Intergenerational Transmission of Islam in England and Wales: Evidence from the Citizenship Survey', *Sociology* 46 (2012), 91-108.

Scott-Baumann, Alison, and Cheruvallil-Contractor, Sariya. *Islamic Education in Britain: new pluralist paradigms* (London: Bloomsbury, 2015).

Şentürk, Recep. '*Ādamiyya* and *ʿIṣma*: the contested relationship between humanity and human rights in classical Islamic law', *Islâmi Araştırmalar Dergisi* 8 (2002), 39-69.

Sells, Michael. *The Bridge Betrayed: Religion and genocide in Bosnia* (Berkeley: University of California Press, 1996).

——'Crosses of Blood: sacred space, religion, and violence in Bosnia-Herzegovina,' *Sociology of Religion* 64 (2003), 309-331.

Sereghy, Zsolt. '"Vienna must not become Istanbul": the secularization of Islam and Muslims in Austria', in Yasir Suleiman (ed.), *Muslims in the UK and Europe I* (Cambridge: Centre of Islamic Studies, 2015), 176-85.

Shalabī, Muḥammad Muṣṭafā. *Taʿlīl al-aḥkām* (Cairo: Maktabat al-Azhar, 1947).

Shaʿrānī, ʿAbd al-Wahhāb al-. *al-Mīzān al-Kubrā* (Beirut: Dār al-Fikr, 1432/2010).

Shāṭibī, Ibrāhīm ibn Mūsā al-. *al-Iʿtiṣām* (Cairo: al-Maktaba al-Tijāriyya al-Kubrā, 1332AH).

Shawqī, Aḥmad. *al-Shawqiyyāt* (Cairo: Maṭbaʿat Miṣr, 1939).

Shihadeh, Ayman. *The Teleological Ethics of Fakhr al-Dīn Al-Rāzī* (Leiden: Brill, 2006).

Siddiqui, Sohaira. 'Sunni Authority's Legitimate Plurality', https://www.oasiscenter.eu/en/sunni-islam-many-authorities

Sikand, Yoginder. *Bastions of the Believers: madrasas and Islamic education in India* (New Delhi: Penguin Books, 2005).

Singleton, Brent D. *The Convert's Passion: an anthology of Islamic poetry from late Victorian and Edwardian Britain* (Rockville MD: Borgo Press, 2009).

Smith, Ken and Benson, Judi (eds). *Klaonica: Poems for Bosnia* (Newcastle: Bloodaxe, 1993).

Steiner, George. *Nostalgia for the Absolute* (Toronto: House of Anansi, 1997).

Stetkevych, Jaroslav. *Muhammad and the Golden Bough: reconstructing Arabian myth* (Bloomington: Indiana University Press, 2000).

Stokes-DuPass, Nicole. *Integration and New Limits on Citizenship Rights* (London: Palgrave, 2015).

Stubbe, Henry (ed. Hafiz Mahmud Khan Shairani). *An Account of the Rise and Progress of Mahometanism, and a Vindication of him and his Religion from the Calumnies of the Christians* (Second edition Lahore: Orientalia, 1954).

Sugich, Michael. *Signs on the Horizons: meetings with men of knowledge and illumination* (n.p.: Michael Sugich, 2013).

Suyūṭī, Jalāl al-Dīn al-. *al-Ashbāh wa'l-naẓā'ir* (Beirut: Dār Iḥyā' al-Turāth al-ʿArabī, 2002).

Ṭabarānī, Sulaymān ibn Aḥmad al-. *al-Muʿjam al-Kabīr* (Beirut: Dār Iḥyā' al-Turāth al-ʿArabī, 1984).

Takševa, Tatjana. 'Genocidal rape, enforced impregnation, and the discourse of Serbian national identity,' *Comparative Literature and Culture* 17.iii (2015), art 2.

Taylor, Charles. *A Secular Age* (Cambridge MA: Belknap Press of Harvard University Press, 2007).

Thapar, Romila. 'Ancient History and the Search for a Hindu Identity', *Modern Asian Studies* 23 (1989), 209-231.

Thomas, Raju G.C. (ed.). *The South Slav Conflict: History, Religion, Ethnicity, and Nationalism* (London: Routledge, 2016).

Thurston, Alex. 'Ahlussunnah: A preaching network from Kano to Medina and back,' in Masooda Bano and Keiko Sakurei (eds.), *Shaping Global Islamic Discourses: The Role of al-Azhar, Medina, and al-Mustafa* (Edinburgh: Edinburgh University Press, 2015).

Tolan, John. *Sons of Ishmael: Muslims through European Eyes in the Middle Ages* (Gainesville etc.: University Press of Florida, 2008).

Toland, John. *Nazarenus*, ed. Justin Champion (Oxford: Voltaire Foundation, 1999).

Traherne, Thomas. *Centuries of Meditation* (London: Mowbrays, 1960).

Travison, T.G.. et al., 'A population-level decline in serum testosterone levels in American men,' *The Journal of Clinical Endocrinology and Metabolism* 92 (2007), 196–202.

Tüfekci, Zeynep. *Twitter and Tear Gas: The Power and Fragility of Networked Protest* (New Haven: Yale University Press, 2016).

Tusler, Robert L. *Music: Catalyst for Healing* (Alkmaar: Drukkerij Krijgsman, 1991).

Valiuddin, Mir. 'The way to control anger – the Qur'anic approach', *Islamic Culture* 46 (1972), 63-73.

Van Ess, Josef. 'Political Ideas in Early Islamic Religious Thought', *British Journal of Middle Eastern Studies* 28 (2001), 151-64.

Vanhoozer, Kevin J. *Nothing Greater, Nothing Better: theological essays on the love of God* (Grand Rapids: Eerdmans, 2001).

Velikonja, Mitja. *Religious Separation and Political Intolerance in Bosnia-Herzegovina* (College Station: Texas A&M Press, 2003).

Verskin, Alan. *Oppressed in the lands? Fatwas on Muslims living under non-Muslim rule from the middle ages to the present* (Princeton: Markus Wiener, 2013).

Walasek, Helen. *Bosnia and the Destruction of Cultural Heritage* (London: Ashgate, 2015).

Wāqidī, Muḥammad al-, ed. Marsden Jones, *al-Maghāzī* (London: Oxford University Press, 1966).

Warsi, Sayeeda. *The Enemy Within: a tale of Muslim Britain* (London: Penguin, 2018).

Wegner, Donald. *The Illusion of Conscious Will* (Boston MA: MIT Press, 2017).

Wehrey, Frederick. *The Burning Shores: Inside the Battle for the New Libya* (New York: Farrar, Straus and Giroux, 2018).

Weiler, Joseph H.H. *En christliches Europa. Erkundungsgänge* (Salzburg: Verlag Anton Pustet, 2004).

Winter, Michael. *Society and Religion in Early Ottoman Egypt* (London: Transaction Books, 1982).

Winter, Tim. *British Muslim Identity: past, problems, prospects* (2nd edition (London: Muslim Academic Trust, 2013).

——'America as a Jihad State: Middle Eastern Perceptions of Modern American Theopolitics', *The Muslim World* 101 (2011), 394-411.

——'"Nations like yourselves": some Muslim debates over Koran 6:38,' in Andrew Linzey and Claire Linzey (eds.), *The Routledge Handbook of Religion and Animal Protection* (London: Routledge, 2019), 163-172.

Wisnovsky, Robert. *Avicenna's Metaphysics in Context* (Ithaca NY: Cornell University Press, 2003).

Woldemariam, Michael. *Insurgent Fragmentation in the Horn of Africa: rebellion and its discontents* (Cambridge: Cambridge University Press, 2018).

Wolfreys, Jim. *Republic of Islamophobia: The Rise of Respectable Racism in France* (London: Hurst, 2018).

Wymann-Landgraf, Umar F. Abd-Allah. *Mālik and Medina: Islamic legal reasoning in the formative period* (Leiden: Brill, 2013).

Yahya, Abd ar Razzaq. *La papauté contre l'islam : Genèse d'une dérive* (Paris: Le Turban Noir, 2011).

Yazıcıoğlu, İsra Ümeyye. 'Affliction, Patience and Prayer: Reading Job (P) in the Qur'an,' *Journal of Scriptural Reasoning*, 4/I (July 2004); etext.lib.Virginia.edu/journals/ssr/issues/volume4/number1/ssr04-01-e01.html.

Yeğenoğlu, Meyda. *Colonial Fantasies: towards a feminist reading of Orientalism*

(Cambridge: Cambridge University Press, 1998).
Yusuf, Noor-un-Nisaa. *The Soliloquy of the Full Moon* (Birmingham: Noor al-Habib, 2015).
Zilfi, Madeleine. *The Ottoman Ulema in the Post-Classical Age (1600–1800)* (Minneapolis: Biblioteca Islamica, 1988).
Žižek, Slavoj. *Welcome to the Desert of the Real* (London and New York: Verso, 2002).
Zabīdī, Al-Murtaḍā al-. *Itḥāf al-Sāda al-Muttaqīn sharḥ Iḥyā' ʿUlūm al-Dīn* (Cairo: al-Maymaniyya, 1311 AH).
Zarrūq, Shaykh Aḥmad. *Qawāʿid al-taṣawwuf*, ed. Ibrāhīm al-Yaʿqūbī (Tripoli, n.d.).

Analytic Index